First published in 2011 by

Glasnevin Publishing
16 Griffith Parade
Glasnevin
Dublin 11
Ireland

www.glasnevinpublishing.com

A CIP catalogue record for this book is available from the British Library

ISBN: 978-0-9555781-8-2

CONTENTS

i

Preface

In this inspiring and remarkable book you will discover the enduring principles of success that have directed and motivated thousands of people to improve their lives and make a significant contribution and difference to the world. The book is aimed at anybody who wants to improve or make a success of their lives.

Success in any endeavour does not happen overnight or by chance, but takes determination, patience, resilience and guidance. It happens through hard work and the application of sound principles and purposeful actions such as:
- Setting realistic goals
- Making worthwhile plans
- Practising good interpersonal relationships
- Having confidence and self-belief
- Being optimistic
- Developing self-esteem
- Being persistent and resilient
- Being highly motivated
- Developing the habit of lifelong learning and continuous improvement
- Practising good personal values.

In this book you will learn to:
- Set goals and plan your career.
- Break free from negative thoughts and limiting beliefs by replacing them with empowering ones.
- Overcome shyness and become more confident in social situations.
- Make lasting friendships by developing and practising good interpersonal relationship skills.
- Motivate yourself to achieve what you want to do with your life.
- Be resilient and overcome adversity.
- Become optimistic and build up your self-esteem.
- Become a lifelong learner by discovering and applying the skills of learning.
- Acquire the values and principles to help you live a life of integrity and happiness.

This book has an entertaining and eclectic blend of inspirational real life stories from all areas of life including business, sport, science, politics, music, entertainment, exploration and invention. Marvel at and learn from the way many people have overcome scemingly insurmountable handicaps and obstacles in their lives to go on and become successful in their chosen careers or area of expertise. The text is interspersed with quotations, practical tips and techniques, acronyms and activities to inspire and help you acquire the right habits and attitudes, and practise the skills of success.

Each chapter begins with a number of questions to arouse your curiosity and prime your mind to seek out the answers. We learn best when we are actively seeking out answers to questions posed. For maximum retention, recall and learning, readers are advised to read the introduction and summary for each chapter first before they read the actual text. You can start anywhere in the book and dip in and out depending on your needs and what specific weaknesses you may quickly want to address.

The book is underscored by the best scientific psychological research currently available which is made accessible to the reader through clear simple language. By following the principles set out in this book, and avoiding the pitfalls of failure as set out in the last chapter, you will become the happy and successful person you are destined to be. Good luck in your quest for success!

Samuel A Malone, June 2011

Goals

- **Why is purpose so important?**
- **Why do we need a vision and a mission?**
- **Why do people need goals?**
- **Why do some people fail to set goals?**
- **How can SMARTS help you set better goals?**

Introduction

Without goals you are unlikely to succeed. Goals give you purpose and direction to achieve the things you want to do in life. A primary goal is to be happy and successful. Pursuing and accomplishing worthwhile goals will bring you contentment, happiness and success. People without goals never achieve much and aimlessly drift through life operating to other peoples' agenda rather than their own. A vision uses the power of your mind to create the future you desire. A mission transforms the vision into concrete words. Some people fail to set goals because of ignorance or fear or indeed they may not realise the importance of having goals. The SMARTS system of goal setting will help you set inspirational, purposeful, and meaningful goals.

Importance of Purpose

All successful people set goals and pursue them with a passion. Goals become self-fulfilling prophecies when we commit sincerely to them. The more passionate and consumed you are about goals the more likely you are to accomplish them. People achieve and become what they frequently think about. Goals provide a road map of where you want to go. The goal provides the purpose to strive to and the end state for ones actions. A man without a purpose is like a ship without a rudder: directionless. J.C. Penney, the founder of the famous retail store said: "show me a stock clerk with a goal and I will show you the future head of the company. Show me a person without a goal and I will show you a stock clerk."

To discover your purpose, follow your heart, your interests and dreams and be guided by your intuition. Many famous inventions were developed and many corporations were founded by one man with a dream and a sense of purpose. Do what you love to do as your enthusiasm and interest will keep you motivated and energised. People with a passion for what they do are unlikely to fail. What do you want out of life? Do you want to be rich? Do you want to be famous? Do you want to be successful at your chosen job or career? Do you want to leave the world a better place than you found it? Do you want to create something that will be remembered long after you are dead? Goals involving personal growth, relationships, and making a contribution to society will bring you greater satisfaction and happiness than self-centred goals to make money or become famous. You should want to pursue your goals rather than have to pursue your goals. Goals that you want to do are intrinsically rewarding and bring more satisfaction than goals imposed by others. Free will is important to success and happiness. That is why people in the Western democracies who are free to pursue their own goals are generally happier than people living in oppressive autocratic regimes.

Most people want to be happy and content no matter what they choose to do with their lives. Work should provide an intellectual challenge and make a contribution to society. Doing work that you love to do and find inherently interesting is a recipe for job satisfaction and happiness. Some philosophers such as Aristotle maintain that the purpose of life is to be happy. Having goals and progressing steadily towards them is a prerequisite for well-being and happiness. People who reach their goals experience a sense of accomplishment and increased satisfaction with their lives. Most of us like to do things we are good at doing: things we like and are naturally enthusiastic about. If you are interested in what you do and are good at doing it, it is more likely that you will succeed and enjoy the process of getting to your goals. Enjoy the journey as it is the journey rather than the destination that provides most satisfaction, contentment and happiness. In fact there is often a sense of anti-climax on reaching the destination because you miss the excitement of the challenge. Therefore it is important to continually renew your goals and set new challenges.

An ideal life is focused, purposeful, positive and organised, so that you are constantly engaged and moving in the direction of your goals. Some people with average abilities achieve outstanding success because they have self-belief and confidence and are hardworking, focused, enthusiastic and driven to achieve their goals. Others with high intelligence and amazing talents are often unsuccessful because of lack of purpose, drive and commitment. Talent alone will only get you so far, hard work is the key to accomplishment.

People with a purpose focus on what is important to them and thus prevent manipulation by others, fruitless distractions, time-wasting, drifting and sidetracking. They make long term plans and retain a sense of balance. They know what's important in life such as love, family, friendships, relationships and recreation and so make sure these are nurtured. They make sure their personal needs and preferences are met. They know they need goals to achieve their purpose. They know where they are going and know when they have achieved their goals. They make sure their goals are in harmony with their beliefs and values. People with a purpose always have somewhere to direct and consume their energies. They know what they have to do to achieve their goals and thus are never bored. They continually develop and renew their skills and talents in order to succeed. The law of cause and effect says you must set goals and take actions to reap results.

According to the world's leading medical experts it was impossible for climbers to survive above 8,000 metres and the only way to conquer Mount Everest was to bring your own oxygen supply. The air above 8,000 metres is very thin with only a third of the oxygen found at sea level. One mountaineer, Reinhold Messner didn't agree and in 1978 together with Peter Habeler set themselves the objective of climbing Mount Everest without the use of oxygen and thus prove the world was wrong. Despite suffering a series of setbacks they succeeded in reaching the summit without the use of oxygen and thus achieved a physical feat which was deemed medically impossible. Two years later Reinhold Messner repeated the achievement, but this time alone. Messner went on to achieve the incredible feat of climbing the 14 highest mountains on Earth becoming the first man to climb them all. People need a seemingly impossible challenge in life to be successful in whatever they decide to do.

> "We must have a theme, a goal, a purpose in our lives. If you don't know where you're aiming, you don't have a goal. My goal is to live my life in such a way that when I die, someone can say, she cared."
>
> Mary Kay Ash

The Need for a Vision and Mission

A vision is a picture of a desired future state. Einstein claimed that imagination was more important than knowledge. If you can picture and visualise in your imagination what you want to achieve it will direct, inspire, motivate, energise, and propel you forward to achieve it. You should then figure out what steps you need to take to get there and then mentally rehearse them. You are using the power of your mind to create the future you want. As an 8-year old boy Harold Wilson set himself the goal of becoming Prime Minister of England. He even had his photograph taken outside Number Ten Downing Street so that he could continually visualise the event to inspire him on his way to his goal. Psychologists claim that thinking determines actions and actions determine results. In the case of Harold Wilson it certainly appears to be true. Sports psychologists encourage athletes to visualise success and to practise their sport mentally as well as physically. It has been found that practising mentally is almost as effective as actual training.

Leonardo Da Vinci (1452-1519) the original 'Renaissance Man,' envisioned flying machines including a helicopter five hundred years before they became a reality. He even foresaw the need for his flying machines to have a retractable landing gear like modern aircraft to improve their aerodynamics in flight. In 1485 he designed a parachute, three hundred years before it became a reality. The Wright Brothers (Wilbur 1867-1912 and Orville 1871-1948) had a vision of inventing and flying the first motor-powered aeroplane. On the 17th December 1903 they achieved their dream when they flew the first successful powered, sustained and controlled flight in a heavier-than-air machine. Though many were invited to witness this historic event only five people turned up. Leo Baekeland (1863-1944) combined a talent for scientific originality in the invention of plastic and a flair for entrepreneurship. He had the vision to commercially exploit his invention and became a very rich and successful man. In 1909 he launched his product called Bakelite and introduced the world to plastics and the world has never been quite the same since.

Just like these people you too can be inspired by a vision. You too can have an impact on the world even if in a small way. A vision represents something you believe you can achieve. You can create the vision you want. This vision is a picture of what you are passionate about and desire most and what you are capable of doing if you set your mind to it and work hard. It will energise you and make your life purposeful and worthwhile. You should plan backwards from the vision, set out a programme of actions that will take you to your goals and so start with the end in mind. Creating a vision engages the right hand side or creative side of your brain while describing the vision in concrete words will use the left hand side or logical side of your brain. Provided you put in the necessary hard work your subconscious mind will drive you towards the achievement of your dreams and facilitate all the resources that you will need.

All inventions, life goals and business plans are visualised in the imagination first. All successful people think big and start small. All difficult journeys, no matter how long, begin with a single step. If you really want to do something you'll find a way and will not be deterred by obstacles, setbacks or naysayers. If you don't want to do something you'll find an excuse for not doing it. Your brain needs dreams and targets to aim for. Achievers in life have big visions. John F Kennedy, President of the United States, dreamed of putting a man on the moon and did so. Bill Gates dreamed of putting a personal computer into every home and did so. Henry Ford dreamed of making an affordable car for the masses and did so. Martin Luther King dreamed of a USA of equality, free of prejudice and racial hatred. In 1963 in front of the Lincoln Memorial in Washington, D.C., he gave one of the most famous, compelling and inspirational speeches ever delivered, "I had a dream." He laid his life on the line for his ideals and paid the ultimate sacrifice when he was assassinated in 1968. However his work for civil rights changed the face of America forever.

Florence Nightingale dreamed of creating a professional and respected nursing profession and her legacy continues to this day. Emily Pankhurst dreamed of a vote for women and campaigned vigorously to bring this objective about and succeeded after many years of agitation and personal suffering In 1914 she suspended her campaign and urged women to play their part to win the war. During the First World War women had proved themselves equal to men in every way. In March 1918 limited voting rights were extended to women in Britain. Ten years later they got the same voting rights as men and in the modern world have taken their rightful place in society. What do you dream of doing?

A vision needs to be supported by a mission which translates the vision into words. The mission tells you why you are here and what you propose to do with your life in order to achieve your purpose and goals. Your subconscious will adopt the vision and constantly direct your behaviour and actions to achieve it. Any thought you accept as true in the conscious mind will be accepted as true by the subconscious mind. Use the power of suggestion through the use of affirmations to program your subconscious mind. The mission which supports your goals will be expressed in general terms and be more inspirational rather than specific. On the other hand, goals tend to be concrete and specific with a time frame and targets to achieve them.

"The person with a fixed goal, a clear picture of his desire, or an ideal always before him, causes it through repetition, to be buried in his subconscious mind and is thus enabled, thanks to its generative and sustaining power, to realise his goal in a minimum of time and with a minimum of physical effort. Just pursue the thought unceasingly. Step by step you will achieve realisation, for all your faculties and powers become directed to that end."

Claude M. Bristol

Why People Need Goals

Research by Richard Davidson at the University of Wisconsin found that patterns of brain activity indicate we achieve our most positive states of mind when we are striving toward some goal.

When a goal is in sight we work extra hard, using all our energies and resources to make the last final surge toward it. Goals give us something to aim at in the future. Without goals you will end up where random chance will take you. Goals will help you take control of your life. So it is vital to know where you are going. If you don't know where you are going you're going nowhere and indeed you may finish up somewhere else, somewhere you don't really want to be. All successful people have clearly defined goals and they know what they have to do to achieve them. Once focused on your goals your inner geographical positioning system will keep you on track and provide the resources to get you there.

There is a part of the brain called the reticular activating system (RAS) which is critical in helping you achieve your goals. When you buy a particular model of car you suddenly see them all over the place. This is the minds way of reaffirming how wise you are and confirming to you that you have made a good decision. Similarly once you have committed to a particular goal you will see opportunities and resources all around you to help you achieve it. When you decide on a topic for a book, you tend to come across relevant information from many and diverse sources such as books, newspapers, magazines, television, and conversations with others to help you achieve your goal.

To reach your targets you need to maintain momentum. One way to keep up the momentum is to break larger goals into smaller more achievable ones. Accomplishing these bring you closer to your ultimate goal and thus builds momentum towards the final target. Having smaller goals makes the job of monitoring progress and taking corrective action as appropriate more manageable. The main obstacles to progress in achieving your goals are inertia and procrastination, which may lead you back into your comfort zone. People who procrastinate lack the focused attention to stick to the job on hand and get it done. One of the laws of physics states that a body in motion tends to stay in motion. You are like a plane on lift-off. You will need a large amount of energy to get you started but thereafter a small amount of energy will keep you going. Once going, you will need to continuously monitor and adjust your position so that you stay on track.

Daily priorities are the building blocks for achieving lifetime goals. Our priority goals should include career, family, finance, health and education. An interesting career will bring us joy and satisfaction. Making time for our family will bring us happiness, contentment and support. Money doesn't bring happiness but it will ensure that we can enjoy a comfortable lifestyle. Beyond a reasonable standard of living money will bring you less and less happiness. Looking after our health is likely to ensure a long productive and sickness free life. A good education will help us progress in our careers and live an interesting and fulfilling life and lifelong learning will help us keep up to date.

On the journey towards your goals be prepared for setbacks, obstacles and failures. From Abraham Lincoln to Steve Jobs, nearly every highly successful person has failed, lost or been rejected at some point in their lives. Don't dwell on past failures and negative experiences. Move on and learn from your experiences and mistakes. During our lifetimes we should be continually trying to reach goals and become the best we are capable of becoming in whatever we decide to do. Turn your goals into written affirmations so that they are always in the forefront of your mind. Review these affirmations daily. These affirmations should be expressed positively, in the present tense and should be personal.

> "The victory of success is half won when one gains the habit of setting goals and achieving them. Even the most tedious chore will become endurable as you parade through each day convinced that every task, no matter how menial or boring, brings you closer to fulfilling your dreams."
>
> Og Mandino

Smarts For Goals

SMARTS is well known acronym standing for Specific, Measurable, Achievable, Rewarded, Timely and Supported. It provides a memorable cue for bringing these critical factors to mind which are so essential to the achievement of worthwhile goals. Let's look at each of these:

S **S**pecific. Goals should be clear and in writing. People who write down their goals are more likely to stick to them and achieve them. Vague goals create vague results. Goals start as a thought but must be made specific, concrete and tangible. Goals must be supported by actions, programmes, timetables, schedules, resources and routines as otherwise they are mere wishful thinking. Optimists tend to set more specific goals than pessimists because they believe that they are achievable. Footballers know their aim is to score goals. To do this they must be highly trained and fit, have self-belief, adopt the right tactics, synchronise with their team-mates, outsmart the opposition, beat the goalkeeper and stick the ball in the net. You need three types of goals: daily, short-term and long-term. Daily goals are what you focus on right now. Prepare a 'to do list' and delete items from this list as you make progress. Achieving short-term goals inspires you to keep going. For example my long-term goal is to complete this book within twelve months and find a publisher. My short-term goal is to complete my first chapter within two weeks. My daily goal is to write sentences, paragraphs, sections and pages.

M **M**easurable. You will need to monitor the progress towards your goals. A plane is off course 99 per cent of the time. A pilot must continually take corrective action to keep the plane on course in order to reach the planned destination. Similarly you must take corrective action to keep you on target. Therefore it is important that you have interim targets on the journey to your goal. If you can't measure your progress you can't manage it. Meeting your daily goals will keep you on track. The control system says that when you set targets, you compare actual results with the targets, you then ascertain the variance or difference between the actual and the target and finally you take corrective action to put the actual situation back on target again. It is by a continuous process of feedback and corrections that we finally achieve our goal. Immediate feedback is important like in sport so that you can quickly take corrective action to rectify mistakes or inappropriate actions. This ensures that we keep on track to a successful outcome.

A **A**chievable. Goals should be realistic but challenging. Don't set yourself up for failure by having unrealistic goals as failure to achieve them may have a devastating effect on your morale. Goals should motivate you by stretching your abilities. They should be difficult but not too difficult to achieve as otherwise you will get frustrated, stressed and give up. Athletes are particularly good at setting themselves challenging goals. They constantly set themselves new personal bests improving on their existing performance standards. They are never satisfied with their existing standards but always strive to do better and better. You must have the ability in terms of competence, skills, and IQ to succeed and the time, resources and energy. You may have to acquire additional knowledge, skill and expertise to help you achieve your goal.

R Rewarded. Goals should inspire you. Think of the benefits, rewards and personal satisfaction that achievement of your goals will bring. Ask yourself regularly why you want to achieve a particular goal. This will help you keep motivated in times of difficulties and setbacks. Celebrate interim successes with your friends and compliment yourself on your success. Rewarding progress towards interim goals will keep you inspired, energised, confident and motivated.

T Timely. Organise your time by setting time targets to reach interim goals. Be specific; decide that you want to achieve your target by next week, next month or by next year. For example, if you want to lose weight by Christmas then you can work back from that date to set yourself a series of interim goals. There is an old saying that life is hard by the yard but by the inch it's a cinch. If you are falling behind you may need to invest extra time to achieve your goals on schedule. Time targets will help you gauge your progress and give you something concrete to aim for. Time constraints concentrate the mind and create a sense of urgency. Things that can be done at any time are never done at all!

S Supported. Your values and beliefs must be congruent with your goals. Obviously if one of your values is honesty you shouldn't contemplate making money by unethical means. Most of us are not completely self-sufficient so that we are likely to need the support of others to help us achieve our goals. A mentor or coach may encourage you, provide you with vital information and keep you focused on task. From time to time you may also need to reassess your goals. If you experience repeated failures it may be time to disengage and try something else. You may need to adjust the time frame in which you hope to achieve your goals because of changed circumstances. Sometimes you may even need to abandon certain goals and establish entirely new ones. It is healthier to give up and switch to a new goal if an existing one is unattainable for whatever reason.

> "The goal you set must be challenging. At the same time it should be realistic and attainable, not impossible to reach. It should be challenging enough to make you stretch, but not so far that you break."
>
> Rick Hansen

Summary

Having goals and pursuing them energetically is probably the most important ingredient to a successful and fulfilling life. Research shows that those who make goals and write them down are more successful than those who don't do so.

Pursuing goals plays an important part in leading a contented and happy life. Goals give you hope and a purpose to strive for. Life without hope is not worth living. As soon as one goal is achieved we should replace it with another. Life should be a continuous process of pursuing worthwhile challenges and goals.

Visions use the power of your mind to create the future you want. A mission crystallises the vision into concrete written terms. All acts of creativity, invention and initiative start with a vision.

In our formal education we are not taught how to set achievable worthwhile goals. They don't realise the importance of goals to achieving success in life. Ignorance or fear of failure is a real obstacle to setting goals. The SMARTS system of goal setting will help us set more meaningful and purposeful goals.

Five Activities to Improve Your Goal Setting Skills

1. Decide on an action plan to achieve your goals. Decide what you want, plan what you need to do to get it, take the necessary action, compare the result you get with what you want and then vary your actions until you get the result that you want. Practical tools to help you get what you want would include to-do-lists, schedules, timetables and action plans. Action plans are the practical things you need to do in the short-term and long-term to achieve your goals.

2. Consider a vision of the future person you want to become. Convert this into a mission statement by translating the vision into words. Write these words down and pin them up in a prominent place to continually remind you and inspire you about your mission.

3. Compare your core values with your vision, mission and goals. Make sure they are congruent.

4. Apply the SMARTS system to your goals. Make sure your goals are specific, measurable, achievable, rewarded, timely and supported. Research shows you are more likely to achieve your goals if you write them down and feel you are being held accountable. So let family and friends know about your goals.

5. Pursue goals that interest you, meet your needs and that use your talents. Draw up goals for the important areas of your life such as career, family, health, recreation and finance. Write these down on cards and consult them frequently.

Planning

- **Why should you plan?**
- **What is a contingency plan?**
- **What's involved in the process of planning?**
- **Why career and financial planning is important?**
- **Why plan for retirement?**

Introduction

Without plans goals will never be achieved and you will drift aimlessly through life without achieving anything worthwhile. You need more than good intentions, wishful thinking and vague commitments to achieve a goal. Just like goals you will need to draw up plans for all the important areas of your life including finance, career and retirement. Our plans should be proactive, flexible and subject to a time limit. Contingency plans should be drawn up for different scenarios so that if things go wrong you will be able to cope. Draw up a personal timeline to get an overall perspective on your life to date and your dreams for the future. Plan your career so that you do not drift aimlessly through life. Finally, plan for your retirement, so that you will be financially secure, and have peace of mind when you retire.

Plans

A plan is a systematic way of achieving a goal. It is a method of doing something that is worked out in detail and written down before it is begun. You need a written plan so that you can think things through in detail, and review the accomplishment of targets as you go along. You will need plans for different areas of your life including finance, career and ultimately retirement. In practice people spend more time planning their holidays and weekly grocery spend than they do planning the important and critical aspects of their lives. In the modern materialistic world the importance of planning to a successful and prosperous life is not acknowledged and postponed gratification like doing without or saving is not encouraged. The convenience consumerist economy creates the psychological attitude of wanting it now rather than planning, saving, preparing and waiting. Marketing people exploit this human failing to their own advantage by encouraging us to spend and spend. Credit cards facilitate the process of instant gratification.

The importance of planning is not something new. Even thousands of years ago the pyramids of Egypt, the only one of the Seven Wonders of the World still standing, were planned in detail before they were built. Rome planned to take over the known world and succeeded in establishing the Roman Empire through conquest and great feats of civil engineering such as roads, bridges and aqueducts. All great battles in history were meticulously planned before they were undertaken. Great military leaders such as Napoleon came to prominence because of their great planning abilities. Great mountaineers and explorers such as Edmund Hillary and Ernest Shackleton spent many months planning and procuring the necessary manpower, provisions and resources, and getting benefactors for their hazardous adventures. In successful companies planning for the future in the form of strategic plans is now the norm.

A goal without a plan is just a wish. No worthwhile goal just happens. It must be planned and action taken to make it happen. For example, many months of preparation and training would go into planning to reach the North Pole or climbing Mount Everest. People would need to be acclimatised for the uniquely cold weather conditions, in top physical condition and mentally and physically prepared for the potential hazards that may arise on such journeys. These difficult tasks must be planned in detail, practised in simulated conditions and action steps taken to make it a reality. Sponsorships will be needed to cover the considerable cost of such undertakings. All of this must be combined with hard work, dedication and determination to make it happen.

"Four steps to achievement: Plan purposefully. Prepare prayerfully. Proceed positively. Pursue persistently. "
William A. Ward

Famous Meticulous Planners

Roald Amundsen (1872-1928) was a Norwegian explorer with ambitions to be the first man to reach the North Pole. He successfully navigated the North-West Passage in 1903 with a crew of six. As a youth in Norway he slept with the window open in order to acclimatise himself to the cold in preparation for the day when he would explore the Polar Regions. He became fascinated with Antarctica at 25 when he first saw its frozen terrain. He abandoned the objective of being the first to reach the North Pole when news broke that Robert Peary had got there first. He then set his eyes on the South Pole. In 1911 he became the first man to reach the South Pole ahead of Robert Scott. Earlier Shackleton had attempted to reach the South Pole but was forced to abort the attempt just 97 miles short of his goal. Amundsen had carefully studied Shackleton's attempt in order to learn from his mistakes before meticulously planning for his own expedition.

Amundsen was known for his superb organisational, planning and logistical skills. Like Shackleton he was careful to pick the appropriate personality mix for his polar expedition with planned activities to keep them occupied during the cold and dark Antarctic winter. When they reached base camp, depots of stores and equipment were set up in preparation for the trek to the South Pole in spring. Unlike Shackleton, Amundsen was known to be a taciturn character, but at the same time regarded by his men as firm but fair. He knew that the sled dogs would be crucial to the expedition and so picked dogs that were equipped by centuries of natural selection for survival in the Antarctic. In addition, Amundsen's ship The Fram was specially built for polar conditions. Shackleton's ship was not suitable for purpose and had been crushed by the ice leaving him and his men stranded on floating seasonal ice. The Fram was a round bottomed ship that was about a third as wide as it was long and this design was meant to prevent it from being crushed, and it performed perfectly as planned.

Just like Amundsen people who undertake degrees or professional qualifications must plan meticulously if they want to succeed. The plan will be based on the yearly programme of studies set down by the college or professional institute. In response to this the student will set down a programme of study to achieve the examinations set at the end of the academic year. In addition assignments may have to be completed and a thesis done in the final year. All of these have to be planned for in the form of appropriate time management and resource commitments for research and compilation. Plans should be broken down into manageable steps. We should set short-term indicators as interim targets to check we are still on course to our goal.

Our plans should not be set in stone but should be flexible and capable of revision and change. On the way to our targets we should try to anticipate and overcome problems and learn from our mistakes. If something is not working we should do something different. If you keep on doing the same thing you'll get the same results. We should not become creatures of habit and get stuck in a particular way of doing things. Einstein's definition of insanity is when you continue to repeat over and over the same practice, hoping to get different results.

The three basic questions of planning are: Where do you want to go? When do you want to arrive? And how do you get there? Learn from what others have done in the past. There is no point in reinventing the wheel. No matter what your goals are in life people somewhere have planned, pursued and accomplished similar goals. If you need help, ask for it. In the Bible it states: ask and you shall receive, seek and you shall find, knock and it shall be opened. It is surprising the amount of help and support that is available if you only ask. Knowledge is power, so seek out the knowledge and expertise you need to reach your goals. However, you must act on it. Remember most people are willing to help if asked.

"He who every morning plans the transactions of the day and follows out that plan, carries a thread that will guide him through the maze of the most busy life. But where no plan is laid, where the disposal of time is surrendered merely to the chance of incidence, chaos will soon reign."

Victor Hugo

Contingency Plans

If things go wrong you need back up plans for each eventuality so that you can take corrective action to put them right. While you are still employed create a fallback position such as doing some consulting work or freelance work on a part-time basis so that you have something to do when the unexpected happens. Job threats like redundancies, new responsibilities, pay cuts, divestments, mergers and acquisitions are commonplace in the modern business world. You should think through potential problems and work out solutions so that you are not caught off-guard if things don't work out according to plan. On a national level civil authorities have contingency plans for major disasters such as hurricanes, storms and floods; and ship, road, rail and air plane accidents. They rehearse these plans so that people are efficiently trained and know exactly what to do in the event of such emergencies and disasters.

Most successful people have experienced failure on their journey to their goals. They are ultimately successful because they pick themselves up, learn from their mistakes and start all over again. In addition, contingency plans should enable you to cope with unexpected opportunities that may come across your path. It is important that worthwhile opportunities when they come along, even if not planned for, are exploited to your advantage. As you are no doubt aware everything in life cannot be planned for as it is impossible to foresee the future and provide for every eventuality. It would be foolish if good opportunities were ignored just because they did not feature in your original plans.

Some of 'Murphy's Laws' are timely to bring to mind in this context. One states that whatever can go wrong will go wrong. Another states that the worst thing that can go wrong will go wrong at the worst possible time and cost the most money. Still another one states that anything you decide to fix will take longer and cost more than anticipated. Although humorous there is a grain of truth in these laws. In practice you must be capable of handling the good and the bad things that happen on the way to your goals.

No matter how bad you feel things are at the moment they are likely to get better. In Ireland we are currently going through

(2011) the worst recession in living memory. Three years of constant bad news on the economy is colouring our perception, leading us to gloss over the positives and focus on the gloom and doom. Psychologists call this the "recency bias" or the tendency to believe that what happens in the future will look similar to what happened in the immediate past. Also, because of the complex way our brains comprehend risk, it takes far more good news to build our confidence than it takes bad news to destroy it. Our brains are naturally programmed for negativity. In the past few years we have lost faith and trust in institutions that were pillars of society such as the banks, government, church, medical, police and legal professions. These feelings have affected our ability to analyse things in a logical way. Just make sure your contingency plans cover you if bad things happen in the future.

> "Expect the best, plan for the worst, and prepare to be surprised."
>
> Denis Waitley

Process of Planning

The process of planning can be thought of in a systematic way as follows:

1. Identify your goal as set out in chapter one. Plan backwards from your future long-term goals. As you approach the present time your plans will become more specific. Detailed plans are needed to achieve your short-term goals. These are daily and weekly plans. Less detailed plans are needed for medium-term goals and outline plans are needed for long-term goals.

2. Develop a timeframe. Have a start time, completion time and interim stages for review. A timescale will ensure that you achieve things on target. The time scale will be in three parts: short-term covering up to 1 month, medium-term covering up to 1 year and long-term covering the period of more than a year and up to five years. Consider the resources you will need to make it happen such as time, money, materials and equipment

and help from others. Also, consider what expertise you will you need to acquire to bring your plans to fruition. To do this you must identify your existing competencies with those you will need to accomplish your purpose. You may need to learn additional knowledge and acquire more expertise to achieve what you want to do.

3. Identify the stages between the start and finish. Stages should be broken down into small manageable steps so that you know the actions you need to take each day. Goals are accomplished through the systematic and successful achievement of steps.

4. Identify challenges and solutions. There will always be setbacks and obstacles to your goals. Some of these can be anticipated and planned for. Others will come out of the blue but nevertheless will have to be dealt with and solved to your satisfaction as they arise.

5. Have rewards for achieving each stage. Acknowledging and celebrating your success with others at each stage will inspire and motivate you to keep going.

6. Revisit your plan and goal daily to ascertain what needs to be done to keep you on track.

7. Adjust as necessary. If things are not going according to plan you may have to make adjustments and take corrective action to get you back on track again.

8. Make a commitment to keep going until you reach your destination. Reflect on the benefits of achieving your goal as thinking about these will keep you motivated. Consider the good feelings and pride you will experience when you get to your destination.

"Planning is bringing the future into the present so that you can do something about it now."

Alan Lakein

Personal Timelines

Timelines are a useful method of recording the major events in your life. The timeline will give you a quick overview of the past, present and proposed future stages of your life. It is a good way of seeing what you have accomplished to arrive at your present stage in life and what your dreams, hopes, aspirations and goals are for the future.

If you use the personal timeline for planning for the future many life events are highly predictable. For example young people finish secondary school in their late teens. Those who go on to university and graduate are in their early twenties. They then go on to start a career. Many people settle down and get married, and start a family in their mid or late twenties. During your thirties you are likely to make rapid progress in your career while middle age is a period of consolidation and brings the peak earning years. This also marks the end of child bearing for women and the start of the process of children leaving the family home and starting their own families. Most people retire in their sixties.

As we get older we are likely to experience more health problems. Grandchildren and, if we live long enough, great grandchildren will enter our lives. Eventually, we will reach the end of our life cycle and die. If you ever want to write your memoir or life-story and leave a legacy for your children a timeline is a good starting point.

How to Do a Personal Timeline

The following are suggestions for creating your own personal timeline:

- Divide your life into decades. For example if you are now 40 years old divide it into four segments. The first segment will be from birth to age 10. The second segment will be from 10 to 20. The third segment will be from 20 to 30 and the fourth segment will be from 30 to 40.

- Now consider five major events that happened to you in each decade and the major decisions you took to deal with them. These can be happy events, traumatic events, illnesses and major transitions in your life such as your birth, starting school, entering college, graduating, your first job, your first love affair and first promotion, the date you got married and so on.

- Start with the earliest significant event and move forward to the present time. For each significant event record the date and a few words explaining why it was important in your personal history. It is essential to keep the events in correct chronological order so that you can group and overview significant stages. Write the dates on the line from left to right. Bringing past events to mind, no matter how difficult, can have a soothing affect on your mind. To make the timeline more memorable you could illustrate each date with photos, diplomas, achievements, symbols or cartoons.

- It may take you more than one sitting to complete your timeline. Then you can update it periodically. The personal timeline should not be just about the past but should project forward into the future. List the events you hope to happen in the future guided by your dreams, hopes, aspirations and goals. As your future evolves compare it with what you anticipated.

- Your personal timeline should be for your eyes only.

"If you don't design your own life plan, chances are you'll fall into someone else's plan. And guess what they have planned for you? Not much."

Jim Rohn

Personal Financial Planning

The vast majority of people are not financially literate. Many people have a deep aversion to maths and figures. The financially aware tend to budget carefully and live within their means while the financially unaware spend recklessly and get into debt. Some people are so financially illiterate that they don't know what they have in the bank from day to day and are often surprised when their bank rings them to say that they are overdrawn. If you feel you need help in understanding finance reading a book or taking a course in personal finance may be beneficial.

One of the chief sources of marital disharmony and unhappiness is arguments over money issues and these are more likely in a recession. There are many toxic financial behaviours including compulsive spending, excessive frugality, serial borrowing and hoarding money, as well as feelings of guilt and shame about poverty and wealth. In many instances these could be avoided if people became more sensible and disciplined in dealing with their financial affairs. The following are some useful tips to help you manage and control your finance:

• Calculate your net worth. Your net worth is the difference between your assets and liabilities. If your assets exceed your liabilities you have equity. On the other hand if your liabilities exceed your assets you have negative equity. Falling property prices means many people are in negative equity for the first time because their mortgage exceeds the current market value of their house. To calculate your net worth list all your assets and liabilities. Your assets include items like your house, car, furniture, domestic appliances, personal computers, jewellery, current account balances, deposit accounts, shares and investments. Calculate what these would be worth if you cashed them in or sold them in the morning. Follow the same process for your liabilities. Liabilities include mortgages, car loans, hire purchase, credit card balances owed and other debts you may have incurred. Subtract your total liabilities from your total assets. The result is your net worth. If this amount is negative, it means that you are living beyond your means and should take immediate action to rectify the situation. Your objective should be to create assets and wealth rather than incur liabilities. It is a good idea to build up cash reserves to help you overcome difficult times and pay for luxury items rather than relying on a loan secured on the equity of your house especially for ordinary consumption items such as holidays and flat screen televisions. If property prices fall you could end up bankrupt. The great recession of 2008 has taught us that when it comes to building wealth you can't rely on rising stock markets and property prices. We now realise that property prices and stocks and shares can fall as well as rise. Some retirees overinvested in financial stocks such as bank shares and found their retirement fund decimated. They hadn't followed the basic rule of investment and spread their risk over a variety of investments such as cash deposits and different shares.

- Construct a cash budget. Calculate your income and expenditure and show them on a spreadsheet. A good way of doing this is to look over a year's worth of bank records and credit-card receipts. If you don't keep good records you could track your expenses for a few weeks to get a handle on your actual expenditure. The cash budget should be done on a weekly basis if you are weekly paid or on a monthly basis if you are monthly paid. Your income would include your wage or salary, bonuses, dividends received, royalties received, interest received and any other sources of income. Your expenditure would include mortgage repayments or rent, upkeep and maintenance of your home, car repayments and running costs including motor tax, insurance, petrol and servicing, food costs, electricity, heating, insurance, television license, phone, mobile phone, cable charges, internet charges, postage, stationery and so on. Subtract your expenditure from your income and the result will be a surplus or a deficit. If the result is a deficit you should review your expenditure and cut back on non-essentials especially in these times of job cuts and pay cuts. Suggestions include cutting back on dining out, spending less on clothes and hobbies and reducing your electricity consumption by investing in energy saving devices. You can also cut down on the use of the car for short journeys and walk instead saving fuel with the added bonus of keeping fit and healthy. Consider getting books on loan from a public library rather than purchasing them and save a considerable amount of cash. If you are lucky to have a surplus you can invest and increase your savings with the added bonus of earning some interest.

- Credit cards. Some people have multiple credit cards which is an incentive to spend. Holding fewer credit cards reduces the chances that you will miss a payment and get hit with a substantial penalty. Consider getting rid of some or all of your credit cards. They are convenient but contribute to the "spend, spend, spend" mentality. A debit or laser card could be substituted for them which will help you live within your means. With a laser card you must have money in the bank before you can spend. Credit cards attract substantial interest charges if the credit terms are exceeded. Paying by cash will make you more aware of the value of money and living within your means, how finite money is and how much you can spend at any given time. If you haven't the money you must do without. This creates the financial discipline of buying the things you really need rather than the things that you want and can't afford. It therefore cuts out impulse buying. Generally, it should be your aim to save for the things that you can't afford immediately rather than funding them through loans and incurring penalty and interest charges. If you have multiple sources of loans it would be sensible to consolidate them into one and thus save on interest and administrative costs. Money matters are one of the chief sources of stress particularly in times of recession. You can eliminate this stress by practising financial frugality and discipline.

- Save a proportion of your earnings. It is a good idea to save about 10 per cent or even more of your income if you can afford it. Saving is easier if it's automated such as a deduction at source scheme from your monthly salary. Money you never had will not be missed. This strategy is effective because it gets around the psychological phenomenon known as loss aversion. We hate any loss, but as we never see the money deducted at source, we won't experience the feeling of loss. You should increase your savings as your income goes up rather than living up to your income. Simplify your investments by reducing the number of accounts you invest in. This will reduce the amount of paperwork and help you manage and control your financial affairs more effectively while reducing administrative charges. Don't touch this money but leave it on deposit to grow with compound interest. You may need a reserve fund if hard times come your way. In the future, poor health, negative equity, redundancy, separation, divorce, bereavement and so on may drain your financial resources. It is times like these that you will appreciate the fact that you have put money away for such contingencies. Put aside enough money to cover job searching and living expenses for at least six months in the event that you become unemployed. A lot depends on how secure your job is. Obviously a job in the public sector is more secure than one in the private sector. The greater the risk of unemployment the larger your emergency fund should be.

- Getting value for money. When buying items like shoes, clothes, furniture and equipment buy quality. It lasts longer, and such purchases will save you money in the long-term. Bargains look attractive but they are often fool's gold. They often look great and entice you to buy things that you don't really need but feel that you have to in order to avail of the great deal offered. For example recently I bought a pair of shoes that looked like a great bargain but they fell apart after only a few weeks. Get at least three quotations if you are planning to get major work done on your house or garden. You'll be surprised how estimates differ for the same work! Shop around for your car insurance. If you add your home insurance you may save a considerable amount of money on a package deal. Have a similar strategy for your major utility expenditures such as electricity, heating and phone charges. Cutting down on the costs of everyday living, such as bringing a prepared lunch to work rather than eating out can yield substantial savings over time. Eliminate impulse buying from your life such as buying clothes or shoes that initially seem attractive and then never wearing them. For your weekly groceries, shop around for greater value. It may be worthwhile to avail of online bill-paying through your bank. It eliminates travel time and cuts down on postage and stationery. Buying on the internet is often cheaper than buying directly in shops. Renting a house is better than buying when property prices are falling. On the other hand buying a house is better value for money when property prices are rising. If you decide to buy a house stick to the rule of thumb that a mortgage of up to three times your gross annual salary is affordable. Also you should have accumulated about 10 per cent of the price in personal savings. During the boom years of rising stock markets and property prices, this rule of thumb was ignored by borrowers and suspended by the banks who often covered up to 120 per cent of the entire price of a house with a loan, causing financial distress to many when the good times came to an end as property prices collapsed.

"Becoming wealthy is not a matter of how much you earn, who your parents are, or what you do. It is a matter of managing your money properly."

Noel Whittaker

Career Planning

Career planning includes setting goals, exploring options, and formulating plans to steer your career in the desired direction. Just like any other area of your life your career should be purposefully planned rather than left to chance. Start with a mission statement which is a statement of what you want to accomplish with your life. Set down your career goals and decide how you are going to achieve them. It will probably be by a combination of getting the right experience, having regard to your interests and aptitudes, acquiring the right qualifications, being guided by a good mentor, and making the right career choices and job moves at the right time. Career planning is about:

- Seeing the big picture and knowing what you want, deciding how you will achieve it and focusing on where you want to go. Even though my day job was as a financial controller I always had a compelling desire to lecture in a third level college. So when an opportunity came my way I took up a part-time post lecturing to business and professional accountancy students at night. Moonlighting is a way of testing the waters and acquiring skills and experience and to sample what the work will be like before you burn any bridges. Preparing lectures and handouts also gave me an opportunity to develop my writing skills. When the opportunity came up for early retirement I was able to avail of it and get a full-time lecturing position and develop further my interest in non-fiction writing.

- Plan significant events in your life such as career and job moves and promotions. Make sure these events are taking you towards your ultimate goal. Switching jobs without purpose is not a good strategy even if it enhances your salary in the short-term. Switching jobs must be part of a purposeful career development strategy to help you acquire the experience and skills that you will need to achieve your long term ambitions.

- Acquire the right experience and the right qualifications having regard to your capabilities, interests and aspirations. Anyone thinking of returning to college will have to decide between daytime and evening programmes. Evening programmes take longer to complete but will permit you to work during the day. These programmes may be very flexible offering evening, weekend and online schedules.

- Be guided by a good mentor and take a Myers-Briggs Type Indicator test to ensure that you understand what motivates you and that your career ambitions are compatible with your personality. This is a popular questionnaire used by some organisation to assess the type of personality you have and is available on the internet. Many successful people attribute their success to having a good mentor and being aware of their unique strengths. Studies show that four out of five promotions are influenced by a mentor higher up in the company. In addition take an aptitude test to confirm that your choice of career is validated by the facts.

- Know where you want to be at different stages of your life. As you progress through life your needs and aspirations will change and so will the type of jobs that suit these needs.

- Plan your career moves by making sure that job switches and promotions take you in the direction you want to go.

- Try to be in the right place at the right time so that you can exploit opportunities as they arise.

"Choose a job you love and you will never have to work a day in your life."

Confucius

Aspire Model of Self-Development

The value of a strategic plan for an individual is the same as that for an organisation. It provides a clear sense of direction and sets out a series of steps that will take you to your desired future. It will help you exploit future opportunities and successfully deal with future setbacks and so keep you on track to your future goal. ASPIRE is a personal career strategic plan and an acronym which stands for Assess, SWOT, Plan, Implement, Review and Evaluate. It is a strategic and systematic process of self development in that it looks at and plans for the long term. It matches your career aspiration and expectations with the strategic path you must take to achieve them. It matches your personal career objectives with the organisation's strategic human resource needs and objectives. It prepares you to anticipate and cope with a turbulent competitive job market. Let's now examine each of these steps in more detail:

A   Assess your current position. Decide where you are now and the resources you currently have such as skills, experience and qualifications. Decide on your future desired state – where you want to be in a few years time. Consider how you can get there such as acquiring additional skills, experience and qualifications, and how long it will take. Successful people think about missions, roles, values, visions and goals and these will be an essential part of your career plan. A mission is discovering the purpose of your life. Your mission might be to become the best you can be in your chosen profession and to make a difference in the world. A role is the various identities you have to assume to achieve your mission. Values are the things that are important to you such as the level of independence a job allows or the chance to be creative or use your initiative. Vision translates your life purpose into images specific enough to inspire. Without a vision, you don't know where you are going and without assessing your current position you don't know where you are starting from. To develop your vision you will need to do research. Read relevant books and journals, search the internet, talk to others who have done what you would like to do, and try to develop a detailed sense of what the life you want really involves. Goals are the specific results you want to achieve to fulfil your mission. The goals should be consistent and congruent with your values.

S   SWOT. This stands for strengths, weaknesses, opportunities and threats. These are part of the strategic planning process but can be successfully adapted to career planning as well. Strengths might include your positive can do attitude, determination, resilience, presentation skills, experience, qualifications, and good analytical abilities. Weaknesses might include a lack of certain critical skills essential for career advancement, a tendency to harbour negative thoughts, be reactive and procrastinate. An opportunity might be an offer of promotion or an overseas assignment while a threat might be the possibility of company contraction, closure and redundancy. Your aim is to do jobs and work assignments that will help you achieve your career goals. Carry out a SWOT analysis of your capabilities. Try to turn weaknesses into strengths and threats into opportunities. Redundancy has often been turned into an opportunity where people have become successfully self-employed, releasing hidden talents that they never knew they possessed. Do a skills self-assessment to discover the skills you have and those you need to succeed in your chosen career. Don't ignore the skills you have acquired through hobbies and volunteer work as these may be useful in helping your career or even in finding a new job if your existing one disappears. Match the skills you will need with the anticipated changes in the company and external environment. Acquire those skills that will differentiate you and give you a competitive advantage in the working environment.

P   Plan. Draw up an action plan to achieve your long-term and short-term goals. Be as specific as possible with time, money and other resources clearly set out. You are primarily responsible for your own development. If you don't make it happen, nobody else will. In the long term you may need to acquire specific experience or do an MBA or professional qualification to give you the competitive edge and help you get ahead in the future. Draw up a schedule to determine the time you will need to devote to this goal. Generally, the more you learn the more you'll earn. In the short-term, you will need to continually update your knowledge, skills and experience. Upgrade your skills by attending courses, networking with experts in your field, listening to educational CDs and watching educational DVDs, and reading self-development books.

I Implement. Without taking appropriate action nothing gets done. Decide the steps to be taken and the deadlines that will make them happen. Reduce it to manageable (daily/weekly) steps. Focus your concentration by doing one thing at a time. Write daily "to do lists" into your diary. Tick them off as you accomplish them. This will concentrate your mind, give you a sense of purpose, accomplishment and satisfaction and inspire you to continue.

R Review. Write down the rewards to yourself when you have achieved your goals and sub-goals. Compare your actual performance and achievements against your goals. Vividly imagine your success. What will you feel, hear, see and do on the achievement of your goals. What praise, compliments, recognition and respect will you earn? See yourself graduating with that MBA or professional qualification! Experience the elation and pride of the occasion! See yourself winning that long awaited and desired promotion! Imagine the scene and sense the feelings of happiness and pride associated with the promotion!

E Evaluate. How successful have you been in achieving your personal development goals? What can you learn from your setbacks, rejections, disappointments and mistakes? What corrective action do you need to take in the future to put things right and get back on target again? Evaluation is an ongoing process of continuous learning and personal improvement against targets until you achieve your desired outcomes.

> "Change is the law of life, and those who look only to the past or present are certain to miss the future."
>
> John F. Kennedy

Take Responsibility for Your Career

Don't wait around for other people to do things for you. If you do you will be sorely disappointed. Take responsibility for your own career. People have their own interests at heart rather than yours. Determine the direction of your own career and make it work for you. In life everything comes to an end. This means you should be prepared for the day when your current job ends by being equipped to move to the next stage of your career. The following are some points you should keep in mind:

- Keep your CV up to date. Review your CV every six months so that the most recent job experiences and accomplishments are recorded.

- Maintain and build a strong network with business and professional colleagues. Attend professional institute meetings and network with professionals from other organisations. Become actively involved in your professional institute and become known as a person who gets things done. Develop a data base of people who have the potential to help you in your career and stay in touch with them. These contacts may provide you with emotional support, information, career advice or even recommend you for employment or promotion. You may never know when you need to call on them for help. Some people are so obsessively focused on their current jobs that they become very inward looking, and fail to maintain contact with the outside world and keep up to date with trends and developments.

- Create a personal brand. Just like a product you should consider what differentiates and makes you stand apart from the competition. What are the unique strengths, skills, characteristics, qualifications and achievements that distinguish you from others? Perhaps you have very good communication and interpersonal relationship skills? Perhaps you are good at working in groups and inspiring and motivating people? Perhaps you are a good problem solver and creative thinker? These are the type of labels you want people to associate with you when they speak your name. Build up a reputation for being dependable, trustworthy, approachable, co-operative and delivering work on time. Outside of work make a name for yourself by presenting papers at professional conferences and writing articles in professional journals.

- Know when it's time to move on. If you have achieved what you want to achieve in your current position and realise

31

your career is beginning to stall, then perhaps it's time to reassess your position by exploring the options and move on to new challenges. Even a career change may be possible. If you enjoy reading, learning, debating, critical thinking and sharing ideas, a teaching or lecturing position may be a good job fit.

- Become a lifelong learner. Make sure you keep up to date by attending courses, reading journals and books and keeping in touch with the latest trends and developments in your field of expertise. When you achieve goals, set new ones so that you are continually stretched and challenged.

- Do the appropriate research when considering career moves. Consult with career management experts and research on the internet. Talk to people who are currently in the field. Undertake skill and personality assessments to identify the career moves that are appropriate for your unique talents. We are all born with unique gifts and most of us gravitate towards our areas of aptitude and strength.

- Have regard for the competition and make sure you are ahead of them. Find out what they are doing and match and exceed their qualifications and expertise.

> "An intelligent plan is the first step to success. The man who plans knows where he is going, knows what progress he is making and has a pretty good idea when he will arrive."
> Basil S. Walsh

Retirement Planning

People should prepare for the psychological and social aspects of retirement as much as the financial aspects. Due to increased longevity retirement is no longer a short trip on the way to the grave. Improved medical treatments for heart disease, stroke, cancer and other diseases has expanded the life span and extended individuals ability to remain healthy, socially involved and active. Improved education, diet, hygiene, exercise and health care have also improved the longevity of people. Retirement should now be viewed as a potentially substantial life stage involving the need to restructure time, change role identities, redefine social and interpersonal relationships, and set new goals and purpose in life. After all you are likely to spend 20 years in retirement, equivalent to about half of your previous working life. So make the most of the opportunity to create a career in retirement and do the things you really want to do by planning for it!

Retirement should be viewed as an opportunity to pursue things you are really interested in but previously hadn't time to do because of work and family commitments. It is an opportunity to be active and involved, to start new activities, to meet new people, to pursue your interests and hobbies, to spend more time with your family, to visit new countries and to set new goals. People most satisfied in retirement are those who made the decision to retire themselves, and who view retirement not merely as an escape from the stress of everyday work, but as a challenge and the start of a new opportunity. Work provides us with a sense of identity and gives us a chance to mix with other people, fill our time productively and make a contribution to society. We want to remain useful and productive and mentally challenged. So it's important that you continue to work after retirement even if it's only on a part-time or volunteer basis.

Retiring from a job can create a great void and sense of loss, especially for those strongly committed to work, and can lead to depression, confusion and unhappiness in retirement. Research indicates that people who continue working full time after retiring from their career jobs are significantly less satisfied with retirement that those who work part-time. Also retirees who are married report greater happiness than those who are not. This finding applies equally to men and women and is consistent across cultures. People who do pre-retirement courses are better prepared intellectually, emotionally and psychologically for the challenge and happier when they retire than those who don't. Retirement planning is essential for professional sportspeople who retire in their mid-thirties and are often faced with a very difficult transition to the "real" world of work. As sportspeople they were probably very well paid and treated as celebrities. They will miss the excitement of the roar of the stadium crowd and the camaraderie of their teammates. They are now just unemployed people with no particular skills looking for a job. They probably have poor educational and social skills as many footballers start their apprenticeships very young and so are deprived of a formal third level education. When they retire many choose to get a job related to sport such as sport management and coaching but few are successful in this area. For example, Roy Keane the former captain of Manchester United has found the transition to management traumatic and a less than successful experience. It doesn't automatically follow that because you were a very successful footballer that you are going to be equally successful in the stressful and demanding job of sport management as a different skills set is needed.

> "Age is only a number, a cipher for the records. A man can't retire his experience. He must use it."
>
> Bernard Baruch

The Importance of a Pension

Invest in a retirement fund as early in your working career as possible. The earlier you do so the greater the fund you will have built up. You should aim to save at least 15 per cent of your gross income, including the contribution from your employer. Your aim should be to be able to afford the same lifestyle in retirement that you currently enjoy. This should be invested in a diversified portfolio. Financial security has a powerful impact on retirement contentment, peace of mind and satisfaction. Research shows that having no financial worries in retirement is correlated with positivity, better health and happiness, while financial strain is correlated with stress, depression and a negative self-concept.

In the 2008 recession many retirees lost money by investing in a narrow range of shares such as financials and property. In Ireland some retirees who invested all their retirement savings in Allied Irish Bank and Bank of Ireland lost all their savings even though these were considered blue chip investments a few years previously. Similarly those who invested in property incurred substantial losses when property prices collapsed. This highlights the importance of applying the portfolio concept to your investments and so diversifying and spreading your risk.

Many companies now have their own pension schemes and in some cases they are compulsory for employees to join. These schemes usually provide for a reduced pension for a surviving spouse. The pension contributions are deducted at source from your salary which means saving for your retirement is automated and painless. Remember, the state pension will only provide you with a subsistence level existence in your old age. Research shows that retirees who have a reliable source for a pension are happier than those who don't have one. You don't want the stress of financial worries to upset your peace of mind in your retirement.

There has been a move away from defined-benefit retirement schemes to defined-contribution retirement plans in the last few years. Defined-benefit retirement schemes are index linked and give you a guaranteed pension for life. They usually give a pension equivalent to half of final salary plus a lump sum of one and a half times final salary. They are thus very expensive from an employer's point of view especially as people are now living longer and so employers are trying to move away from them. In a defined benefits scheme the employer underwrites the vast majority of costs so that any shortfall in the fund will have to be made up by the employer. Defined contribution schemes shift the risk away from employers to individuals. This has made the level of retirement income far less certain.

One of the best ways of reducing your living costs when you retire is to pay off your mortgage before you retire. Eliminate your loan over the final years by making extra payments if necessary. In addition, you should consider paying off any other debts you have such as credit card balances. Credit card payments can be a dead weight in your retirement as the payments have to be met irrespective of your more straightened financial circumstances. The more debt free you are in your retirement the greater your peace of mind and the happier you will be. It is a good idea to build up a cash reserve before you retire to draw down for emergencies.

If you are self-employed you can invest in your own pension scheme and get generous tax reliefs. When retired your pension will be taxed at the normal rate but you will be entitled to a tax free lump-sum. Your fund should be a judicial mix of shares, bonds and cash deposits. In any event you should consult a good financial planner to advise you.

A good financial planner is trustworthy and honest, thorough, experienced, objective, easy to get along with and unbiased. You should also consider joining a good deduction at source medical insurance scheme. Once you pay for your medical bills and submit receipts for costs incurred your medical insurance will reimburse you. Although expensive, medical insurance is a small price to pay for peace of mind. Retirees normally can contribute to the health insurance scheme of their former employers.

With your children reared you should consider downsizing the family home as this will achieve considerable savings. You should also consider trading in your present car for a smaller more fuel efficient one and thus save motor tax, insurance, servicing and petrol costs. If your children have left the family home and your house is paid for you may not need life insurance anymore. Retirement will give you an opportunity to switch from full-time work to part-time work and start a new career.

"Life is full of uncertainties. Future investment earnings and interest and inflation rates are not known to anybody. However, I can guarantee you one thing; those who put an investment program in place will have a lot more money when they come to retire than those who never get around to it."

Noel Whittaker

What Are You Waiting For?

Change begins with one small step and then another. So it is important to get started on your plan by taking the first step. Change starts with you. The only person you can change is yourself.

Summary

A good plan should be proactive, flexible and subject to a time limit. Proactive means that you take a series of actions in the future to achieve your goals. Flexible means your plan can be changed as needed in line with changing circumstances. A time limit provides targets and a sense of urgency. You will need contingency plans to deal with the unforeseen issues that will inevitably happen in your life. A personal timeline will give you a perspective on your life to date and on your dreams for the future. Financial planning will help you keep solvent. Career planning will help you achieve the career you desire. Retirement planning will help you feel secure and bring you peace of mind in the autumn of your years.

Five Activities to Improve Your Planning Skills

1. Calculate your net worth. List down all the assets you own. Then list down your liabilities or what you owe. Subtract your liabilities from your assets; the difference is your net worth. A minus figure means you are technically bankrupt and should take immediate corrective action to rectify the situation and make you solvent.
2. Get a grip on your day to day spending by preparing a cash budget and always living within your means. List down the sources of your total income for a month. Then list down all your expenditure. Subtract your expenditure from your income. If you show a surplus well done! If you show a deficit you are living beyond your means and you should take remedial action to reduce your outgoings.
3. Commit the ASPIRE model of career planning to memory. Follow this model to plan your future career.
4. Start paying into a pension scheme now! You'll need to be investing at least 15 to 20% of your earnings including your employer's contribution (if you are lucky enough to have a company pension scheme).
5. Create a personal timeline. For example if you are 30 years old divide your timeline into segments of 10 years. Think about and record on a timeline the important events in each decade of your life. Now project forward the things you would like to achieve in the next decade. Include here your dreams, hopes, aspirations and future goals. Draw up an action plan to bring these dreams, hopes and aspirations to fruition.

3

Interpersonal Relationships

- *Why are IPR, communications and feedback skills so important to success?*
- *What is the JOHARI model?*
- *How can I develop my EQ?*
- *How can I influence others?*

Introduction

An important ingredient of a successful life is the ability to get on with others. The JOHARI model is a practical tool designed to improve personal awareness and interpersonal communications. Managers maintain that listening is the most important communication skill for career success. Being aware of the barriers to listening will help you become a better person and a better communicator. Many people with a high Intelligence Quotient (IQ) but low Emotional Quotient (EQ) fail to succeed in life or progress in their careers. Being able to influence people to do what you want them to do will help you succeed in your personal life and in work. Without feedback you can't improve your behaviour or correct your mistakes and thus you can't improve and become better at what you do. Good manners cost nothing but will help you get along with others. Learn to accept your own limitations and those of others. Remember nobody is perfect!

IPR and success

An important aspect of a successful life is establishing and maintaining good relationships with others. This includes your family, friends, work colleagues and those you come in contact with everyday. Money can't buy happiness but good relationships do. In a world dominated by consumerism and materialism more is never enough. If you want to be happy make others happy and they in turn will make you happy.

Nobody likes being around someone who is always moaning and groaning. People like to be around those who are positive and friendly and make them feel comfortable, accepted and wanted. Making friends is one thing but putting in the time and effort to maintain them is another. In the modern world people spend more time online and watching television than they do socialising. Many people who live very busy and chaotic lives forget the importance of maintaining and nurturing human contact and so eventually lose their friends. Friendship needs to be appreciated, nurtured and looked after if it is to last. In addition to making new friends it is important to keep up contact with your old friends. Exploit modern media such as the internet, texting and Facebook to do this.

People like those whom they can trust. People who are trustworthy are positive, consistent, credible, capable, honest and reliable. People trust you because they know that you tell the truth, mean what you say, keep your promises and stick to your commitments. Trust means that people will take risks for you, do things for you, and stand by you in difficult times. We naturally trust experts and we show this every day by putting our lives in the hands of others when we board a plane, bus or train, hire a taxi or undergo surgery. Dishonesty and being unreliable undermines trust as does a failure to keep promises. A common mistake in interpersonal relationships is to overpromise and under-deliver as this causes disappointment and resentment. It is better to surprise and delight people and so under-promise and over-deliver. Win trust and respect by doing more than expected.

"Interpersonal communication and other so-called soft skills are what corporate recruiters crave most but find most elusive in MBA graduates. The major business schools produce graduates with analytical horsepower and solid command of the basics – finance, marketing and strategy. But soft skills such as communication, leadership and a team mentality sometimes receive cursory treatment."

Wall Street Journal

Relationships and your expectations about them can become a self-fulfilling prophecy. If your first serious relationship is a negative experience you could become trapped over and over again in self-destructive relationships and be primed for a lifetime of disappointments. The reverse is also true and you could be primed for a lifetime of happy relationships if your first relationship is a positive experience. You will expect people in the future to be similarly friendly and trustworthy and thus be more favourably disposed towards them. As trust increases you will disclose more about yourself making it more likely that they will react similarly and you are thus likely to become more emotionally and intimately involved with the other person.

Self-Awareness

The JOHARI model was developed in 1969 by Joe Luft and Harry Ingram (hence the name Johari which is derived from combining 'Joe' and 'Hari'). It has stood the test of time and is still widely used in training and coaching. It is designed to improve personal awareness and interpersonal communications. Breakdowns in relationships are the major reason for disputes and conflicts between people. A general law of interpersonal relations suggests that understanding between two people is best when they are both of the same minds. This means their awareness, attitudes, feelings, and communication styles are similar. The Johari window is only effective if people have an ongoing relationship with each other and are prepared to learn. It is divided into four windows called open, blind, hidden or closed and unknown.

- The open part is our public persona. This is the part of our personality including beliefs, behaviours, feelings and motivation which we share with others and is thus known to the outside world. Studies show that traits like extroversion, talkativeness, and dominance are easily observable both to the self and to others. The more we share information and understand each other the better, more productive, and mutually beneficial our interpersonal relationships will be. On the other hand, hidden agendas, lies, concealment, denial, deceit, or defensiveness hinder effective communication and trust between people.

- The blind part is the part of our personality including beliefs, behaviours, feelings and motivation known to others but not known to you. These may include thoughtlessness, defensiveness and inappropriate unconscious habits. This is likely to damage our personal relationships because other people will not understand the reason for our actions, concerns, thoughts and feelings. In addition, we are not aware of what is happening ourselves.

"Everything that irritates us about others can lead us to an understanding of ourselves."

Carl Gustav Jung

Sometimes eavesdropping may be an opportunity to discover what other people really think about you. I once had a manager who was usually in a bad mood in the mornings but whose mood improved in the afternoons. This was known by staff who were able to exploit this information effectively by approaching the manager in the afternoon knowing that they were more likely to get things approved or agreed.

	Your view of yourself (Known)	Your view of yourself (Unknown)
Other's view of you (Known)	Public Area	Blind Area
Other's view of you (Unknown)	Closed Area	Unknown Area

Figure 1: The Johari Window

- The hidden part or closed area is that part of our personality including beliefs, behaviours, feelings and motivation which is known to you but kept hidden from others. These may include your tendency to get anxious in crowds or your contempt for your work colleagues. People may feel if others knew certain negative things about them it would damage their image and reputation. People may feel ashamed of certain things that happened in the past or that are currently going on in their lives and so don't want others to know about them. We retain information about ourselves because it is a source of power and control.

- The unknown part is that part of our personality including beliefs, behaviours, feelings and motivation not known to others or to you. It is the unconscious part of our personality often developed and strongly influenced by our parents and peers when we were young children. It may include deep unconscious motives that drive your behaviour, such as the fact that your fierce ambition is fuelled by the need to prove wrong your parents' assumption that you will never amount to much. People have idiosyncrasies and annoying habits which they are unaware of but are very obvious to other people. If we are prepared to accept feedback about these from other people and take corrective action we will become better, more effective and more sensitive persons.

As time goes on and trust increases people become more transparent and begin to disclose more of themselves to their friends and close acquaintances by revealing secret or confidential information about themselves. This means that the blind area decreases and the open or public area increases. Poor communication and interpersonal relationships arise because our open window is small and so we are not in touch with our feelings and cannot respond appropriately to what we hear. In general people don't like others who are withdrawn and secretive.

Importance of Listening

Communications experts maintain that on average we spend 45 per cent of our time listening, 30 per cent speaking, 16 per cent reading and only 9 per cent writing. Managers rank listening as the most important communication skill for success in the workplace. Most people are poor listeners. Our ears enable us to hear but not necessarily to listen. Listening involves interpretation and understanding. Even if we listen intently we are only liable to remember half of what we hear. For example after listening to a lecture the average student will only remember about 25% of what was said. With the passage of time they will remember very little unless they review what they heard occasionally.

A wise person said that the reason we have two ears is that we should listen twice as much as we speak. A basic problem of listening is that we think much faster than we talk. The average person talks at the rate of 125 words per minute but thinks at a much faster rate. This means that while listening we have a lot of spare capacity for mental doodling creating a communications barrier that detracts from our ability to concentrate and listen. You can use this spare capacity to good effect by:

1. Thinking ahead and anticipating ideas while not prejudging what the speaker is planning to say. Active listening means drawing reasonable conclusions from the words spoken up to that point.

2. Evaluate the evidence for the points made so that you are listening in a critical way.

3. Review and mentally summarise the key points as grasping the gist of ideas is a key skill of a good listener. Demonstrate your understanding by nodding, saying 'uh-huh' or 'I see' at intervals. Staying silent for long periods of time can unnerve the speaker. Acknowledge the emotional content of the message by reflecting back with empathy what has been said such as 'you felt angry because they didn't return your call.' People feel acknowledged when others validate their feelings and demonstrate that they are listening. People who ignore feelings and fail to empathise are likely to erode the relationship.

4. Take notice of things not said but that may be inferred by the body language such as demeanour, facial expression, gestures, degree of eye contact and tone of voice. Body language is often more meaningful and can tell a different story than the words spoken.

"A wise old owl sat on an oak; The more he saw the less he spoke; The less he spoke the more he heard; Why aren't we like that wise old bird?"

Unknown

43

Some people think that interrupting saves time particularly if the other person is not saying anything worthwhile or new. Listening means focusing on what the other person is saying in a thoughtful and attentive way. Some people are so preoccupied with figuring out what they are going to say next and so self-absorbed that they fail to hear what the other person is saying. Sometimes what the other person is saying sparks a good idea and you can't wait to interrupt and say your piece. Interrupting is rude and shows a lack of respect for the other person. It gives the impression that what you have to say is more important than what they have to say. Those who interrupt are less likely to follow the gist of the conversation and thus more likely to request that the speaker repeat what has been said. This of course demonstrates that you haven't been listening and is very annoying and frustrating to the speaker. A fundamental principle of good dialogue is give and take so that we allow others to finish speaking before we take our turn and have our say.

People like to feel important and feel resentful when they are ignored. One way of demonstrating your attention is to show interest and support by actively listening to what the other person is saying. Demonstrate this interest by maintaining eye contact and nodding occasionally. Show by your body language, tone of voice and facial expression that you are keenly interested and engrossed in what the other person is saying.

> "I know that you believe you understand what you think I said, but I'm not sure you realise that what you heard is not what I meant."
>
> Robert McCloskey

Closed questions are those which elicit a yes or no response. These are useful if you want to check facts and establish the current status of an issue. Ask open questions which explore issues and options to keep the conversation going. If you are unsure ask for clarification of what was said. Check and verify so that you have received the correct message rather than what you wish to hear. Don't jump to conclusions but instead establish the facts by checking them out with the person concerned. Demonstrate your interest in what the speaker is saying by the way you stand or sit, focusing on the person talking and maintaining eye contact while looking directly at the person who is speaking. However, don't stare as too much eye contact can be perceived as threatening and make the speaker feel uncomfortable.

Barriers to Listening

There are many barriers to listening. When you consider that people may have different experience, religion, education, background, motivation and come from different cultures one wonders how any two persons can understand each other. An awareness of the barriers to listening will help us become better communicators. The key barriers can be recalled by the acronym PUBLIC:

P **P**oint of view. Some people have fixed viewpoints and are highly opinionated. They become emotional or excited when the speaker's point of view differs from their own. They disagree or argue outwardly or internally in their minds with the speaker so that they find it difficult to hear clearly what was said. They may have a negative view of the speaker and have their mind made up in advance irrespective of what the speaker says. A more positive view of the speaker and more interest in the content and logic of the other people's point of view would help reduce this barrier.

U **U**nattentive. They concentrate on the speaker's mannerisms or delivery rather than on the message. Poor delivery distracts listeners from the message of the content and consequently reduces the impact of the speech. There is a link between strong delivery and credibility. Speakers are thought to be more credible if during delivery they maintained eye contact, smiled, used positive body language and had good fluency. More concentration and focused attention on the part of the listener on the core message would reduce this barrier and improve their listening effectiveness.

B **B**oredom. They lack interest in the speaker's subject and thus switch off mentally. They may become impatient with a long-winded and jargon loaded speaker. They may daydream or become distracted or preoccupied with something else when listening. Looking for interesting points in the speech to use as an anchor would help to reduce this barrier.

L Laziness. They are mentally lazy and avoid listening if the subject is complicated, challenging, difficult to understand or too long to keep concentrated on. To improve motivation the listener should reflect on the benefits and reasons why they should listen to the speech and expect to learn something new.

I Insincerity. They avoid eye contact with the speaker while listening and thus give the impression that they can't be trusted. They pay attention only to the speaker's words rather than the emotional content of the speech and thus only get half of the message. Concentrating on the emotional content of the speech as well as the words will ensure that you get the total message.

C Closed mind. They are prejudiced against the views of the speaker who they may have stereotyped and thus refuse to relate to and benefit from the speaker's ideas. Having a more open mind and thinking constructively how the speaker's ideas might benefit and be used would eliminate this barrier to listening. After all everybody has something to contribute and you may learn something new!

> "If A equals success, then the formula is A equals X plus Y and Z, with X being work, Y play, and Z keeping your mouth shut."
>
> Albert Einstein

Building Good IPR -Communication

Good communication and good interpersonal relationships are intrinsically linked. It is very difficult to develop good interpersonal relations if you are a poor communicator or a poor listener. Specific skills if practised regularly will produce real change. If you practise the following you will enhance your interpersonal relationships:

• The meaning of any communication is in the response you get. This places the responsibility for clear communication on the speaker because if the receiver fails to understand you, then it's your fault and nobody else's fault! Good communication is an important element in positive interpersonal relationships. In this era of email, texting, blackberry, iPods and other electronic methods of communication, face-to- face communication is still the best. Email is great for conveying factual information but is one dimensional and open to misinterpretation. Academics claim that email and texting has contributed to the current deterioration in the standard of written English particularly amongst students. In fact in the modern era, with the pervasiveness of electronic media, we are also in danger of losing our ability to write clear good English and communicate on an intimate basis. When you communicate face-to-face you build up rapport, trust, and get valuable information and feedback which is difficult to get by other means with those you come in contact with. In face-to-face communication there is a more natural exchange of information and a greater facility to build up warm social relationships and prevent misunderstanding. Winston Churchill knew the power of words and galvanised the English public with his radio broadcasts to withstand the threat of Germany during the Second World War. Like other great speakers he used analogies, metaphors, stories, anecdotes and simple short concrete words to inspire his audience, capture their imaginations and keep them emotionally involved.

- Body language. Language is only about 50,000 years old. Before language people communicated non-verbally by grunts, signs and gestures. Become a student of human behaviour by observing and studying body language. Look for facial expressions and tone of voice that will tell you whether or not the person is happy, engaged, enraged, indifferent, frustrated or bored. Maintaining eye contact while leaning slightly towards the speaker indicates that you are keenly interested in what they have to say. On the other hand, standing too close to them may make them feel uncomfortable as they may feel that you are invading their territorial space. The amount of personal space acceptable varies from culture to culture. For example, Italians like to stand closer whereas English people tend to keep their distance. When people cross their arms it may suggest defensiveness. Yawning may mean a person is bored or indeed just tired from the night before. A frown may mean that a person is confused or worried. A raised eyebrow may indicate disbelief. Blushing may indicate shyness. On the other hand paleness may indicate a state of shock. Your hand shake can be an indicator of how confident and friendly you are. A firm hand shake is the best, whereas a limp hand shake may indicate indifference while a bone crusher can be painful to the recipient. Males tend to be less skilled at interpreting body language than females. An interesting fact about communication is that you are always communicating. Even when you say nothing it may be a sign that you are displeased or disinterested. The silent treatment can communicate negative feelings more effectively than strong words as anyone in a relationship knows.

- Network. Your network may be more far-reaching than you think. In 1967, psychologist Stanley Milgram coined the phrase "six degrees of separation" to highlight the fact that everyone is on average only six steps away from anybody in the world. Even Barrack 4 didn't realise that he was only six steps away from his Irish roots until genealogists discovered the fact. Take every opportunity to meet other people. Spending time with people you are trying to influence builds trust and gets people on your side. Take a genuine interest in others and enjoy their company. Be natural and sincere and avoid a false persona. If people don't like you, don't take offence and just move on. Nobody is loved by everybody. Nevertheless we do like to be liked as we are by nature gregarious social animals. The most feared punishment for prisoners is solitary confinement. Similarly infants deprived of human contact fail to thrive. Get actively involved in your professional institute and attend their conferences and meetings. Use the opportunity to build up contacts. Win friends by being generous in sharing your knowledge, time and talents. Offer help to those who need it. Being generous with your time and obliging will help you make friends. Under the law of reciprocity this will have a boomerang effect in that they are more likely to help you in return when you need their help. If we genuinely respect other people these feelings will be reciprocated. Some people are reluctant to break the ice so introduce yourself to other people and get the conversation going by using small talk such as making an observation about the weather or the latest political crises.

Observe others who are good at interpersonal relations and copy their style. We can use others as role models to enhance our influencing skills by copying what they do successfully in social situations.

- How to avoid conflicts. Conflicts are caused by differences of opinion, competition for scarce resources, unclear lines of authority, personality clashes or just simply because people can't get along with each other. Conflicts if left to fester create barriers of distrust and hatreds between people and so something should be done to solve them. You can't prevent conflicts from arising but you can reduce their frequency and duration. Show understanding for the other person's point of view. Ignore insults as reacting to them in anger will only make the situation worse. Be careful what you say as intemperate language spoken on the spur of the moment cannot be undone and may cause lasting emotional pain and irretrievable damage. Better to stay calm and silent and let the situation get off the boil by allowing the other party to let off some steam. Bring differences out into the open by asking questions and addressing them rather than ignoring the situation and letting it fester. You must understand the nature of the problem if you want to remedy the situation. If it is possible to meet the other person's requests, do so. If you are in the wrong, apologise! 'Sorry' can be the most difficult word to say but often the most effective to diffuse a situation.

> "My talent lies in my ability to ask very simple, yet very powerful, questions like 'What if...'
>
> Albert Einstein

Building Good IPR – Friendship

If you practise the following you will win and retain friends:

- Smile! Practise acceptance and friendliness by smiling more often. Smiling creates a sense of warmth, support and positive feelings between two people. It takes 112 muscles to frown but only 13 muscles to smile. So smiling is easier, more positive and beneficial. Forcing a smile actually puts you in a better mood. You can think yourself happier by smiling. Smiling is contagious, so spread a little happiness about by smiling and make a few friends in the process. Ebenezer Scrooge the central character in Charles Dickens classic novel, A Christmas Carol underwent a personal transformation after being confronted by the three ghosts of Christmas to change his selfish and miserly ways. He changed from being a mean, greedy and grumpy person to become a generous, smiling, happy and considerate individual.

- Empathise. This means seeing life through the eyes of the other person. It means getting inside their heads and feeling the way they feel and seeing things from their perspective. Actors spend months studying the quirks, behaviours, idiosyncrasies and mannerisms of the people they portray on screen. For example, the actor Dicaprio read every book he could find on Howard Hughes the reclusive multi-millionaire when preparing for the part. He carried out extensive research by interviewing people who knew him and watched newsreels to get inside the idiosyncratic persona of Hughes. He also consulted with a specialist on the obsessive compulsive disorders that Hughes was known to suffer from in order to make his portrayal more unique and realistic. We all have a special way of looking at things influenced by the way we were brought up, our beliefs and values, and our life experiences. Many disagreements arise because people fail to understand the other person's unique point of view because of their different perspectives. You don't have to agree with the other person but you should try to understand how they feel and where they are coming from. The great Henry Ford believed that there was only one secret of success and that lay in understanding the other person's point of view.

- Getting people to like you. Project your warm personality by being open and friendly with people and they'll reflect it back to you. Adopt a happy outlook on life. Optimistic people are fun to be around. If someone asks you how you are, say, wonderful, fantastic, terrific, marvellous, incredible or great rather than all right. When people ask you how you are they don't want your medical history and a list of your ailments. Being self-pitying, pessimistic, gloomy, critical, resentful, defeatist and overly introverted is not going to help you win friends and influence people. You should be warm and supportive rather than critical and dismissive of others. Avoid schadenfreude or the natural human tendency to take delight in other people's misfortune. Instead you should empathise with their loss and realise that we all share the human condition.

- Making friends. We are more likely to make friends with those we meet frequently in our everyday lives. Thus our friends tend to be neighbours, work colleagues and people we run into at the supermarket. We tend to bond with those that we have something in common with such as religion, ethnic background, sporting interest, membership of the same club, occupation, hobbies or a similar sense of humour. We become best friends with those who boost our self-esteem by affirming our good points and by sharing membership of certain groups such as clubs and sports teams. Similarly survivors of breast cancer often become great friends after experiencing a common traumatic event and thus understanding each other's unique perspective on life. This is often a wake up call for people to realise that life is short and we should live every day as if it is our last. Self-disclosure is the thing that cements friendship. In the early stages of friendship one person takes the risk of disclosing personal information and intimacies with the expectation that the other will reciprocate. Reciprocity is the key. If this does not happen the friendship is likely to wither and die. Friendships last because of common interests, emotional ties, followed by unconditional acceptance, loyalty and trust. True friends last a lifetime and are there for us in good times as well as bad. In fact, you will quickly discover who your real friends are in times of difficulty, personal crisis, bereavement, trauma or illness. Friendship will only last if people keep in touch. The main ingredient in keeping a friendship going is positivity. People must enjoy each other's company and be prepared to invest the required energy in the friendship to keep it fresh and alive. Dale Carnegie believed that you can make more friends in two months by becoming interested in other people that you can in two years by trying to get other people interested in you.

- Improving relationships. The golden rule is to treat others the way you would like to be treated. Addressing people's wishes, needs, concerns and expectations will win their trust. Be agreeable. Don't tell people directly they're wrong especially in front of others as they will lose face. It upsets them and will undermine their self-confidence and self-esteem. You may win the argument but lose your friend. If you have a disagreement, don't argue but you could introduce a third party perspective and thus give the impression of neutrality by not being personally involved but at the same time bringing their mistake diplomatically to their attention. If there is a difference of opinion don't turn it into an argument but accept the difference and move on. People are entitled to have different opinions. If you made a mistake admit it. We are all human and prone to make mistakes and none of us are infallible.

- Mirroring is a way of building up rapport. This is done by matching and synchronising with certain behaviours of the person you are trying to influence. These behaviours can be gesture, head tilts, voice tone, volume and speed, words, facial expressions, breathing and body posture. Obviously mirroring should be done in a subtle way so that it appears natural and does not draw the attention of the other person. Most people do not like to feel that they are being manipulated by others. Mirroring may be used by job interviewers to establish rapport with job applicants. On the other hand, a job candidate could build up rapport with an interviewer by mirroring. The interviewer would feel favourably disposed towards the interviewee without being conscious of the reason.

- Humour. Create a positive atmosphere by the use of humour. The humour should be harmless, neutral and acceptable, and not cause offence. Humour releases tension and promotes collaboration. People are more inclined to trust and agree with those who make them laugh. People can often say in jest things which in a different context might cause offence. A positive mood helps people relax their barriers so that they can accept other's arguments more readily.

- Building self-esteem in others. Avoid destructive criticism as the damage done is very hard to rectify. Keep your mouth shut instead. If you must say something say something nice and complimentary. Complaining undermines your own self-esteem and that of others. Your policy should be: what can't be cured must be endured. If you have a problem, fix it or solve it rather than complain about it as no one likes a moaner. Avoid negative attitudes such as contempt, condemning or patronising. Be very reluctant to condemn people as you do not know their personal problems or circumstances and you certainly wouldn't like others to condemn you. Some people may be going through a bad patch at the moment and require your support rather than your criticism. Patronising or stereotyping others such as minority groups or women will certainly get you into a lot of trouble.

- Remember people's names. The sweetest sound to a person's ear is the sound of their own name. Remember people's names and address them correctly. Always introduce people to each other when in a position to do so. Respond with grace, patience and good manners when dealing with rude people. Always keep your cool. Just because they're rude and unmannerly doesn't mean you have to be likewise.

- Dress smartly. They say you shouldn't judge a book by the cover. Nevertheless people are often judged by the way they dress. Your appearance says a lot about you including confidence, taste, dress sense and self-respect. So dress smartly and appropriate to the occasion. Lasting impressions for good or bad are often made within a few seconds of an introduction.

"Today the most useful person in the world is the man or woman who knows how to get along with other people. Human relations is the most important science in the broad curriculum of living."

Stanley C. Allen

Exceptional IPR Skills

Sir Ernest Henry Shackleton (1874-1922), was born in County Kildare, Ireland. He was a great explorer and leader, and motivator of men. Like other explorers he was prepared to risk his life to expand human knowledge and go where no man had gone before. Throughout his expeditions he won and retained the respect and admiration of his men, showing exceptional loyalty and support for his men even in the most life threatening and demanding circumstances. He served in the British merchant navy where he mastered his seafaring skills and joined Scott's first Antarctic expedition (1901-1904). In 1902 Scott, Shackleton and Wilson reached within 400 miles of the South Pole: the furthest south reached by anybody at that time but was forced to turn back because of hunger and scurvy. In 1908-09 he commanded an expedition in the Nimrod, and reached a new furthest south: just 97 miles from the South Pole. Unfortunately, he had to abandon the effort due to a shortage of food and poor planning but pledged to learn from his mistakes and be back.

Shackleton's next adventure was to attempt the first crossing of the Antarctic Continent. In his own words, "After the conquest of the South Pole by the Norwegian, Amundsen who by a narrow margin of days only, was in advance of the British Expedition under Scott, there remained but one great main object of Antarctic journeyings: - the crossing of the South Pole continent from sea to sea". In 1915 during his attempt to cross the 2000 mile Antarctic continent his ship Endurance was strangled in pack ice and drifted north on ice floes for months. The ship was eventually crushed to smithereens by the ice and had to be abandoned, leaving 28 men on the ice with 3 small boats. They had to leave most of their possessions when the ship sank but Shackleton with uncanny foresight insisted that one crew member save his banjo because he believed in the power of music to lift spirits during the months ahead. They then spent 5 months on an iceberg floating away from the continent. Luck was on their side when they landed on Elephant Island on the 15th April 1916: a small inhospitable, godforsaken island of rock and ice with a few penguins and seals for food. Shackleton knew that his men would not survive very long in such a hostile and inhospitable environment.

His next move would turn out to be one of the most courageous, daring and incredible small boat journeys of all time. He set off in search of the island of South Georgia to get help with 5 others in a 22 foot boat. Shackleton was a great judge of human character and picked the right mix of personalities to leave behind and for the perilous journey ahead. He had the prescience of mind to take two toxic personalities with him so that they could not infect the morale of the men left behind on Elephant Island. Two of the others in the boat were from Ireland: Tom Crean from County Kerry and Tim McCarthy from County Cork. Tom Crean was strong, courageous, good humoured and experienced: having previously served on Scott's expedition. Tim McCarthy was famous for his happy, even-tempered and optimistic outlook, even in the direst and most challenging circumstances: a trait that would lift the spirits of all on board. It was McCarthy that spotted South Georgia, 16 days after leaving Elephant Island.

The six men had spent 16 days and over 800 miles crossing the ocean in freezing and hurricane conditions and then trekked across the island over mountainous terrain for a further 10 days to a whaling station. They returned to Elephant Island and rescued the remaining 22 crew on 30th August 1916. The rescue faced many setbacks and obstacles before they reached their destination and took four months. Amazingly, all his crew had survived, no doubt kept going by the belief and hope that Shackleton, a true gentleman and leader of men, would return and rescue them. Wild, the person he had left in charge, had followed Shackleton's example of keeping the routine going with entertainment and celebrations, fending off depression by keeping everybody busy and mentally occupied.

Some people might consider Shackleton's life a failure. He had led or been involved in three ambitious polar missions, all of which had to be abandoned before his objectives had been achieved. His greatest failure and greatest triumph was his attempt to cross the Antarctic. He lost his ship but successfully led all the members of his crew to safety, after the most gruelling and harrowing two-year fight for their survival while demonstrating exceptional leadership skills. Having jettisoned his ambition of crossing the Antarctic he then concentrated all his efforts on getting his men back safely. He didn't become rich but did open new worlds, new paths and new possibilities for others to follow. However, his true grit, determination, endurance, perseverance, resilience and concern for others in the most trying and hazardous circumstances, won him worldwide fame and respect, and have inspired managers, leaders and others over many decades since.

Psychological Insight

Shackleton demonstrated a great psychological understanding of his men and did everything possible to maintain a harmonious group. He displayed empathy to his men through his kindness, concern and consideration for their health, welfare and safety. He walked the talk by living up to his promises and commitments. He built up rapport by creating and maintaining a spirit of camaraderie amongst his men. He never expected anyone to do anything that he wasn't prepared to do himself and did menial tasks just like anybody else. He broke down the status barriers between the officer staff and the ordinary crew members. He was never standoffish with his men but still managed to retain discipline and retain their respect and loyalty. He created a common bond of friendship and trust between himself and his team.

He was also able to use his considerable interpersonal relationship and diplomatic skills to get money from his benefactors. He used his personal charisma to get large sums of money to fund his expeditions from heiresses and wealthy businessmen. He knew how to please his patrons and immortalising them by naming places he discovered after them. For example, he named 200 miles of Antarctic coastline after James Caird, a wealthy Scotsman who gave him $24,000, a significant sum of money at the time. He got public schools to cover the cost of his sled dogs and named the dogs after the schools.

In terms of recruiting the right mix of people with the right skills and personalities for his expeditions he was highly successful. In one instance, 5,000 people applied for just 56 positions on his team with prospects of little reward except glory, honour and fame. People crave recognition more than monetary reward. He always looked for temperamentally happy but ambitious, determined and committed people for his team. They had to have the mettle to survive in the most dangerous and difficult circumstances. When things went well on his expeditions, he encouraged the men to celebrate. When things were going wrong he rallied the men to play football and ice hockey on the ice to lift their spirits. He used the sled dogs for races and diversion and even permitted betting. This kept the men occupied, stopped them from getting on each others nerves, and prevented them from getting depressed. Unfortunately to prevent hunger and starvation the dogs were eaten by the crew. He had a photographer on board to capture the voyage and encouraged his officers to keep diaries, which most managed to do so. As well as doing a worthwhile job this also kept their minds occupied during the dark Polar winters. He used their diaries in writing his best-selling book, "South".

When on the Endurance he developed a personal relationship with each of his crew and knew each of their names. His technique was to keep the ship's library in his cabin, so that he could chat with the men when they came to borrow books. He made sure that everybody got their fair share of the scarce food available, thus preventing conflict, and used mealtimes to chat and joke with his men, to listen to their ideas and relax in their company. His optimism, enthusiasm, self-belief and courage were contagious, particularly when faced with life threatening problems. His motto was: "difficulties are just things to be overcome." He knew how to handle the diverse personalities of his men while keeping their minds focused on what needed to be done to achieve the common objective. He was able to cheer up the perpetual worrier, humour and cajole the pessimist, keep the disgruntled from poisoning the minds of others, prevent boredom and fatigue from developing and bring discipline and success to a chaotic, hostile and dangerous environment while working with limited resources. He knew that optimism was the most potent defence against failure.

Shackleton believed in fair play. He summed up his philosophy on life and leadership as follows: "Some people say it is wrong to regard life as a game. I don't think so. Life to me means the greatest of all games. The danger lies in treating it as a trivial game, a game to be taken lightly, and a game in which the rules don't matter much. The rules matter a great deal. The game has to be played fairly ....and even to win the game is not the chief end. The chief end is to win it honourably and splendidly." Shackleton couldn't resist the lure of the South Pole and after the war he organised another expedition. However, he never completed the project and died on board his ship of a heart attack at the age of 47. Although he worried about the welfare of others he obviously failed to look after his own health. Nevertheless, his memory survives to inspire others to undertake the seemingly impossible.

Develop Your Emotional IQ.

It is only in relatively recent times that the value of emotional intelligence to success in life has been acknowledged. Ancient Egyptians believed the heart was the centre of intelligence and emotion. They were so convinced of this and thought so little of the brain that they removed and discarded it during the mummification of royalty and dignitaries. Similarly, for centuries the Western World believed the seat of intelligence and emotions was in the heart.

Emotional intelligence has been defined as the ability to recognise your own emotions and the emotional states of others in order to improve interpersonal relationships. Many people with a high IQ fail to succeed in life, or progress in their careers, because of a low emotional intelligence and an inability to get along with others. Similarly people who are very technically competent but who lack emotional IQ may not do as well in their careers as they should. We are all aware of celebrities who cannot cope with their fame because of a lack of emotional IQ. They often have inadequate social skills indulging in inappropriate behaviour and getting involved in drug and alcohol abuse.

Emotionally intelligent people are able to keep things in perspective and thus realise what's important in life. They understand that there are different definitions of success and thus know they can be successful in anything they choose to do. They keep a positive outlook on life and thus they are more likely to turn setbacks into opportunities and weaknesses into strengths rather than become dejected, despondent or depressed. The good news is that EQ like any skill can be developed and learned.

Key aspects of emotional IQ are self-awareness, social awareness and self-control. Self-awareness means being aware of your emotions and the impact, whether positive or negative, that they have on other people. Self-aware people are thus able to express their feelings accurately without causing upset to others. Self-awareness includes having an appreciation of your own strengths and weaknesses and using feedback to improve your responses. Self aware people are keenly aware of their personal guiding values. A deep-rooted sense of self will help you understand other people and is the foundation for self-confidence. Social awareness is your ability to understand and get along with other people in work and social situations. It means that you are sensitive and respond to the needs and feelings of others and show respect for the different perspectives of others and take these into account when interacting with them. Self-control is your ability to control your emotions and manage your frustration calmly and effectively. People with self-control can think clearly and stay grounded and composed even in the most provocative and trying situations. Some people are prone to get angry and enraged at the least provocation and this can prove to be a severe handicap in social and work situations. Nobody likes to be around people who are like live volcanoes liable to erupt unpredictably at any moment. Thus it is important to have control of your emotions and to think clearly, calmly and sensibly in difficult situations.

"In the last decade or so, science has discovered a tremendous amount about the role emotions play in our lives. Researchers have found that even more than IQ your emotional awareness and abilities to handle feelings will determine your success and happiness in all walks of life, including family relationships."

John Gottman, Ph.D

The Principles of Influence

Using one or a combination of the following psychological principles will help you influence people to do what you want them to do. Influencing is often a combination of good interpersonal relationship, communication and assertiveness skills. Influencing is not the same as manipulation or coercion. This is forcing people to do what you want them to do often against their will. You may succeed in winning their support but people who have been manipulated or coerced won't forget the way they have been treated. The six principles of influence can be recalled by the acronym SCRAWL:

S   Social proof. People are often persuaded to do something if they think that many others are doing the same thing. If you are told that a number of your friends or colleagues are doing it you are more likely to buy-in to the idea. People like to conform to the norms and mores of society. People's desire to wear the latest fashion is influenced by this principle. Young people in particular tend to mimic the way celebrities dress. We are influenced to buy new innovative products when we see that they have been generally accepted and worked satisfactorily for other people. So if you want to influence people to take a particular decision give them examples of other people who have taken similar decisions and have benefited from doing so.

C   Consistency. People commit to their own decisions especially if confided to others beforehand or if they make them in writing. People like to be consistent with their words, values, beliefs, attitudes and promises. Remind people what they have done in the past which proved to be successful or effective. If you want people to do something, get them to make a public commitment or pledge to do it. In such circumstances people are extremely reluctant to break their word. This phenomenon is well known to charities who manipulate people to commit to making monthly contributions by standing order.

R   Reciprocity. You scratch my back and I'll scratch yours. People are more likely to return a favour because it creates a sense of obligation. Neighbours help farmers bring in the harvest with the knowledge that the favour is likely to be returned in kind. People who give compliments are more likely to get compliments in return. Accept compliments graciously. People with low self-confidence tend not to believe compliments. Sales people who give small gifts are more likely to make a sale as they create a sense of obligation to buy in order to return the compliment. Medical doctors who are taken away for a luxury weekend or even to lunch by a drug company are more likely to prescribe their particular brand of drugs to patients rather than the cheaper generic equivalent. Politicians who accept large political donations from companies are more likely to implement favourable policies for them. This practice though prevalent is unethical as it creates favouritism and a conflict of interest.

A   Authority. People in positions of authority are more believable than others. People have more confidence in the views of an expert. Some detergents on television are often promoted by people in a white coat creating the illusion that they are doctors and thus have high credibility. Other products are often endorsed by well-known celebrities giving the impression that they are users of the product. To protect ourselves against the persuasive effects of this principle we should verify that the authority is really an expert and that what is put forward is factually true. We sometimes defer to the symbols of authority such as status or position rather than the substance and logic of the argument. So if you want to influence others you should put forward your case from a position of strength.

W We crave scarce things. It is a well known psychological phenomenon of marketing that people often want things that they don't really need. We value things more that are in short supply or scarce. A basic law of economics is that when demand exceeds supply the price goes up. Hence the premium price for antiques. Think of sales promotions such as 'last day of sale' and 'only five items left.' This creates a sense of urgency and mild panic in that people are likely to fear missing out and feel deprived if they don't make the purchase. The scarcity principle can also be applied to information. Confidential information is valued because it is seen as exclusive to the person receiving it and thus can be used to make them feel very special.

L Liking. We tend to like those people who are like ourselves. We are more likely to like those we are frequently in contact with or easily accessible to. Similarly we tend to like those who have helped us in the past. Initially physical attractiveness can act like a magnet to draw us to people. However, in the long term other characteristics such as friendliness, genuineness, transparency and reliability become more important. We can communicate more effectively with those who are on the same wavelength as ourselves: people with similar interests, values, beliefs and attitudes.

"Our attitude toward life determines life's attitude towards us."
John N. Mitchell

Giving and Receiving Feedback

There are two types of feedback. Positive feedback encourages us to continue doing what we have been doing. Negative feedback Is a warning that we should moderate or discontinue what we have been doing in order to improve the situation. There is a positivity/negativity ratio which suggests that our positive feedback should exceed our negative feedback if we want beneficial results. For example, it has been found that marriages that flourish have a positive to negative ratio of 5 compliments to 1 criticism, while those that end in divorce have significantly more negative feedback than positive. This means that partners who demean or criticise one another frequently are unlikely to be happy and have a long lasting marriage. Feedback helps us to improve and correct our mistakes and refine our behaviour. What you heard may not be what they meant and the only way to know for sure is to ask clarifying questions and receive feedback. Seek feedback from people who will give you constructive criticism rather than flattery and insincere praise. Ask trusted friends, family and work colleagues how they would rate your interpersonal relationship skills. Brainstorm specific ways to improve these abilities.

Without feedback you can't improve your skills, knowledge, work performance or relationships. Some people are too direct, abrupt, and insensitive, condescending, patronising, argumentative, arrogant and opinionated. Arrogant and argumentative people tend not to listen which aggravates the problem. Without feedback you can't rectify personal faults caused by inappropriate behaviour, attitudes or beliefs. Without feedback you can't correct mistakes caused by lack of information or misunderstanding. Thus feedback about errors should be accompanied by clear information about how to correct them. Ideally it should be linked with some form of coaching or assistance to improve performance.

Decide how you can improve your behaviour or performance the next time based on what you now know. Acknowledge that you did your best at the time with the information you had and in the circumstances you found. Some people are very sensitive and are not prepared to take critical feedback. If you are a sensitive person you are hurt more easily than others and react more emotionally to disappointments, even minor ones. You should keep in mind that feedback is simply information and should be treated as such. So don't take it personally and shoot the messenger as he may have your concerns at heart. Be gracious and thank the person for the feedback. If several people are telling you the same thing there is a high probability that there is some truth in it and you should take remedial action to put it right.

In a corporate context the beauty of 360 degree feedback is that it provides feedback from the different perspectives of managers, work colleagues, customers, suppliers and others. Self-perceptions are often quite different from those made by others. We think we see things objectively but in fact only see what we want to see. Feedback helps us become aware of these differences. More importantly, once we know what they are we can change our behaviour if appropriate. Take and use personality type assessments to highlight your weaknesses so that you are able to create opportunities for personal development. These will give you good insights into your own and others communication and interpersonal relationship style and equip you to identify and manage them more effectively. Mentors and coaches may also be a great source of feedback and advice on your personal shortcomings. The majority of leaders attribute their success to having a good mentor. Benchmark your behaviour against others to highlight your deficiencies. Take a training course to address negative behaviour as these will enhance your personal development and improve your attractiveness to employers.

To be understood by others is the first step to understanding ourselves. When giving negative feedback try to link it with something positive. Reinforcing positive behaviour is the key to getting more positive behaviour in the future. The feedback should be about observable behaviour only. Don't pass judgement on internal attitudes and personality traits. The feedback should be specific to a particular problem and suggest a solution. Follow the negative feedback with friendly conversation highlighting positive things to maintain the relationship. Even bad news can be tolerable if given sensitively as any priest or policeman will tell you. If you are lucky enough to get a compliment, always thank the person for it rather than give the impression that you don't deserve it.

"Champions know that success is inevitable; that there is no such thing as failure, only feedback. They know that the best way to forecast the future is to create it."

Michael J. Gelb

Importance of Good Manners

Good manners are the sign of character and good upbringing. Make it a habit of using the common courtesies such as 'please' and 'thank you.' Just because you are busy this is no excuse for being rude. Bad manners seem to be fashionable these days. Rudeness is widespread. Not returning people's phone calls and not responding to social invitations is the norm. Keeping people waiting who turn up at the appointed time is not unusual and gives out the message that their time is more important than yours. It is good manners and shows consideration and respect for others to turn up on time and be prepared for meetings. Being subjected while waiting on the telephone to long periods of easy-listening music or advertisements and then when finally you get through the "service provider" is unable to solve your problem. Unfortunately, these days this is typical of bad customer service.

Treat your customers with incivility and contempt and they will leave you. Bad customer service is a prescription for the ultimate downfall of a business. Discourtesy between work colleagues, humiliating people by reprimanding them in public in front of customers, patronising women, low level bullying and bad language is fast becoming the norm in many organisations. Rude behaviour to customers is unacceptable but not uncommon. If employees are civil to one another they are likely to be courteous to customers as well. Good manners are a sign of class no matter the wealth, status or position of the person. They are an important ingredient of personal success in life generally and in business in particular.

These days the more obnoxious celebrity chefs appear to behave in dealing with employees the more famous they become in the popular media. People think its okay to be rude, abrupt and interrupt others continually during political debates on TV. Even prime ministers can be bereft of emotional IQ skills.

Gordon Brown the ex Prime Minister of England had a dour and unmannerly demeanour. He was once caught off camera using inappropriate language when describing a constituent and a subsequent apology proved futile, false and too late. This incident caused irreparable damage to his image and reputation. Unlike Tony Blair his emotional IQ was poor and this contributed to his eventual political downfall. You need more than a high intelligence to succeed in life. A pleasant manner showing sensitivity to the feelings of others and a personable disposition will often go a long way. Similarly, office rage is often caused by incivility and has a detrimental impact on office relationships and work performance. Displaying consideration for others by leaving things the way you got them is a good principle to live by. A common irritant to office workers is inconsiderate people who leave paper jams in photocopiers for others to fix and who fail to replenish paper in the feed.

Manners cost nothing but make living civil and pleasant. Good manners can give you the competitive advantage in social and work situations. Give credit where credit is due. People in general are quick to criticise but slow to praise. When someone does a good job praise them in a genuine way. The praise should be specific, personal and sincere and done as near to the event warranting the praise as possible. General praise has no impact on people and false praise will sound patronising and will prove counterproductive. An occasional compliment is always worthwhile as people like others to genuinely praise them and boost their confidence.

If someone does you a favour always express your gratitude and appreciation. Send 'thank you' notes to those who have helped you. Saying thanks is not only polite, but also good for your health. These are a rare gesture these days and so will catch people's attention and make a big impression. Women are more likely than men to express gratitude. Some psychologists maintain we should keep gratitude journals to regularly record all the positive things in our life and what we should be grateful for. List the people and things you take for granted in your daily life and then consider what your life would be like without them. This exercise will highlight what you should be grateful for. Those who regularly count their blessings, exercise more, complain less and feel happier and better about their lives overall.

"Let us rise up and be thankful, for if we didn't learn a lot today, at least we learned a little, and if we didn't learn a little, at least we didn't get sick, and if we got sick, at least we didn't die; so let us all be thankful."

The Budda

Accepting Yourself and Others

The following is based on a book titled "I'm Okay, You're Okay by Thomas A Harris MD (1969). Life style positions indicate how you feel about yourself and others and the importance of good communications and interpersonal relationships with others. How we view ourselves and treat others is often influenced by our perspective and attitudes. Most interpersonal relationship problems are caused by feelings of personal inadequacy and an inability to understand and accept the shortcomings of others.

1. I'm okay – You're okay. People who hold this position see themselves and others as competent and interdependent with others and their environment. They possess high self-esteem and are self-confident and comfortable with themselves, and take a similar view of others. They are kind and considerate to other people and value their opinions and wishes. They are more likely to seek social support, collaborate and network with others, and have no difficulty being assertive, open and discussing their problems. This position assumes that most problems can be solved, that conflicts, though inevitable can be worked through and resolved, and that people are responsible for their own actions. They are prepared to compromise with others and incorporate others' ideas in win-win outcomes. Because they see others as okay, other people will reciprocate in a similar fashion. This is a realistic adult healthy positive position of mutual recognition and respect. This is the most functional position and one that we should all strive for. A manager who adopts this position will trust and delegate to staff and invest in their training and development.

2. I'm okay – You're not okay. People who adopt this position feel arrogant and consider that they can't rely on or trust others because they are incompetent and thus tend to

ignore them. They perceive other people as worthless, untrustworthy and potential enemies and so they may try to dominate and bully them. They are suspicious and blame everybody else for their problems and so consider it pointless to speak out, as they believe nobody will do anything to help them. They feel problems can't be solved by cooperating with others because people can't be trusted to be responsible and that conflict is predominately caused by others. A manager who adopts this position has no faith in his staff and will be reluctant to delegate. If forced to delegate he will exercise close control and supervision. He will not invest time and resources in the training and development of his staff because he believes that they have no potential.

3. I'm not okay – You're okay. This is the most common position and it is often instilled in childhood. When we are little children we see adults as big, powerful and competent and ourselves as small, weak, helpless, powerless and prone to make mistakes. So we conclude that 'I'm not OK' and 'You're OK. Adults who adopt this life position feel powerless, helpless and unworthy, and have an inferiority complex. This is a feeling of insecurity and worthlessness. They compare themselves unfavourably with others and lack self-confidence and have low self-esteem. Because they see others as superior they rarely set themselves challenging objectives and are generally risk averse. If they have problems, they blame themselves because they consider themselves incompetent or lack sufficient influence to change events.

4. I'm not okay – You're not okay. This is the most dysfunctional of the four life positions. People with this life position feel hopeless, irrelevant, and consider themselves and others equally worthless and are consumed with negative feelings. They feel disconnected from others and from their environment and tend to be introverted and obsessed with their own thoughts, problems and concerns. Consequently they are likely to be depressed and lack motivation and interest in life. They keep a low profile and their main concern is 'not to rock the boat'. This is a position of despair by one who wants to give up on life. This position is not sustainable in an organisation because a manager

who does not trust his own abilities and those of his staff will not survive long in a competitive environment.

I'm Ok You're OK **Happy**	I'm Ok You're not OK **Angry**
I'm not Ok You're Ok **Helpless**	I'm not Ok You're not OK **Hopeless**

Figure 2: Life Positions

From an individual's viewpoint, adopting the first position means you're positive, self-confident and assertive. This is the healthy position that everybody should strive for. The other three life positions do not make a happy, effective and productive person. Feeling angry, helpless or hopeless is not a recipe for success but rather a recipe for self-destructive behaviour.

"Consideration for others is the basis of a good life."

Confucius

Summary

The ability to get along with others is an important part of a successful life. Successful people are good communicators and know the importance of developing active listening skills. Studying the JOHARI model will improve your self-awareness and interpersonal communication skills. Developing empathy skills will increase your popularity with others. Networking will help you develop useful contacts to make your life more interesting and progress your career. Many technically qualified and competent people with a low EQ may not go as far in their careers as they should. This highlights the importance of developing EQ skills. Influencing skills will help you get what you want and is a combination of interpersonal relationship, communication and assertiveness skills. Getting feedback from trusted others will help you develop into a better and more self-aware person. Good manners are an important social skill. You should accept your own limitations and those of others.

Five Activities to Improve Your IPR Skills

1. Study body language and become an amateur behavioural psychologist by observing others, because the meaning of communication is a combination of words and non-verbal signs.

2. To develop your EQ skills read a good book on EQ and attend an EQ course. Study the behaviour of people who display a low EQ, such as lack of empathy skills and a quick temper, and learn from their inadequacies.

3. Make a habit of smiling, saying 'please' and 'thank you'. Return phone calls promptly and reply with courtesy to social invitations. Keep your appointments and don't keep people waiting. Pay sincere compliments to others as appropriate.

4. Ask trusted others to give you constructive criticism about your everyday interpersonal relationship skills rather than look for insincere praise. Constructive criticism may help you to challenge unhelpful beliefs. Use this information to improve your IPR skills.

5. Memorise the six principles of influence by committing the acronym SCRAWL to memory. This stands for **S**ocial proof, **C**onsistency, **R**eciprocity, **A**uthority, **W**e want scarce resources and **L**iking. Use any one of these or any combination to influence people in future encounters.

4

Confidence and Self-Bellef

- *What is confidence*
- *How can I become more confident?*
- *How can I acquire empowering beliefs?*
- *How can I get rid of disempowering beliefs?*
- *What is the comfort zone?*

Introduction

Confidence is about being self-assured and having the competence, judgement, persistence and resources needed to succeed in whatever you decide to undertake in life. Those with an internal locus of control believe that they are in charge of their lives and can influence the direction that it takes. Those with an external locus of control believe that outside forces shape and control their lives. Shyness can be overcome by adopting the appropriate strategies to counteract it. Being aware of and asserting your rights will make you a more confident person. Confidence can be acquired like any other skill if you actively practise confidence building skills. Self-belief and confidence are interlinked as strong self-belief is an essential ingredient of confidence. Empowering beliefs will enable success while disempowering beliefs will facilitate failure. To be successful and more confident we must move out of our comfort zones.

What is Confidence?

The fictional cinematic character James Bond, secret agent, known by the code name 007, is the epitome of confidence. He is portrayed as having a suave, sophisticated, courageous, charismatic and confident persona: the type of person we would all like to be in a fantasy world. He drives fast cars, drinks vodka martinis, stays in beautiful 5 star hotels, captivates the hearts of glamorous women, has a sharp wit, and rescues the planet from tyrannical scheming monsters. However, unlike James Bond we live in the real world but nevertheless can learn something about the art of being confident from his screen portrayal. Just like Bond you are unlikely to be successful in your chosen profession if you lack the confidence and self-belief to pursue your aspirations, dreams and goals. Many people who begin with enthusiasm to follow their dreams give up at the first sign of a difficulty or obstacle. Confidence is about being self-assured and having the competence, judgement, persistence and resources needed to succeed in whatever you decide to undertake in life.

Confidence comes from within while exuding self-assurance outwardly to others. Confident people feel comfortable and happy in their own skin. You are unlikely to get along and inspire others if you are not happy and at peace with yourself. Confident people value and respect themselves and others and regard themselves equal to others. They are not afraid to make mistakes and so do not beat themselves up when they get things wrong. They know their strengths and weaknesses and are aware that it's human to make mistakes. It's a sign of self-confidence when you can accept your limitations and weaknesses rather than be defensive about them. People who are aware of and accept their shortcomings can work to improve them and are also more likely to learn from their mistakes.

Because confidence is infectious, other people feel happy and comfortable around confident people. Confident people are considerate and in tune with other people's feelings and concerns. They strike a balance between fairness and consideration for others with a determination to succeed. They are not intimidated by other people and know when to assert themselves without being aggressive or domineering. They are able to express with sensitivity what they think, what they feel and what they want. Confidence is evident through body language, demeanour and speech. Confident people have immense energy, drive and infectious enthusiasm. They have a confident posture, speak with assurance, dress well and know how to greet people in a convivial way. When they enter a room they are relaxed, make eye contact, have a friendly smile and acknowledge people warmly. On the other hand, people who slouch or avoid eye contact are seen as lacking confidence. However you cannot feel confident all the time and most people will only feel confidence about topics that they are competent in. That is why you should be aware of confidence strategies such as the process of acting as if you are confident even if you feel the opposite. The more you 'act as if' the more confident you will become.

How to be More Charismatic

People with great self-confidence are known as charismatic. Charisma has been defined as a magnetic personality with the ability to inspire devotion, enthusiasm, interest or affection in others through personal charm or influence. People with charisma seem to have a powerful aura which draws people closer to them. Fame doesn't automatically confer charisma, as we all know many famous people with zero charisma. Charisma draws people towards you but character gets people to trust you. Lack of character can get people to ridicule and disown you. Therefore, for real success charisma must be combined with character.

President John F. Kennedy was probably the most charismatic president of the United States but his character was flawed while President Jimmy Carter, a man of exceptional character ranks among the least charismatic. Similarly, Brian Cowen, the ex Prime Minister of Ireland was a man of great character but had no charisma, and was unable to connect with the people of Ireland on a personal level and this led to his resignation in early 2011. On the other hand the late Charles Haughey, a former Prime Minister of Ireland, was a man of great charisma but little integrity. He was forced to resign in disgrace because of a financial scandal. President Richard Nixon had some charisma and considerable political acumen but lacked character and like Charles Haughey this proved to be his political downfall. He was linked to the break-in of the Democratic National Committee headquarters at the Watergate office complex. He used lies and deceit in an attempt to cover up his involvement. The effects of the scandal eventually forced him to resign on the 17 June 1972, becoming the first and only US President to do so.

People with charisma tend to use words that evoke images in the minds of their listeners. Charismatic leaders are able to articulate a compelling vision that captures the imagination of their followers. Image based words arouse the senses and thereby engage more fully listeners or readers. The acronym CAME will help you remember the critical skills of charisma:

C   Comprehension. If people do not understand what you are saying they cannot do what you want. People with charisma use short concrete words because they are easier to process and understand than long abstract words and thus make a better impact. People appreciate political leaders who use simple words that they understand.

A   Attention. You must grab peoples' attention if you want them to hear your message and be totally interested in others. People who dress to impress, have a good appearance and manner and use vivid speech are more likely to hold attention than those who are not. They use words that connect with the everyday experiences of people. They have strong convictions and are not afraid to use humour when appropriate. These people are seen as friendly, enthusiastic, dynamic, positive, powerful and influential.

M   Memory. Charismatic people know how to tell a good story. What they say is memorable because they want people to remember and act on their message. Words that evoke images are easier to remember and retrieve than abstract words. Words expressed in images are stored in more places of the brain and in richer detail than comparable concept words.

E   Emotions. Words must resonate at a deeper emotional level to leave an impact on the listener and to inspire them to take appropriate action. It is well known that imagery and emotion are closely connected. Leaders, who pepper their speeches with vivid images, evoke stronger emotional responses and a greater chance that followers will embrace their visions and act.

A Charismatic Character

Eva Peron (1919-1952) was a controversial, attractive, confident, charismatic character and a great orator. She is a symbol of emancipation for women and is remembered for her charitable and humanitarian work and her great public speaking which captured the hearts of the Argentinean poor. She was the wife of President Juan Peron. She was born to an unmarried mother and her father never really acknowledged her. She was reared in very poor circumstances, had little formal education and left home at 15 to follow her dream to become a famous actress. From such humble beginnings she was able to become one of the most famous women of her generation and in Hollywood style a rags to riches success story.

During the next ten years she appeared in some minor film roles but made a name for herself especially on radio where she developed her oratory skills and became nationally famous. She met Juan Peron in 1944 at a charity function and they became lovers. At this stage she was independently wealthy from her radio and other work. He was 48 and she was 24. The two were married the following year and in 1946 Juan Peron became President. She was idolised by the Argentinean poor with religious fervour. They considered her a saint and a saviour and gave her the type of devotion normally reserved for the Virgin Mary. Even today in many Argentinean homes her picture appears alongside that of the Madonna.

She exuded self-belief, charisma and confidence, dressed to impress and wanted to re-brand herself as a person of class and distinction and to quote her own words: "the poor like to see me lovely; they don't want to be championed by some lady who doesn't dress well. They dream of me and I cannot disappoint them". She dyed her hair blond and sought advice on fashionable elegant clothes from women of high society, and from Europe bought Dior Dresses and expensive perfumes. She liked wearing expensive jewellery. She set up her own charity foundation and was very generous to the poor. She also believed in the personal touch and set aside a few hours each day to meet poor people. She played a big part through her support in getting the vote for Argentinean women which was finally conceded in 1947. She said that she demanded more rights for women because she knew what women had to put up with. She was extremely ambitious and at one stage put herself forward for the Vice-Presidency of Argentina but the army was opposed to this and the idea was dropped. In any event at this stage her health had deteriorated and she was not well enough for the role. She said that what she wanted was to pass into history and she eventually got her wish at the young age of 33.

She became ill in 1950 with ovarian cancer and died in 1952. To promote her dream of immortality she ordered that her body be embalmed. Shortly before her death she was given the official title of "Spiritual Leader of the Nation." When she died she was given an official state funeral despite the fact that she was not an elected head of state and Argentina went into an official period of mourning. For many months after she died the radio stations of Argentina interrupted their broadcasts every evening at 8.25 p.m. to remind their listeners that it was exactly at that time that Eva had died. The Vatican received 40,000 letters requesting that she be canonized but they didn't consider her a candidate worthy of sainthood. Even in death she was controversial. In 1955, Juan Peron was overthrown by a military coup. Eva Peron's body was taken away in secrecy from the country and interned in Milan in a grave under the name of a nun. They feared her legacy would provide a focal point for opposition to the military regime. In 1973, Juan Peron was returned to power and Eva's body was repatriated and finally put into its last resting place in Argentina.

Since her death, Eva Peron has become an iconic and mythological figure with film, books and countless articles written about her. She is hugely venerated or indeed despised depending on your perspective and political allegiances. She is condemned by association because of Juan Peron's oppressive and undemocratic regime. It is hard to imagine that she was unaware of what was going on. When in power he ruthlessly put down opposition to his regime; some were jailed, others were tortured and sometimes killed. Juan Peron was pro-Nazi and after the war hundreds of war criminals were given a safe haven in Argentina. Nevertheless, a fair judgement on her would be that she achieved a lot and did much good especially for the poor and dispossessed during her short sojourn on this planet. She is remembered as a charismatic person who came from humble beginnings to achieve considerable fame.

> "The nation's government has just handed me the bill that grants us our civil rights. I am receiving it before you, certain that I am accepting this on behalf of all Argentinean women, and I can feel my hands tremble with joy as they grasp the laurel proclaiming victory."
>
> Eva Peron

Confidence and Locus of Control

Confidence is also related to the locus of control. This is where people perceive the control centre of their lives to be located. Those with an internal locus of control believe that they are in control of their lives and that what they do can influence outcomes. They believe that they can make things happen and are in control of their destiny. They are inclined to make up their own minds about things and are not easily influenced by the opinions of others. These people live happier, healthier and more successful lives. They are more achievement oriented and get better jobs. They are more likely to be proactive in regard to their health care taking exercise and following the advice of medical experts. College students with an internal locus of control believe their grades are achieved through their own preparation and efforts. They are thus more motivated and likely to learn.

Those with an external locus of control believe that outside influences such as fate, chance, luck, the government and others determine the direction of their lives. They believe that they have no influence on events and thus become despondent, indifferent and unhappy with their lot. They often adopt a victim mentality blaming others and adverse circumstances for their plight. Since they believe they are less in control of their lives they are more likely to suffer doubt, uncertainty, stress, anxiety and depression. They are more likely to feel cynical about politics, and because they believe they are powerless to influence events are less likely to vote. They tend to be reactive in their approach to life waiting for others to take the initiative or events to unfold before they take any action. They are easily led and influenced by the opinion of others. In matters relating to health it may be too late at that stage. College student with an external locus of control attribute low grades to bad luck, the unusual difficulty of the exam paper, or the incompetence of the examiner. They are likely to believe that their study efforts are pointless and therefore they are less likely to work hard for grades.

"Without a humble but reasonable confidence in your own powers you cannot be successful or happy."

Norman Vincent Peale

Why Confidence Matters

Confidence leads to a happier, calmer and a more fulfilling existence for you and for the people you come in contact with. We need to set goals and be confident that we will succeed in achieving them. In a competitive world it is confident people who influence others, win respect, inspire others, get things done, make an impact on the world and succeed. Confidence enables you to take calculated risks and participate actively, productively and fully in society. You will never know what you are capable of doing unless you are prepared to take some prudent risks.

A confident person knows what they want and can assert their needs without upsetting others. While meeting their own needs they are also sensitive and help meet the needs of others. Confident people inspire confidence in others because they appear more credible and self-assured. They are more likely to be seen as role models for others. Children who lack confidence find it difficult to stand up for themselves and thus often become victims of bullying.

Lack of Confidence and Shyness

There is no doubt that a lack of confidence is a terrible handicap in life. Without confidence we will lack the motivation to use our initiative and pursue our goals. Lack of confidence manifests itself in many ways such as anxiety, uncertainty and lack of self-belief. People who lack confidence give off negative vibes which makes others doubt them. They tend to sound unconvincing and thus tend to be overlooked and ignored. Lack of confidence may come from our early childhood experiences. If you were not encouraged by your parents to be independent and outgoing then you may have difficulty doing so when you mature. If you were part of a family where favoured brother and sisters were made to feel more important than you, then this might have generated feelings of inferiority and inadequacy that continued into adulthood. Parents or teachers who set impossibly high standards may have convinced you that you will never measure up or achieve anything worthwhile.

People who are extremely shy find it very difficult to socialise and assert their needs in the company of others. They find it difficult to do the normal day to day activities like going shopping, making appointments to see the doctor or attending meetings. If you find it difficult to make friends you will become isolated and lonely. Consequently you will not be able to develop and exercise good interpersonal relationship skills and so shyness will become a self-fulfilling prophecy.

18/40/60 Rule

Shy people feel embarrassed, self-conscious and awkward in the company of other people and think they are always being observed and evaluated by others. Dr. Daniel Amen's 18/40/60 rule is relevant here because it suggests that young immature people are deeply immersed and obsessed with their own thoughts. He maintained that when you're 18 you think everybody is thinking about you. At 18 the part of the brain dealing with rational thought called the prefrontal cortex is not fully developed and is still immature. When you reach 40 you don't care what anybody thinks of you and may adopt the attitude of accept me as I am or leave me alone. Deep down you still need the approval of others but just don't care as much. When you're 60 you realise that nobody has been thinking about you all along and you realise that you have been wasting a lot of time worrying about nothing. Evolution has ensured that the brain is hard wired to be negative and so it is normal for the brain to focus on worries and for gloomy thoughts to dominate.

We are socialised to please other people such as our family, friends, work colleagues and boss. We want to preserve and even to enhance the reputation we have built in the eyes of others. However, shy people are so self-consciously focused on their own shortcomings that they fail to realise that most people are just like them with their own thoughts, concerns, preoccupations and issues. When you realise that most people just think about themselves it may help you become less shy and self-conscious and become more outgoing and assertive. It is advantageous if you do so as insensitive and ruthless people may take advantage of your shyness and treat you like a doormat. The good news is that you don't have to reach 60 to become more self-assured. You can do so right now by adopting the right perspective and attitude and acquiring the right skills.

Many famous people were shy including Robert Frost the American Poet who won four Pulitzer Prices for Poetry, Eleanor

Roosevelt first lady of the United States who campaigned for the equality of women, Albert Einstein the most famous scientist in history for his theory of relativity and Charles Darwin for his work on evolution. Moderately shy people have often positive traits such as empathy, perceptiveness, intuition, sensitivity and drive which may more than compensate for their shyness.

Becoming More Confident

To overcome shyness you must take every opportunity to go out, socialise and meet people as it is only through interacting with others that we practise and acquire social skills. Building confidence is like learning to play golf. You must be aware of the critical skills and practise them frequently. Even Tiger Woods the world famous golfer still practises for hours each day. Shy people tend to be obsessed with themselves and how they appear to other people. They consistently rate themselves as less attractive than others do because they are so self-conscious and critical of themselves. Replace critical thoughts with more positive ones. Act "as if" you are outgoing and full of joy and laughter. See yourself as warm, interesting, sensitive, competent and engaging enthusiastically with others, as in the long-run these are more important characteristics than physical appearance.

To become more outgoing shy people must stop dwelling on their own insecurities and become more aware of and concentrate on the people around them. They must realise that other people have their own insecurities, fears and problems. It is only by engaging with them that you will see that they are just like you with their own sensitivities and vulnerabilities. It is only by thinking of other people that you forget about yourself and become less self-conscious. Once you become more outwardly focused on the lives of others and less focussed on yourself, shyness will no longer control and dominate your life.

When buying their daily newspaper at the local newsagents, instead of just putting the money on the counter, they should focus on the shopkeeper maintaining eye contact and thank them for the service provided. This creates a favourable environment for a positive social interaction. Also seek random opportunities to engage in small talk with people while waiting on the checkout line in the supermarket. This will do wonders for your social skills and make you less self-conscious.

> "Confidence is that feeling by which the mind embarks in great and honourable courses with a sure hope and trust in itself."
>
> Marcus T. Cicero

Strategies for Overcoming Shyness

The following are further useful strategies to overcome shyness and become more confident:

- Socialise as much as you can. Practise makes perfect, even for the socially accomplished. Even famous musicians and sportspeople practise every day. The more they practise the better they get. Socialising will give you plenty of opportunities to practice your social skills and observe the good social behaviours of others so that you can improve on your own. However simply showing up is not enough. Shy people often expect others to approach them to engage in conversation and take all the initiative. Unfortunately this is not the way things happen in reality. You must make an effort and approach others, start a conversation and learn how to talk to other people. When joining a group at a party, always introduce yourself. To start the conversation, engage in small talk as this breaks the ice and shows you are willing to talk. This reminds other people to introduce themselves as well. Arrange to meet people that you would like to know better.

- Research the people who are likely to be there and what their interests are before you attend social events or meetings. Plan what you are going to say and rehearse appropriate questions. Arrive early so that you can acclimatise to the situation. At the event focus your attention outward by observing other people and listening actively while maintaining eye contact. You can't be obsessed with yourself if you are thinking about others as the mind can't think of two things at the same time. Non-verbal cues such as facial expression, level of eye contact and tone of voice will help you recognise the interest level, concern and emotional state of others so that you can react appropriately. This will help you gauge situations and know when it is time to engage, withdraw or move on. If a person starts to yawn while you're talking it may be a signal to switch the conversation. On the other hand, if you tell a joke and somebody laughs it may be a sign that they are enjoying your company. Good conversationalists make comments that are in tune with or add to what is being said and ask open-ended questions to keep the conversation alive. Answering questions with one word answers is a conversation killer. You don't have to be interesting to make your mark socially; all you have to do is to show interest in others, engage and listen.

- Think positive thoughts and see yourself as a worthwhile person with unique abilities and talents. Self-assured people expect others to respond to them positively. In life, you often get what you expect.

- Don't take rebuffs personally as they may not be your fault. They can be due to many causes such as incompatibility, thoughtlessness, someone else's bad mood, a misunderstanding, lack of consideration or just plain rudeness. Rejections are a part of life. You are not going to like or be liked by everybody. Just mark it down to experience and move on until you find a more agreeable and compatible person or group.

- Learn to control your emotions by not reacting aggressively to the negative emotions and insensitivities of others. Ignore the rudeness of others by acting calmly and politely. Defuse difficult situations by explaining your point of view, compromising, apologising, if appropriate or sometimes by just changing the subject. Generally it is best not to judge ideas as they come up as it encourages other people to participate more freely if they feel what they say will not be evaluated or criticised. People prefer to be told they're right rather than they're wrong. Saying they're right affirms their intelligence and values, and shows that you like them which makes them feel good about themselves and good about you.

- Try to see the humour in situations. Laughter is contagious and will lighten up a situation and defuse a negative atmosphere. Smiling sends the signal that we are open, friendly and fun to be with and thus encourages others to engage and converse with us.

"Self-confidence is: knowing that we have the capacity to do something good and firmly decide not to give up."

Dalai Lama

You Can't Be Confident All the Time

Most of us will experience a lack of confidence at times during our lifetimes. People can experience a crisis of confidence during difficult times such as redundancy, a breakdown in a cherished relationship, a serious accident, incapacity or death of a loved one. During such times your self-esteem can be extremely undermined or severely tested with feelings of self-doubt, uncertainty and fear dominating your every thought. However, these are cycles we go through and healthy people will pull out of them and recover to become their former confident selves again. You do this by refocusing on the positive and rediscovering your sense of self-worth. In a minority of cases some people may need the help of a psychologist or counsellor to make a full recovery.

Being introverted is not the same as being shy. Some people are deep thinkers and prefer their own company to that of others. In fact many successful people are introverted and this is not a disadvantage in certain vocations such as science, writing and computer programming as introverts tend to be preoccupied with their thoughts. Nevertheless extroverted people are more outgoing and find it easier to make friends and operate successfully in a team; skills that are becoming more and more crucial to a successful life. In addition, they are often perceived as being more intelligent and approachable whether they are or not.

Where Does Confidence Come From?

Confidence is probably attributable to an equal mixture of genetics and experience. It helps if you have confident parents as nature may pass the genes on to you. Parents, teachers and religious leaders will imprint rules and norms, principles and values and 'musts, oughts and shoulds' in your child's subconscious when you are still impressionable. Some of these will help you progress successfully in your life while others will be detrimental and hold you back. Reflect and examine where they came from and recognise those that are no longer appropriate to a responsible adult and eradicate them. After all as an adult you are supposed to be a rational responsible human being thinking for yourself, making up your own mind and using your knowledge and experience in a critical, thoughtful and sensible way.

Confidence comes from being successful. The old adage that "nothing succeeds like success" is true. There is a cycle of success where one successful outcome is likely to lead to another. Overcoming a major obstacle, passing an exam, winning at sport or getting a book published is associated with feelings of euphoria and pride. Success makes you feel confident and happy and ready to take on new challenges. To make yourself more confident, think back to a moment when you were feeling supremely confident and create a trigger, such as touching your forefinger and thumb, to recall that feeling. Any experience can be anchored through sounds, words, touch or context and prompted by engaging the appropriate cue. When you want to feel confident engage the trigger to revive the feelings of confidence.

Confident people know they can achieve what they want and they persist until they succeed. They may experience setbacks but always learn from these and they do things differently until they achieve their purpose. Developing self-confidence is all about overcoming situations in which you feel anxious, afraid and insecure. The more you challenge yourself the more self-confident you will become. Ask yourself what would you dare to do and dream if you weren't afraid of doing anything in the world? At the end of your life you will regret the things you wanted to do but for whatever reason were afraid to do.

The nurture part of confidence can be learnt and developed through training and lifetime experiences. It is important to realise that you can become more self-confident through your own determination and efforts. Become an expert in a specific subject as this will build your confidence. Study the behaviours of confident people and use them as role models. Read the autobiographies and biographies of famous and successful people and see how their behaviours contributed to their success. In fact, many famous people themselves, including Winston Churchill and George Patton, have said that biography was their favourite form of reading as a source of information and inspiration. Similarly, you should adopt those actions and behaviours that will help you live a fruitful and successful life. John Hume the civil rights activist in Northern Ireland and Nobel Prize winner for peace admits that he was strongly influenced and inspired by the life of Martin Luther King who won civil rights for the black population in the USA.

> "You have brains in your head.
> You have feet in your shoes.
> You can steer yourself in any direction you choose.
> You're on your own.
> And you know what you know.
> You are the guy who'll decide where to go."
>
> Dr. Seuss

Exercising Your Rights

You have a right to reach your potential and a right to be confident. Others have rights as well as you. Realising this will ensure that you treat people with respect and prevent you from being self-centred. Knowing you have rights helps your self-respect and enhances your confidence. The basic human rights include:

- You have the right to ask for what you want. Other people have the right to refuse.
- You have the right to express your opinions. Other people have the right to have different opinions and to disagree with you. You have the right to say no.
- You have the right to change your mind. Circumstances change, knowledge changes, people mature and therefore you have the right to change.
- You have the right to be fairly treated and not to be discriminated against.
- You have the right to make decisions. However, you must take responsibility for the consequences of your decisions.

- You have the right not to get involved in other people's problems. They are primarily and ultimately responsible for their own lives.
- You have the right to make mistakes. However you should admit your mistakes and be prepared to learn from them.
- You have the right to get what you paid for. When you return goods for replacement or refund you have the right to be treated with courtesy and fairness and on your part you should also be mannerly and civil to others.
- You have the right to privacy.
- You have the right to grow and develop and be successful.

Competence and Confidence

Competence is your ability to do something. You are more likely to be confident when operating within your area of expertise. A doctor may have competence in medical matters but lack competence and indeed confidence when dealing with financial matters. An accountant may have confidence in financial matters but lack confidence when dealing with legal issues. Without competence confidence can be dangerous, misleading and unjustified particularly if you are operating outside your area of expertise. However a realistic belief in your own ability to get things done will take you a long way. Without self-belief you are unlikely to have the confidence to even get started or take the calculated risks needed to succeed. Building confidence is like learning to acquire any skills. It's about knowing what the critical skills are and practising them every day. Just like any other skill confidence has four levels of competence as follows:

1. Unconscious Incompetence. At this level you are shy and do not possess the skill of confidence and you are unaware how useful it could be to living a happy and successful life. One could be extremely shy and not realise how beneficial confidence could be as a trigger to success in any area of life you choose. If you are shy all your life you may accept shyness as a natural way of being and do nothing about it. You are incompetent about confidence not realising how you can learn to be confident as confidence is an acquired social skill.

2. Conscious Incompetence. At this level you are becoming aware of your shyness and how it is holding

you back in life. Awareness of the problem now means that you have an opportunity to do something positive about it by acquiring confidence building skills. By observing confident people you know what confidence looks like, feels like, sounds like and how it has contributed to their success. You realise that the more you work on your shyness the more you will move towards becoming more confident.

3. Conscious Competence. At this level you have acquired the skill of confidence but are conscious and uncomfortable about it. The skill is not yet habitual as you will need to practise confidence skills for at least 21 days (the time psychologists have found that it takes to acquire a new habit). Remember practise makes perfect and practise make permanent! Nothing worthwhile is achieved without hard work, repetition, persistence and dedication.

4. Unconscious Competence. At this level you have acquired the confidence habit. Confidence is now part of your persona and you can be confident without thinking about it. You now wonder how you ever functioned in life without the benefit and calm self-assurance of being confident. Without confidence you have an overwhelming fear of change, don't like mixing socially, and are unlikely to take any risks and therefore unlikely to live a successful life.

> "If we all did the things we are capable of doing, we would literally astound ourselves."
>
> Thomas Alva Edison

Self-Belief

People with strong self-belief set and achieve stretching goals. They are able to take, accept and learn from criticism. They have a balanced perspective on their strengths and weaknesses and take remedial action to overcome their shortcomings. They are prepared to take realistic risks and so don't suffer from fear and self-doubt of being wrong or making a mistake when pursuing goals. They bounce back from setbacks and create a positive future for themselves. They anticipate and know how to deal with the stresses in their lives because they know that life will not always run smoothly. They follow their heart and don't worry what others think about them. They realise that other people are wrapped up in their own concerns and interests and think very little, if at all, about them. They know that it's up to them if they want to succeed. People who believe in themselves are more likely to be trusted, respected and believed in by others. Those lacking in self-belief give out negative vibes which makes other people doubt them resulting in their being overlooked and ignored. It was his strong sense of self-belief and the winning mentality that helped Sebastian Coe, two times Olympic 1,500 metres gold medallist, win the 2012 Olympic Games for London against strong opposition from Paris, Madrid and New York.

Your beliefs are strongly influenced by your parents, teachers and significant others in your life. They are laid down in your subconscious as a child when your critical faculties are not fully developed and so you accept them without question. Beliefs are not necessarily true or even useful. Some are empowering while others are limiting. Empowering beliefs will aid your success while limiting beliefs will facilitate your failure. Children reared in a supportive, egalitarian, loving and nurturing environment and instilled with the value of education and learning and respect for others, are more likely to prosper and develop into self-sufficient and successful human beings.

Children who are encouraged to set achievable but stretching goals are more likely to become confident and to challenge themselves with difficult undertakings when they mature. The more they accomplish the more confident they become. Those brought up in a negative environment may never mature psychologically and reach their full potential. Things we are told as children are imprinted on our minds and stick with us for a lifetime. Beliefs can spur you into action or hold you back. However irrespective of the circumstances of upbringing people have overcome their past and gone on to achieve great things because we are the only ones who truly know what we want and what we are capable of achieving. Children can overcome the most dire childhood circumstances and go on to live prosperous and successful lives.

"Keep your dreams alive. Understand to achieve anything requires faith and belief in yourself, vision, hard work, determination, and dedication. Remember all things are possible for those who believe."

Gail Devers

Empowering Beliefs

It's aerodynamically impossible for the bumblebee to fly as his wings are too short and his body weight too high. However, nobody has told this to the bumblebee and so he just goes on flying. Great things are often achieved by people who are unaware of or just don't accept their limitations. The following are empowering beliefs which you should adopt as part of your philosophy of life:

- You are primarily responsible for where you are right now in life and for your own destiny. Some people go through life blaming their parents, teachers, circumstances, luck and other people for their lack of success in life. Some people blame their lack of formal education for holding them back but we all know people with little formal education who went on to become highly successful in life. Attributing blame to others for your circumstances does not lead to empowerment or control over your life and behaviour. Instead you should be taking action right now to change the direction of your life in a positive way.

- Learn from your mistakes. View failure as a learning experience on the road to achieving your ultimate goal. There is no failure only feedback. Become a lifelong learner by continuously undertaking learning and training experiences. Learn also from your successes so that you can apply the success principles you have learned to future enterprises.

- You mostly get what you expect. Expect to achieve what you desire and you are more likely to do so. Expect to be happy and you are more likely to be happy. Expect to be liked and you are more likely to be popular. Expect to be successful and you are more likely to succeed. For many years the conventional wisdom and self-limiting beliefs held athletes back from breaking the four minute barrier until Roger Bannister came along on the 5th May, 1954 and broke it. By 1999, 955 athletes had run a sub 4 minute mile which proved that it was not physiologically impossible as previously thought but was merely a self-imposed psychological barrier. Good runners now achieve the sub 4 minute mile as a matter of course. Similarly it was thought that there was an upper limit of 500lb in weightlifting until Valery Alexis was tricked into thinking he was lifting a slightly lighter weight.

- Psychologists maintain that if you want to acquire a new behaviour you should fake it until you make it. Act as if anything you want to do is possible and it is more likely to become a self-fulfilling prophecy. Anytime you hear your inner voice saying 'I can't' ask 'why not.' It is more positive and productive to spend your time trying to figure out how you can do something rather than have doubts about it. Another approach is to say to yourself; "I can't yet." This opens up possibilities such as if you take appropriate action such as undergoing mentoring, coaching, training or reading up on the subject matter you may succeed. "I can't" is a self-sabotaging belief that robs you of your energy, hope and motivation. You must question your limiting belief in order to get rid of it. Modify or discard the beliefs that are not serving you well. Experiment with new beliefs supporting what you know you are capable of doing if you really put your mind down to it.

- Irrespective of the outcome you are still a worthwhile person. Success is often due more to persistent effort rather than inherent ability. If you make the best use of what you have you have all the resources you need to succeed.

- You are more than your job or your performance on a given task at a given time. People who get too much wrapped up in their jobs or careers find it very difficult to cope when their job is made redundant or their careers come to an end as they inevitably will. Develop other interests as a fallback position.

- Control your thoughts and attitudes to control your destiny. Attitude makes a more significant contribution to success than skills and knowledge. Some psychologists maintain that 85 per cent of our success is determined by attitude. So view things in a positive light. Change your beliefs to change your thoughts, attitudes, behaviour and actions You become what you think about all day long. If you think you can succeed you will, and if you think you can't succeed you won't. Changing your attitude to life by taking the 't' out of can't and making it 'can' creates motivation and encourages effort. Thoughts have a massive impact on your life. Change the way you think to change the way you live. Either you shape your thoughts for the better or your thoughts will shape you for the worst. We all move in the direction of our dominant thoughts; so make sure they are positive, energising and constructive. Visualising and thinking about the changes you want to make is the first step to making improvements in your life.

- Psychotherapist Albert Ellis invented the term 'musturbation' for a person who thinks that they must, should, ought, or have to. He maintained that a healthy response would be to change these to 'I want to' or 'I choose to'. If you want to do something you are empowered and in control of your own destiny. If you feel you have to you are disempowered.

- Money can't buy happiness but it may provide security and peace of mind. Pursue your passion and the money will follow as night follows day. You will be far more fulfilled and happier in a job that you are interested in and passionate about than spending your whole life in a job that you hate.

- When things go wrong, keep your problems in perspective by reframing and refocusing. Things are never as bad as they seem. It could be worse. Reframe problems as challenges to be overcome. Develop a healthy balanced perspective by questioning any negative thoughts. Imagine thinking, focusing, believing and acting in more constructive ways. To build a positive self-belief, think about your strengths and past successes which will inspire you to keep going.

- If you want to know another person, study their actions rather than their beliefs. Believe what they do rather than what they say. We all have different perspectives on life. Be aware that you cannot change another person, you can only change yourself.

> "Men often become what they believe themselves to be. If I believe I cannot do something, it makes me incapable of doing it. But when I believe I can, then I acquire the ability to do it even if I didn't have it in the beginning."
>
> Mahatma Gandhi

Limiting Beliefs

Some people are hindered and hampered by unhelpful beliefs imprinted deep in their subconscious which hold them back from achieving their desires. Your subconscious doesn't know the difference between what is true and what is untrue. It imposes rules on us and then operates as if they are true. Question your limiting beliefs as they will lead you to failure and substitute empowering beliefs for them as they will lead you to success. Change your limiting beliefs one at a time and change your life. Circus fleas are trained to jump to a certain height by being trained in a limited space such as a jar with a lid on top. After a while they believe that they can only jump a certain distance so that when the lid is removed they jump to the expected height. Similarly baby elephants are restrained from breaking free with a steel chain. After awhile they believe they can't escape from their tether and so can be restrained by a twig when they mature. They have literally given up!

The following are some examples of limiting beliefs which you should question:

- You are too ready to take responsibility for things over which you have no control. You cannot control other people. You can't control their actions, reactions, incompetence and behaviours. On the other hand you have control over your actions, reactions, attitude, perspective, thoughts, feelings, emotions and goals.

- You feel that everybody must love and approve you when in fact you should realise that you can't please everybody. Seek out the people who will support you and who are compatible with your personality, attitudes, beliefs, values and interests. Avoid those who are incompatible with your views and lifestyle.

- You feel that other people must do what you want them to do, or agree with what you say, or with what you perceive to be the truth. This has given rise to fundamentalists willing to kill those who disagree with their dogmas and has led to feuds, atrocities, wars and genocides. It has also led to disagreements, conflicts and rifts in family life.

- You are too concerned with what others may think. Charles Darwin delayed the publication of his famous work on the theory of evolution called The Origin of Species fearing he would upset his wife who was a devout Christian and the Church of England because it challenged the biblical story of creation. He was pushed into publishing his great work when he become aware that another evolutionist Alfred Russell Wallace was about to publish a similar theory. The greatest thinker of the 19th century could have become a mere footnote in the study of evolution because of his anxiety and fear of disapproval and public scorn.

- You exaggerate the importance of a particular outcome. People who make a catastrophe out of every little setback focus on the worst possible outcome. It's not the end of the world if things do not work out as anticipated. Don't catastrophise but rather put things in perspective. Things are never as bad as they seem and most things work out okay in the end.

- You feel that you must always be competent, adequate and achieving. You must be perfect in everything you do. We are all burdened with imperfections and idiosyncrasies. Nobody is perfect.

- That the past is all important and determines your feelings and behaviour today. The reality is that even though we can't change the past, we can learn from the past, free

92

ourselves from the past and move on with our lives. It is now and the future that we should focus our minds on.

- We are too focused on negative possibilities. Most of our worries never materialise.

- You feel that you must serve other people's needs before your own. Your primary responsibility is to serve your own needs first; then serve the needs of others.

- You believe that you are too old to achieve what you desire. Age didn't stop people like Ronald Reagan from becoming at 69 the oldest ever President of the United States or Winston Churchill from becoming Prime Minister of Great Britain for the second time at the age of 77.

- You feel that you are too small, too tall, too thin or too fat. Wayne Gretzky one of the greatest hockey players of all time was told he was too small and too slow to make it as a professional ice hockey player in the National Hockey League. However he didn't accept this self-limiting belief and went on to become a great hockey player nicknamed 'The Great One'.

- You find it difficult to make decisions without getting the approval of others. At the end of the day you are responsible for your own life and so should take those decisions which you feel are in your best interests and stand by them.

- You feel you have to do everything yourself and believe nobody can do work as efficiently and effectively as you can. A successful person is one who can delegate appropriately to other people and thus free himself to concentrate on the important tasks.

- You feel that you must not take risks. Life is a series of risks such as accepting a challenging work assignment, taking a promotion in a different city, raising a sensitive issue with your friend, or confronting an abusive manager about his conduct. We must be prepared to take prudent risks if we are to change and succeed in life. In fact there is nothing more empowering and confidence building than taking a risk and succeeding.

- You believe that people cannot be trusted. Trust but verify, should be your motto. Modern society and business in particular could not operate without trust.

> "People are disturbed not by events that happen to them, but by their view of them."
>
> Epictetus

Moving Outside Your Comfort Zone

The comfort zone is where you feel most comfortable and safe. We like familiar places, people and things. Notice the way people go on holidays to the same location year after year. When they go out for a meal or a drink some people like to sit in the same spot in their local restaurant or pub. When they go to church on Sunday they like to sit in the same pew. We associate with the same people and we are extremely reluctant to challenge or change our beliefs, values and attitudes. Some people work in the same job all their lifetime and some never leave the town in which they were born and marry their childhood sweetheart. They will never know if they have reached their true potential.

We all have a desire for conformity, routine and familiarity where we settle for the mundane because we are afraid to take risks. We are creatures of habit often sticking to the same daily routines. Everyday becomes indistinguishable from the day before. If we stick to the same routine we get fixed in our ways and only see what we expect to see. Some wise person said; if you keep on doing the same old thing you are going to get what you always got. On a similar note, the definition of insanity is doing the same thing over and over and expecting to get different results. Your brain is like a muscle; it needs to be used and challenged in different ways to make it grow. So engage in lifelong learning and continuous improvement to keep it in top shape.

Even successful people may become victims of their own success and refuse to change until it is too late. An example would be a business man who refuses to react to competition or new technology. In your comfort zone you feel competent, confident, safe and unchallenged. This then becomes a comfort trap where you become set in your ways and are reluctant to undertake anything new even if it means your eventual downfall. It's like the frog in the pot of water that gradually gets accustomed to the heat and boils to death when he could have just jumped out of the water before the critical boiling point was reached. To succeed in life and stay successful you must be prepared to create new challenges, overcome your fears and move outside your comfort zone. In fact, the best way to develop people is to move them from the familiar to the strange.

For changes that are difficult to make try making incremental steps that gradually take you outside your comfort zone. Small successes give us the confidence and motivation to do so. Immigrants to a new country such as the USA find themselves challenged by a new entrepreneurial and democratic environment and have to be innovative, competitive and hard working to survive. They are willing to start at the bottom, work hard and do the menial tasks that others are reluctant to do. This in no small way has contributed to the economic success of the USA and made it the leading commercial and political force in the world.

People have a problem moving outside their comfort zone because the perceived risk can make them feel anxious, insecure and stressed. The negative feeling experienced may overwhelm them and outweigh any possible rewards. Your motto should be 'feel the fear and do it anyway.' Life is about expanding your experiences and horizons and living every moment as if it is your last. After all in this uncertain and brief life, you never know what's around the corner in terms of poor health, crippling accidents, misfortune, adverse financial circumstances and even death.

Understand what's important to you and so what's worth feeling uncomfortable about and taking a risk for. Look for the positives in new opportunities rather than thinking about the possible problems and negatives. The new comfort zone eventually becomes your comfort trap unless you eventually push it out further. New opportunities and a burning desire to change and progress in life will energise you to break away from your existing cosy situation. If you are a lifelong learner you will be continually challenged and out of your comfort zone.

> "Move out of your comfort zone. You can only grow if you are willing to feel awkward and uncomfortable when you try something new."
>
> Brian Tracy

Opportunities to Move You Outside Your Comfort Zone

The following are examples of opportunities that will move you out of your existing comfort zone:

- Undertaking part-time degree programmes such as MBA or professional qualifications while working fulltime. This is not easy to do as it requires determination, dedication and commitment. In addition to the syllabus subject matter such as finance and strategic thinking, you will learn study and research skills, time management, problem-solving, writing skills and networking (with new class mates).
- Accepting an overseas assignment. It will give you the opportunity to learn a new language, meet new people, experience a new culture and stretch you in ways that you never thought possible.

- Accepting a new promotion. You will learn how to cope with new responsibilities such as decision-making, problem solving and leadership.

- Moving between departments such as from finance to marketing or from engineering to operations. You will learn to adopt a new perspective, acquire a new discipline, learn a new technical vocabulary and develop yourself for general management.

- Becoming self-employed after losing your job. This will force you to learn new disciplines such as finance, taxation, marketing and entrepreneurship. In this instance the move out of your comfort zone is involuntary. However, many people choose to downshift from a high level stressful executive job to opening up a bed and breakfast in a rural location to fulfil a dream or indeed just to simplify their lifestyle.

- There is an uncomfortable period of adjustment when learning new processes or procedures or adapting to new work practices but such changes are beneficial despite the initial human reaction to resist because they will keep your mind sharp, improve your powers of concentration and teach you how to cope with change.

- Experiencing a 360 degree appraisal may take senior managers out of their comfort zone by learning from feedback from numerous sources and taking corrective action to improve their behaviour or management style.

- Leaving home to go to college in a different town. This will force you to make new friends, become independent and take responsibility for your life, learn budgeting and cooking skills and adapt to a new environment.

- Being transferred to a new city or town in a different part of the country. This will force you to adapt to new circumstances, make new friends and learn about a new topography.

- Being asked to make a verbal presentation to a group of managers especially if you do not usually speak formally in front of people. This will give you the opportunity to learn presentation skills such as planning, preparation, delivery and answering questions.

- Acquiring a new hobby. This may help you develop creativity and other skills. People who are made redundant often turn their hobbies into profitable enterprises.

- Moonlighting such as part-time lecturing in a local college. This will force you to learn research and presentation skills and give you the confidence to talk knowledgeably about your area of expertise and handle questions competently.

"If you're in a comfort zone afraid to venture out, remember that all winners were at one time filled with doubt."

Author Unknown

Summary

You need confidence to live a happy and successful life. Many people give up on their dreams because they lack the confidence to pursue them. Confidence is linked to the locus of control. Those with an internal locus of control are more confident because they believe that they are in control of their lives and can do things to influence outcomes. Those with an external locus of control lack confidence because they believe that external influences such as fate, the government and others determine the direction of their lives.

A lack of confidence is a terrible handicap in life. People who are extremely shy find it difficult to socialise, make new friends and assert their needs. There are useful strategies that you can learn to overcome shyness and become more confident. Confidence is probably attributable in equal measure to genetics and experience. Knowing and exercising your rights will make you more confident. Just like any other skill confidence can be learned through practise and application. Get rid of your disempowering beliefs and replace them with empowering ones. Move outside your comfort zone if you want to become more confident and successful.

Five Activities to Improve Your Confidence Skills

1. When you meet someone for the first time actively engage with them and consciously focus your attention on them. By thinking about them and less about yourself you will become less self-conscious and self-obsessed.

2. Plan before you attend a social event. Think about who you are likely to meet, what the subject of conversation is likely to be and prepare with these in mind.

3. Familiarise yourself with the basic human rights and assert them appropriately as the need arises.

4. Adopt the empowering beliefs as part of your philosophy of life as listed in this chapter.

5. If you feel you are getting too settled in your ways do something unusual to move you out of your comfort zone. Consider a foreign adventure holiday, a new hobby or undertaking an educational qualification.

5

Optimism & Self-Esteem

- *What are the dangers of unrealistic optimism?*
- *What is the downside of self-esteem?*
- *What is narcissism?*
- *How is self-efficacy and self-esteem linked?*

Introduction

Optimists are hopeful and positive about the future. They are positive thinkers seeing opportunities where others see problems. Unlike optimists, pessimists have negative expectations about the future. Self-esteem is the value we place on ourselves. People with high self-esteem have more initiative and are happier than others. There is a downside to self-esteem. Too much self-esteem can be bad for you and for others. Many murders are caused when self-esteem is undermined by insults and humiliation. Self-efficacy is a constituent of self-esteem and is the belief that we have the skills and competencies to do a particular task.

Optimistic Traits

An optimist is a person who tends to stay hopeful and positive about future outcomes. Optimists believe or expect things to work out well. They see the glass as half full rather than half empty. The American belief that the future can be better has given hope to the people and contributed in no small way to the entrepreneurial spirit and economic success of the USA. Optimists have a can do attitude and believe anything is possible. Unfortunately, their wishes aren't always met. After becoming the richest man in the world, Andrew Carnegie, tried to stop World War 1 by building peace temples throughout Europe. Needless to say he didn't succeed in stopping the war. After founding Silicon Graphics and Netscape, Jim Clark started Healtheon, a company he predicted would solve the American health-care crisis but it failed to do so.

Entrepreneurship, which is good for the economy, may be financially bad for many individuals as most start-ups fail. Psychologists' estimate that optimism like confidence is derived one half from our genes and one half from our experience. People with an optimistic personality are likely to remain relatively optimistic in many areas of their lives and remain so over their entire lifetime. If you want to become an optimist act like one as optimism is a matter of practise. Optimistic behaviours create a positive feedback loop which means that over time these behaviours will be reinforced and so you will become more optimistic.

Successful people expect the world to support them and present them with opportunity. Psychologists have named these kinds of people Inverse Paranoids. It is the opposite of being paranoid or thinking the world is out to get you or do you harm. Inverse Paranoids expect good things to happen to them and the world to be supportive. They expect good interpersonal relationships, rewarding careers and to be happy and successful. However, they do not leave this to chance but take the necessary steps to make it happen. They do everything possible to improve themselves by reading, taking courses, and attending lectures and seminars. They mix with others who have achieved the things that they want to achieve and so can learn from them.

Optimists are positive thinkers. They see opportunities where others see problems. They look for the silver lining in every cloud and ultimately believe that the future is bright. We think more creatively and intelligently about the future when we are hopeful and happy. Optimists focus on their successes rather than their failures. Even when confronted by adverse circumstances they make the best of a bad situation by actively tackling problems rather than thinking that things will be fine on the day and doing nothing. They believe that they can change their circumstance through their own ideas, actions and hard work.

Optimists measure themselves against their own standards rather than other people because they know this is the correct philosophy to adopt as comparisons to others can be invidious and de-motivational. If you compare yourself to other people who have more material goods you may conclude that they are living better and happier lives, not realising that spending time accumulating wealth may just mean that you have less time to enjoy what you have. In any event comparisons are always erroneous and undermining as everybody experiences things differently. Optimists know that changing their thoughts can change their destiny and thus realise the value of changing negative thoughts to positive thoughts.

Optimists are healthier and when they get ill they recover faster. They are able to cope with bereavement better than less optimistic people, as do people who come from strong supportive family backgrounds. It is their ability to engage with the world and to persist in the face of adversity that makes the difference. In 1993 and at 22 years of age Lance Armstrong became the youngest road-racing world champion. In 1996 he was diagnosed with testicular cancer. He showed his true grit, optimism, determination and resilience by making a comeback and winning the Tour de France in 1999. He viewed adversity as an opportunity for growth and became even more competitive and committed to his goals. A mere five months after being diagnosed with cancer he was back in training and has won the Tour de France seven times.

Being over-optimistic can lead to disaster. Convinced that the Titanic was unsinkable, Captain Edward J Smith ignored three warnings on 15th April 1912 that he was heading straight into major icebergs. A more realistic appraisal of the situation could have saved more than 1,500 lives. He could have taken a more southerly route to avoid the icebergs or slowed down the speed of the ship to leave room for manoeuvre. Furthermore because the designers believed the ship was unsinkable there were an insufficient number of life boats to cater for the number of passengers on board, resulting in needless deaths.

"Optimism is faith that leads to achievement. Nothing can be done without hope or confidence. No pessimist ever discovered the secret of the stars, or sailed to unchartered land, or opened a new doorway for the human spirit."

Helen Keller

Famous Optimistic People

Helen Keller (1880-1968). Helen Keller, who was born in the USA, was a socialist, lecturer, author, and activist on behalf of physically handicapped people. She was also a suffragette, pacifist, a birth control supporter and campaigner for women and workers' rights. She was left blind and deaf at 19 months which is now thought to be due to scarlet fever or meningitis. She showed great determination to learn to read and write, with the help of her devoted mentor and constant companion, Anne Sullivan, who came into her life at the age of seven and stayed with her for 50 years. Her dream of being able to talk normally was never fully realised and her efforts during her speaking tours had to be translated by Anne Sullivan. Before seven years of age, Helen who was clever and had an amazing memory was obstreperous and frustrated because she could not do what other normal children could do. She was virtually locked into her own mind with only primitive physical signals to indicate to others what she meant or wanted. Relatives found her temper tantrums so bad that they felt she should be put into an institution, which was the customary thing to do at the time for people with disabilities, especially those who were troublesome.

Under the guidance of Anne Sullivan, and as the trust and bond between them grew, Helen learned that words represented things and as soon as this link was made in her mind her appetite for learning new words was insatiable. Anne had been blind but had regained her sight after an operation but was still visually impaired and so could empathise with how Helen felt. Helen recalled her first awakening to the meaning of words as: "We walked down the path to the well-house, attracted by the fragrance of the honey-suckle with which I was covered. Someone was drawing water and my teacher placed my hand under the spout. As the cool stream gushed over one hand she spelled into the other the word water, first slowly, then rapidly. I stood still, my whole attention fixed upon the motions of her fingers. Suddenly I felt a misty consciousness as of something forgotten, a thrill of returning thought, and somehow the mystery of language was revealed to me."

Eventually Helen learned to use sign language, to read Braille, to type on both Braille and ordinary typewriters, and to dance and ride on horseback. When she typed she made very few typographical errors which is an outstanding achievement for a blind person. She went on to graduate with a BA from Radcliffe College being the first deaf and blind person to do so, and lived a very active life travelling and lecturing all over the world. Her optimism, self-esteem and determination to live a normal life in the face of such severe handicaps made her a source of hope and inspiration for those with similar disabilities and a source of amazement and admiration for the general public. She had a vivid imagination and a great sense of optimism and humour and said: "I seldom think about my limitations, and they never make me sad." She won the admiration of many throughout the world and Mark Twain maintained that the two most interesting characters of the 19th and 20th centuries were Napoleon and Helen Keller. She was extremely popular in Japan and met every US President from Grover Cleveland to Lyndon Johnson. She met many famous people including Alexander Graham Bell, Charles Chaplin and Mark Twain.

In 1962 a film about her life called The Miracle Worker, which was previously a television and a Broadway play, won two Oscars for the portrayal of Helen and Anne. In 1964 she was awarded the Presidential Medal of Freedom and a year later was elected to the Women's Hall of Fame. She campaigned tirelessly on behalf of people with disability and gave them the hope, optimism and strength to live happy and fulfilled lives. She devoted much of her later life to raising funds for the American Foundation for the Blind. During her time disabled people were frequently treated as freaks, not given a proper education and often abandoned in institutions. She educated the public that they had the same potential as anybody else but needed special support and facilities. In her time Helen was lucky to have the support of a devoted and loyal person like Anne Sullivan. If she was alive today she would be amazed at the technological gadgetry now available to help blind people live a more fruitful and fulfilling existence. In her own words she said: "The public must learn that the blind man is neither genius nor a freak nor an idiot. He has a mind that can be educated, a hand which can be trained, ambitions which it is right for him to strive to realise, and it is the duty of the public to help him make the best of himself so that he can win light through work." Among the many posthumous honours awarded to Helen Keller was the one made in 1999 when she was listed in Gallup's Most Widely Admired People of the 20th Century. Even today she continues to be a source of inspiration for disabled people throughout the world.

Norman Vincent Peale (1898-1993). Peale was born in Ohio, USA and was an ordained minister, famous orator, author and advocate of optimism. His most memorable and famous book titled The Power of Positive Thinking was published in 1952. The book has sold millions of copies and has been translated into numerous languages and was on the New York Times bestseller list for 186 weeks. A 1964 film based on his life One Man's Way was a commercial flop. The book might never have seen the light of day if it hadn't been for his wife's persistence and prescience. He was over 50 years old when he wrote it and felt discouraged on receiving numerous rejection slips. Dejected he threw the manuscript into the wastepaper basket. His wife took it from the wastepaper basket the next day and brought it to a publisher. It became one of the best selling self-help books of all time and is now a classic of the genre. Peale claimed that when he was young he suffered from an inferiority complex and developed his theories of positive thinking to help himself overcome his lack of confidence.

Peale's book was the progenitor of books on positive psychology, optimism and self-esteem. His books are a folksy mix of Christian theology and popular psychology. It has been criticised by mainstream psychologists as being anecdotal and unscientific but nevertheless its easily understood formulas for successful living have helped many people. Peale was an optimist who believed that the difficulties of life could be overcome through belief in one's self and faith in God. In a nutshell he believed in the American dream that people can achieve great things if they work hard and really want to. We all have a purpose in life, and if we have faith God will help us fulfil that purpose. He taught that people had great sources of power within themselves if they just tapped into them. Our attitude determines our success or failure. You can change your destiny by changing your thinking. In the 1930s he began a very popular radio broadcast, The Art of Living, which continued for 54 years. He was awarded the Presidential Medal of Freedom by Ronald Reagan in 1984 for his contribution to the field of theology. He was 93 when he died of a stroke on the 24th December 1993. His book The Power of Positive Thinking has gone through numerous editions and is still in print.

"Those who are fired with an enthusiastic idea and who allow it to take hold and dominate their thoughts find that new worlds open for them. As long as enthusiasm holds out, so will new opportunities."

Norman Vincent Peale

Realistic and Unrealistic Optimism

Most people are optimistic most of the time. Psychologists have found that people tend to exaggerate their own talents and abilities believing that they are better than average in most areas of life such as looks, health, intelligence, driving, job performance and even making love. Most people also consider themselves less prejudiced than their acquaintances, more socially skilled, look five years younger and have unwarranted confidence in their abilities to detect when strangers are telling lies. Of course, this is statistically impossible since 50 per cent of us are likely to be above average and 50 per cent of us are likely to be below. We all couldn't be better than average. People also tend to take credit for positive outcomes and to attribute negative outcomes to external factors. In many cases the positive outcomes are just due to lucky breaks rather than due to any inherent abilities.

Because optimists think optimistic thoughts their positive expectations increase their motivation and effort to achieve. They are more likely to persist and stick to difficult tasks. As we know persistent people are more likely to succeed and overcome setbacks. It is best if optimism is tinged with a little realism so that people know when to persist and when to give up. Optimists may lose a fortune on gambling as they are inclined to believe that the next bet will recover their losses. As optimists tend to see the best in others, they make more friends and have longer friendships. Because they see the best in others, they bring out the best in others. Optimists tend to be enthusiastically adventurous and willing to take risks, and so are likely to actively solve problems and exploit opportunities. They tend to be resilient when confronted with difficult situations or challenging goals.

Unrealistic optimism known as the Pollyanna Effect and inappropriate risk-taking has contributed to the downfall of many during the current economic collapse. A Pollyanna always looks on the bright side of things with the attitude that everything will turn out all right. Some people invested in property and shares in the belief that their value would keep on going up and so when prices collapsed they lost their money. Some people don't realise that investing in shares is gambling just like betting on horses. Shares are just as likely to go down in value as to go up. Because property prices seemed to be going up for so long very few, except some prescient economists, foresaw the collapse in property prices. These were dismissed as merchants of doom and gloom and so people and indeed governments ignored their advice. Consequently people who bought at the top of the market and financed their purchase with lavish loans now find themselves in negative equity and in some cases struggling to meet the repayments on their mortgages. Those who have lost their jobs are in more dire straits with the possibility of losing their homes.

"Feeling positive emotions is important, not just because it is pleasant in its own right, but because it causes much better commerce with the world. Developing more positive emotion in our lives will build friendships, love, better physical health, and greater achievement."

Martin Seligman

Optimistic Bias

In planning major capital projects, executives routinely exaggerate the benefits and underestimate the costs and thus set themselves up for failure. In fact, most capital projects come in late and over budget. Also in everyday life people habitually underestimate the time it takes to finish domestic jobs. Psychologists call this the 'optimistic bias,' as people tend to assume that things will go smoothly and thus overlook potential roadblocks and obstacles. Almost all newly married people expect their marriages to last a lifetime despite the divorce statistics which suggest otherwise. Most smokers believe that they are less at risk of lung cancer and heart disease than others who smoke.

Graduates such as MBA students overestimate the number of job offers and starting salary that awaits them on graduation. People are particularly poor at forecasting their own feelings. The good things are never as good as we think they will be and the bad things are never as bad. For example, people expect a major event such as winning the lotto or a promotion to make them happier than it actually does. They focus too much on the glorious moment not realising that our mundane lives will continue to unfold with their ups and downs whether or not we win the lotto or get promoted. On the other hand, we are more resilient than we think. If we don't get the promotion we will recover quicker than we think from the setback.

Sociologists are also aware of this tendency in that people generally believe that bad things will not happen to them. Survivors of violent crime often say that they believed these things only happened to other people rather than to them. When murders are committed in a particular locality neighbours always say that they didn't expect it to occur so near where they live, maintaining that these violent crime usually happen somewhere else. Some people ignore warnings of a tornado and stay in their homes believing that bad things only happen to other people. The optimistic bias is also evident in young drivers who see themselves as invulnerable despite the fact that they account for a disproportionate share of road accidents. They never expect car accidents to happen to them even though they indulge in risky behaviour such as driving under the influence of drugs, speeding and overtaking when dangerous to do so.

Pessimism

Unlike optimists, pessimists have negative expectations and so don't think things will work out well. This becomes a self-fulfilling prophecy as people who expect to be unsuccessful will achieve their wish. This is likely to decrease motivation and effort so that pessimists are more likely to give up and sometimes not even try initially. They see a negative future and thus don't see the point in expending effort to overcome setbacks. They may thus be consumed with feelings of helplessness because they believe they have no control over the future. Pessimists ruminate about what might be and what might have been. Pessimists have at least one advantage over optimists. They are more likely to make more realistic forecasts and anticipate problems. However, they are less likely to try to solve problems as they believe that they are only wasting their time and will not be successful.

Organisations tend to discourage pessimism. Pessimists are sometimes seen as disloyal and rocking the boat. They may be shunned and ignored by other employees. Optimists are often rewarded while pessimists are ignored because contrary views and critical thought is discouraged. Going against the conventional wisdom is usually bad for a person's career. The views of the minority of economists who warned against the impending property collapse in 2008 were assiduously ignored. Therefore unrealistic optimistic views are often reinforced by others leading to the ultimate downfall of the company. Pessimists are less likely to take risks and get involved in games of chance and gambling. The good news is that pessimism is to some degree learned and a person can be taught to be more optimistic.

Pessimism and indeed optimism are self-fulfilling prophecies. History teaches us that once a civilisation loses a positive vision of its own future, it withers and dies. Roman civilisation died when it lost its sense of mission and its leaders started quarrelling and fighting for power amongst themselves. Without a positive vision of their future, individuals also wither and die. George Lucas spent four years and numerous rejections submitting his script for Star Wars to various studios. If he hadn't a positive vision of his work he wouldn't have finished up with the highest earning film of all time.

> "Both optimists and pessimists contribute to our society. The optimist invents the airplane and the pessimist the parachute."
>
> G.B. Stern

Self-Esteem

Self-esteem is the value we place on ourselves and the sense of how likeable, acceptable and loveable we are. Self-esteem arises when we feel good about ourselves across a range of areas such as intelligence, social skills, appearance, and physical co-ordination. People with high self-esteem believe they are smarter, more accomplished, more popular and likeable and more attractive than others even if this is objectively untrue. This illusion may not be a bad thing provided it is subject to an occasional reality check as it helps people feel positive. People with high self-esteem, who get into a bad mood work very hard to get back into a good one, while those with low self-esteem do the opposite by prolonging their melancholy and persisting with a negative train of thought.

We know that being held in high regard by others is a source of high self-esteem while being ignored or rejected by others is a source of low self-esteem. Even the smallest slight may affect the self-esteem of sensitive people. Sensitive people are inclined to ruminate excessively about adverse criticism and small snubs. People with high self-esteem have a great sense of self-belief and so generally ignore snubs, and have more initiative and are happier than others. They are less likely to get depressed and to get stressed in response to traumatic events in their lives. They are not afraid to talk up in groups to express their views and are more likely to take the initiative in extricating themselves from unhappy relationships. When things go wrong they stay cool under pressure by focusing on what could have gone worse rather than on what might have gone better.

It is a reflection of how we see the world when we feel good or bad about ourselves. The Law of Correspondence states that our outer world is just a reflection of our inner world. If we feel insecure, unhappy and badly about ourselves inside this is going to show up as low self-esteem on the outside. On the other hand, if we feel secure, happy and good about ourselves inside this is going to show up as high self-esteem and confidence on the outside. If you want change in your outer world you must first change your inner thoughts, beliefs and attitudes. There is one thing you can control – and that's the way you think. So eliminate the negative thoughts, beliefs and attitudes that are holding you back and preventing you from thinking positively about yourself.

Psychologists have identified two tactics that people use to enhance or maintain their self-esteem. One is called basking in reflected glory (BIRG) and the other is called cutting off reflected failure (CORF). The BIRG means that we like to be associated with a winning group while CORF means people like to disassociate themselves from a losing group. When their team wins the self-esteem of devoted football fans increases while if they lose it takes a battering. We all love a winner and fans tend to associate more with a successful team than with a losing side. Generally it has been found that people with high self-esteem distance themselves from negative events more so than people with low self-esteem as a tactic to reduce the pain of failure.

Self-Knowledge

Self- esteem is often expressed in feelings of self-worth. Without a belief in our self-worth we cannot love, accept and respect ourselves and are unlikely to be confident and win the respect of others. We should accept our physical and mental limitations and realise that we can't be good at everything. If you are only five feet tall you are unlikely to become a professional basketball player but you might make a very good jockey. If you haven't a note in your head you are unlikely to become a good singer. Keep in mind the old saying; "change the things you can change, accept the things you cannot change and have the sense to know the difference between the two." There is no point in hitting your head against a stone wall by trying to achieve the impossible having regard to your physical and mental limitations.

Self-esteem can be influenced by the self-knowledge or the view you adopt about your past. Each of us has an autobiographical self or a life story from childhood that we have built up about the key influences and experiences of our life, giving meaning and coherence to our life. This story provides us with a bridge to our past and sense of continuity for the future. This story is not static but is dynamic and interactive. You cannot change the past but It can be imaginatively revisited, re-interpreted and revised, so that the way we view the past can be changed and seen in a more positive and inspirational light. This means that our past life does not necessarily have to determine or limit our future. Bad things may have happened to us in the past but it is our attitudes, thoughts, and interpretations to these events that count. We can control our emotions rather than having our emotions control us. So because you were unhappy in the past doesn't mean you can't be happy in the present and future with new people, new experiences and a reinterpretation of the past.

111

Having a realistic self-knowledge about your strengths and weaknesses will help you make more effective decisions. Self-knowledge will help you choose the appropriate course at college and the appropriate occupation to pursue when you leave. Avoiding things that are too difficult will pre-empt failure and frustration. Avoiding things that are too easy will pre-empt dissatisfaction and underachievement. Correct choices will help you live a happy, challenging and fulfilling life. Self-knowledge will also help you choose the appropriate compatible mate rather than pursuing someone who is unsuitable and cause disillusionment and heartache when they reject you.

"If most of us remain ignorant of ourselves, it is because self-knowledge is painful and we prefer the pleasure of illusion."
Aldous Huxley

High Self-Esteem

Parents have a significant influence on our self-esteem. We are more likely to have high self-esteem if we come from loving homes with supportive and encouraging parents where clear standards of behaviour were laid down and where we were taught to take responsibility for our actions and value ourselves. On the other hand, physical and sexual abuse are extremely damaging to the self-esteem of children. Family conflict, breakdown, separation and divorce are also likely to have a detrimental effect on children's self-esteem.

People with high self-esteem won't feel good about themselves all the time. On a daily basis, external circumstances such as successes, failures, mistakes, setbacks and mood will influence our level of self-esteem. Obviously successes will enhance our self-esteem while failures will diminish it. Your self-esteem goes up when you are promoted, pass an exam or win a prize. On the other hand, when you fail to win a promotion or fail an exam your self-esteem plummets. However high self-esteem will help us cope with the vicissitudes of life. It helps people to persist longer in the face of failure and is also associated with knowing the opportune time to quit.

Those with a high self-esteem are more likely to adopt a systematic problem solving approach when confronted with difficult issues. They will objectively appraise a situation, consider alternative solutions, weigh them up and pick the best one in the circumstances and then take the appropriate action. They are more proactive in seeking professional help to solve their problems.

Good looking people are likely to have a higher self-esteem than others. They are perceived by others as kind, nurturing, patient and happy. Even studies of children as young as 18 months show they prefer to look at and are more likely to smile at an attractive face. Attractive people often get preferential treatment from strangers, employers and especially from their own mothers which reinforces their self-concept that they are special. On average, they even get lighter sentences in criminal courts. However, attractive people are not happier than the rest of us as they are subject to the same ups and downs, trials and tribulations, we all experience going through life.

A sense of optimism, good relationships, empathy and living an interesting, purposeful, engaged and meaningful life, have much more influence on your happiness than do your looks. People with high self-esteem are more likely to initiate new relationships and interactions with others but are not necessarily liked any better than people with low self-esteem. An inflated self-esteem is not an endearing characteristic to others who may see you as obnoxious, pompous, self-opinionated, conceited and self-absorbed and therefore someone to avoid.

> "Outstanding leaders go out of their way to boost the self-esteem of their personnel. If people believe in themselves, it's amazing what they can accomplish."
>
> Sam Walton

Low Self-Esteem

The conventional wisdom to use self-affirmations to boost your self-esteem if you have low self-esteem is now thought to be counterproductive as people with low self-esteem don't believe the statements because they have such a low opinion of themselves. Such a strategy may actually make them more demoralised because the affirmation may strengthen their negative view of themselves. It works with people with high self-esteem because they already have a high opinion of themselves while people with low self-esteem need to hear the praise from someone else before they believe it.

If you suffer from low self-esteem it is a good idea to seek out friends with high self-esteem as they are likely to treat you well and thus help you to think more positively about yourself. Otherwise if you surround yourself with low self-esteem friends your negative self-view is getting reinforced. If you're in a job where you are being put down all the time, assert yourself and insist that you be treated with dignity. Otherwise your confidence is undermined by becoming unsure of achieving what you once knew you were capable of doing. Alternatively if assertiveness doesn't work; change jobs. Keep a diary of your successes and read and reflect on these from time to time to boost your positive self-esteem and learn from your experiences.

Success and Self-Esteem

In our present cult of celebrity young people are obsessed with fame and fortune. They see people on reality shows, and becoming famous quickly without achieving anything of substance. People who become famous in such circumstances often suffer from the affects of the imposter syndrome. This means that they find it hard to accept their success and feel they are frauds and undeserving of such recognition. They constantly need reassurance that they really deserve what they have achieved. They attribute their success to luck rather than hard work or special talent. The constant harassment, scrutiny and criticism of the media undermine their sense of self-worth and make them self-conscious and aware of their imperfections. Those who become successful too fast are often too emotionally immature to handle the relentless scrutiny of media and fans. Their sense of low self-esteem often leads to alcoholism, drug abuse and compulsive sexuality and are thus inappropriate role models for other young people to follow.

Even very talented and well established celebrities often spiral into self-destructive lifestyles when they seem to have the world at their feet. Popular culture provides us with many examples such as the film actress Marilyn Monroe, Elvis Presley and River Phoenix, all of whom died before their time. Similarly, Kurt Cobain, famous singer-songwriter and leader of Nirvana was addicted to heroin and killed himself in 1994. When people get to the top they suddenly realise that achieving the goal is not as enjoyable as the process of getting there which totally absorbed and engaged their time. Any character weaknesses and self-destructive habits quickly come to the fore when celebrity status has been achieved. Young people must realise if they want to succeed in life that it requires self-discipline, effort, hard work and persistence rather than luck. They should be determined to avoid the destructive lifestyles of many of the famous celebrities that have gone before them.

There is very little link between self-esteem and high academic performance or job performance. High self-esteem may be the result of doing well academically rather than the other way around and good job performance may lead to feelings of high self-esteem. Factors that are positively linked include intelligence, ability, effort and family background. Your focus should be on lifelong learning and improvement. This will allow you to compare yourself against your own standards rather than competing and boosting yourself at the expense of others.

"You must love yourself before you love another. By accepting yourself and fully being what you are, your simple presence can make others happy."

Anonymous

Women and Self-Esteem

Self-esteem is only moderately influenced by gender. Females on average have slightly lower self-esteem than males, the gap being the widest in the late teens. Young women have often a problem with their body image as they compare themselves with the fashion models, film stars and rich and famous personalities they see on television and in glossy magazines with beautiful faces and thin figures and they think this is the norm. The average person spends more than 4 hours a day watching TV so that these negative comparisons are reinforced and imprinted on their subconscious. In contrast, men and women when evaluating their intelligence rather than their appearance do not compare themselves to Albert Einstein but rather to a more mundane standard such as their close friends.

Viewers don't realise that these people in films or television programmes are not the norm and are often chosen because of their exceptional attractiveness, figures and talent. They then go to extreme lengths with grooming, makeup and diet to stay beautiful and keep their figures. Some have even undergone expensive cosmetic surgery and coaching to acquire their present look. Their photographs are airbrushed to make them seem more attractive still. With more women in the workplace this pressure to look attractive is heightened because they feel that appearance counts when competing with other women and men for acceptance and promotion.

Though women seem to suffer more from a poor body self-image than men, even men are now beginning to feel the pressure to look youthful and as attractive as possible to increase their desirability and marketability in different areas of their lives including their work life. Just like women's magazines the male models in men's magazines represent an impossible standard of perfection, proportion and sculpted muscularity that most men will never meet. These feelings of insecurity are being exploited by the marketing industry that target men as possible customers of fitness clubs and equipment. Even make-up, deodorants and cosmetic surgery is being increasingly targeted at the male population. Women and indeed men, who undergo cosmetic surgery, are often disappointed with the results not realising that self-esteem comes from within rather than from negative comparisons with others. If you have a solid self-concept you will not be constantly looking to others for acceptance and self-assurance.

Low self-esteem is thought to be the motive behind compulsive shopping by women which is a type of addiction and therapy. Compulsive shoppers are consumers out of control, buying things they want but don't really need. Some people buy things that they don't ever use and they remain unwrapped in their packaging. Like people with eating disorders shopaholics are more likely to suffer anxiety and low self-esteem than the average shopper. They are more impulsive than average and tend to be perfectionists. People who compulsively buy may be trying to boost their low self-esteem. Buying, conversing and interacting with retail assistants give them a feeling of power, control and importance. Self-esteem may also influence their purchase decisions. They are more likely to buy things that enhance their appearance and status such as designer clothes, shoes, handbags, makeup, and jewellery irrespective of the cost. Judicial praise may enhance feelings of self-esteem. This does not mean that praising and never criticising is good. Praise should be balanced with constructive criticism. People should be praised for ethical socially desirable behaviour, good job performance and worthy achievements. In contrast people should be criticised constructively for unethical behaviour, poor performance and underachieving without worrying that a person's self-esteem might be damaged. Indiscriminate praise may contribute to narcissism and other forms of inflated self-esteem and prove detrimental to the individual and society.

The Downside of Self-Esteem

High self-esteem is not a panacea for all social problems. Men with high self-esteem in committed monogamous relationships cheat more. Wealth, fame and celebrity magnify the effect with the rich and famous more prone to cheat because they can afford to do so and are exposed to more temptations and feel they are entitled to do what they like. The following two cases are examples of this phenomenon. Tiger Woods, the infamous golfer, had a string of affairs and made a public apology to his fans about his behaviour. This was insufficient for his wife who has left him and filed for divorce proceedings. Wayne Rooney the Manchester United soccer player cheated on his wife while she was in hospital having their baby. In contrast it is women with low self-esteem who are more likely to be unfaithful because it is thought that they are seeking affirmation of their self-worth outside the relationship.

Psychologists use the term self-enhancers for people who have an unrealistically high self-esteem. Self-enhancers tend to be hostile, socially inept, and appear anxious and moody. They are sensitive to criticism and keep people at a distance to protect themselves from negative feedback. They may be deluding themselves but they are not deceiving their friends who describe them as aggressive, impulsive and unable to delay gratification. And when friends see through the facade, self-enhancers engage in more distortion and denial in an attempt to maintain their self-esteem. Positive self-esteem is good but it should be based on reality. If you are not prepared to accept negative feedback about your shortcomings then there is no way to get in touch with reality and improve yourself.

Some people think that the more self-esteem they have the better. In fact too much self-esteem can damage the health of others. To succeed in politics as in many areas of life, high self-esteem is a prerequisite. Dictators and autocrats have high self-esteem combined with a sense of destiny. There is no doubt that Adolf Hitler had a ruthless sense of destiny, tremendous initiative and self-esteem but used it destructively to bring misery and death to millions including his own people. He offered a sense of self-esteem to the German people not on the basis of achievement or ethical behaviour but instead on the false premise that they were members of the so-called Master Race; an idea that was appealing and seductive. Similarly his henchmen the Nazi war criminals tried at Nuremberg showed that their grotesquely inflated self-esteem and hubris prevented them from understanding the evil that they had perpetrated on Jews and other minority groups. Most of them went to their executions unrepentant for their crimes, pleading that they were just following orders.

In modern times Colonel Gaddafi of Libya is one of the longest serving dictators in history being in power for 42 years. In 1979 he relinquished the title of prime minister and is now known as "The Brother Leader" or "The Guide". This megalomaniac is the author of state sponsored terrorism, thinks nothing of murdering expatriate opposition leaders and has amassed a multi-billion fortune for himself and his family at the expense of the Libyan people. A popular uprising (April 2011) is currently in progress to overthrow him and has won the backing of NATO forces.

Many murders and acts of violence are caused by people retaliating, when their self-esteem has been attacked and their pride wounded by insults and humiliation. The consumption of alcohol or an indulgence in drugs can be a contributing factor in arousing passions and loss of self-control. Putting someone down and hurting their pride can have life threatening consequences.

Narcissism

Too much emphasis on self-esteem can encourage a culture of narcissism which is harmful to individuals and society as a whole. Just like in any other area of life moderation is the key. A narcissist is a term used to describe a person who loves themselves too much. They love themselves so much that they are incapable of loving others. Though they may be charming at first they eventually alienate others by their thoughtless, self-centred, selfish and conceited behaviour. Some degree of narcissism is essential for a healthy personality because we need a sense of self-worth.

Negative characteristics of narcissism include a grandiose sense of self, attention seeking, arrogance and a belief that they are better than anyone else. They tend to be manipulative, selfish and unfaithful. Narcissistic people have a need for admiration and a love of power and prestige. They are prone to belittle others in order to make themselves feel superior. Consequently they are unable to engage in meaningful relationships with others. In extreme cases narcissistic people may be prone to violence if they fail to get their needs met or their pride is wounded. In 2009 a New Zealand university lecturer named Clayton Weatherston was convicted of the murder of his girlfriend. He stabbed her 200 times. A psychiatrist diagnosed him as suffering from narcissistic personality disorder where rejection triggers an uncontrollable and violent rage.

People with high self-esteem are more likely to be racist, violent and criminal. Low self-esteem increases the risk of eating disorders, suicide and depression, but despite the conventional wisdom is not a factor in delinquency or drug abuse. It seems that young people who value themselves too much are more likely to get involved in anti-social behaviour with negative consequences for others. They like to experiment and thus are more likely to smoke, drink alcohol, take drugs or engage in early sex resulting in unwanted pregnancies. They are more likely to get involved in risky pursuits such as driving too fast or driving under the influence of alcohol or drugs. Unlike those with high self-esteem those with low self-esteem are only likely to harm themselves. One important exception is that high self-esteem reduces the chances of bulimia in females although other factors may contribute such as poor body image and negative comparisons with others. People with low self-esteem may become more materialistic by investing their time and money in material things to boost their self-esteem. On the other hand, people with high self-esteem may have an unrealistic view of themselves and are reluctant to take good advice.

Too much self-esteem may also turn a person into a snob. Some people consider themselves superior to others because of a better education, social background or prestigious occupation. A snob is a person who has a tendency to patronise others and treat them with condescension. Snobs genuinely believe that they are better than others and do not like to socialise with those they consider to be their inferiors.

Despite what is generally thought most bullies don't lack self-esteem. However they are more likely to pick on people with low self-esteem such as unassertive shy people. Those with high self-esteem are more likely to stand up to bullies to defend themselves and other victims.

Self-efficacy

Self-efficacy is an important aspect of self-esteem and is the belief that we have the skills and competencies to accomplish a particular task. You can't take advantage of an opportunity if you don't have the requisite skills to exploit it. People with strong self-efficacy focus their energies on analysing and solving problems and believe that they will succeed. Those with weak self-efficacy doubt their skills and abilities and anticipate failure and so give up easily. We acquire a sense of self-efficacy in four ways.

- Cumulative. True confidence comes from the gradual accumulation of self-efficacy over many successes. With each success we reinforce our feelings of self-confidence. The old saying that success begets success and that we build on our successes is true. Even as children successful early experiences can have a positive impact on us for the rest of our lives. For example, a single win in sport in contrast to numerous wins may not be sufficient to boost your self-confidence permanently. However, a spectacular first win may motivate and inspire the start of a transformation of your self-concept from "I'm a loser" to "I'm a winner".

- Observation. When we see others with similar abilities to ourselves succeed we realise that we can too. We can learn from the successful behaviours of others and use them as role models to inspire us to achieve similar feats.

- Positive attitude. One simple way to enhance your self-efficacy is to direct your thoughts. A positive attitude increases our self-esteem while a negative attitude diminishes it. To get positive results you must have positive thoughts and follow through with action. Thinking about things is not sufficient. You must take appropriate action to make it a reality. Surround yourself with positive people as these will help you have a positive view on life and encourage you to achieve your aims. Make a list of positive things in your life that you can refer to when you need to.

- Encouragement. We all need the support, encouragement and inspiration of others such as family and friends at different stages of our lives. We are motivated by those who believe in our ability to succeed. Tell them that you believe you can achieve your goals and this will help them believe you too.

"We find that people's beliefs about their efficacy affect the sorts of choices they make in very significant ways. In particular, it affects their levels of motivation and perseverance in the face of obstacles. Most success requires persistent effort, so low self-efficacy becomes a self-limiting process. In order to succeed people need a sense of self-efficacy, strung together with resilience to meet the inevitable obstacles and inequities of life."

Albert Bandura

Summary

Optimists see the glass as half full rather than half empty. They believe or expect things to work out well. Optimists see opportunities where others see problems. Because optimists think optimistic thoughts their positive expectations increase their motivation and effort to achieve. They are more likely to persist and so more likely to succeed and overcome setbacks. Pessimists see a negative future and thus see little point in expending effort to overcome setbacks.

Self-esteem arises when we feel good about ourselves in different areas of our lives such as intelligence, social skills, appearance, and physical co-ordination. Being held in high regard by others is a source of self-esteem while feeling rejected diminishes our self-esteem. Low self-esteem can be caused by issues with body image or making invidious comparisons with others. On the upside high self-esteem produces happiness, initiative and resilience. The downside to self-esteem is dysfunctional behaviour such as snobbery, narcissism, unfaithfulness, bullying and criminality. Self-efficacy is an important aspect of self-esteem and is the belief that we have the ability and competencies to achieve a particular task.

Five Activities to Improve Your Optimism/Self-Esteem Skills

1. Act like an optimist. Change your outlook and behaviour to become more optimistic. See opportunities where others see problems. Actively tackle problems rather than ignore them.

2. List down the positive things you have done in your life to date. Review them each day to reinforce your optimism and sense of self-esteem.

3. When confronted with a problem objectively appraise the situation, consider the alternative solutions, pick the best one in the circumstances and then take the appropriate action.

4. Mix with people who have high self-esteem. They will give you a boost to think more positively about yourself and raise your self-esteem.

5. As part of your plan of lifelong learning and self-improvement acquire new skills as you go through life to

build up your sense of self-efficacy. This could be in an
area that interests you such as gardening, photography,
astronomy or computers.

6

Persistence and Resilience

- *Why is persistence important to success?*
- *What is the link between patience and persistence?*
- *What is the significance of passion?*
- *Why is willpower so important?*
- *What is resilience?*

Introduction

Persistence is the quality of continuing going forward steadily or obstinately despite problems, setbacks, difficulties, failures or obstacles. Persistence, patience and passion are the hallmark of success. Patience is the ability to endure waiting or delay without becoming annoyed, agitated, frustrated or upset and to persevere calmly when faced with seemingly insurmountable difficulties. A passionate person is fully engaged, deeply involved and totally dedicated to whatever they undertake. Willpower is a combination of determination and self-discipline enabling you to do something despite the difficulties encountered. Resilience is the ability to recover quickly and bounce back, survive and flourish from the trials and tribulations of life. Resilient people are successful because they have the facility to pick themselves up from failure and start all over again.

Persistence

Persistence is the quality of going forward steadily or obstinately despite problems, setbacks, difficulties, failures or obstacles. Failure is often due to insufficient application or a lack of belief in ones' self. People fail because they give up even after one attempt. Some people even give up when they are on the threshold of success. Great people overcome great adversity with great mental strength, courage, determination and character. They do have setbacks and make mistakes but they learn from them and keep on going. They never take their eye off the target and are determined to succeed despite repeated failures. Persistence is not about doing the same thing over and over again but may involve changing your habits, accepting new challenges, learning new skills and adopting a different approach to reach your goals.

The Wright Brothers, Wilbur (1867-1912) and Orville (1871-1948) had many setbacks before they became the first to fly in a powered aircraft at Kitty Hawk, North Carolina on 17th December 1903. Orville stayed in the air for only 12 seconds and initially covered just 120 feet but by the end of the day they had both made successful, longer flights. The human brain is designed to solve problems and sticking to the task will eventually achieve seemingly impossible objectives. In the case of flying it took a few hundred years of persistent human endeavour. Leonardo da Vinci had studied the mechanics of flight as early as the 15th century. Although getting airborne in a hot air balloon was achieved in 1783 it took two bicycle repairmen with vision, determination and persistence to achieve powered flight in 1903.

Persistence pays off in the end. Admiral Robert Peary made 7 unsuccessful attempts to reach the North Pole until finally he succeeded on his 8th attempt. NASA failed 20 times during their first 28 attempts to send rockets into space. Robert Pirsig wrote Zen and the Art of Motorcycle Maintenance, a book which became a best seller and sold millions of copies. He claims that the manuscript was rejected 121 times before it was published in 1974 which must be a world record. Tawni O'Dell, the famous author produced 6 unpublished manuscripts after 13 years of writing. Her first novel 'Back Roads' was published in January 2000. In an interview Tawni gave the following advice "Never give up on your dream. Talent is a necessity but only part of what goes into making a successful writer. Perseverance is all important. If you don't have the desire and belief in yourself to keep trying after you have been told you should quit, you'll never make it." Jimi Hendrix was a famous guitarist and rock star. The value of perseverance was instilled in Jimi by his father. He practised playing his guitar so much that he eventually became a virtuoso. This was despite the fact that he was unable to read music; was left-handed and learned to play the guitar with his right hand.

"Just don't give up trying to do what you really want to do. Where there is love and inspiration, I don't think you can go wrong."
Ella Fitzgerald

Patience

Patience is an aspect of persistence. It is the ability to endure waiting or delay without becoming annoyed, agitated, frustrated or upset, or to persevere calmly in the face of obstacles, provocation and difficulties. It is the philosophy that everything comes to him who waits. It is the ability to create calm in our life and stay connected when all around you are panicked and in disarray. People with patience are in control over how they react to situations. Patience is an attitude of mind and a habit you should develop. In times of hardship and disappointment patience will help you put it into perspective and remain in control rather than get annoyed, upset or stressed. Don't get frustrated by things over which you have no control as patience, wisdom and humility go hand in hand.

Patience and dogged determination may see you through in the end. A classic example is Grandma Moses (1860 – 1961) an American, who was self-taught, took up painting in her late 70s and continued painting into her 90s proving that it is never too late to learn. Despite having no formal training her paintings earned worldwide acclaim. During the 1950s, her exhibitions were so popular that they broke attendance records all over the world. Life magazine celebrated her 100th birthday by featuring her picture on the front cover of its September 19th 1960 edition. She received numerous awards including an honorary doctorate from Philadelphia's Moore College of Art. Edna Kenny the current prime minister of Ireland spent 36 years in opposition before becoming prime minister in March 2011. He became the leader of the Fine Gael party in 2002 and has survived several challenges to his leadership from within the party.

Andre Kertesz, (1894 – 1985) the famous photographer was in his 80s before he finally gained public recognition. In his early years his unorthodox style prevented him from gaining wider acceptance and during most of his life he felt unrecognised as a photographer. Today he is considered one of the most prominent figures that photojournalism has ever produced. In 1982 he was awarded the National Grand Prize of Photography in Paris, as well as the 21st Annual George Washington Award from the American Hungarian Foundation the same year. Like Grandma Moses he was also awarded an honorary doctorate for his outstanding contribution to photography.

Ian Fleming (1908-1964) was a British author, best known for his novels about the British spy, James Bond who has been immortalised in film and has fascinated and entertained millions over the years. He had a varied background as a journalist, banker, stockbroker and Naval Intelligence Officer before he became a novelist and introduced the world to James Bond as a late bloomer at the age of 45. He went on to write twelve novels and nine short stories and his books have sold over 100 million copies worldwide. He obviously had got the ideas for his books from his experience as a British Naval Intelligence Officer. His career proves that people at middle age can reinvent themselves and discover and exploit talents that they were unaware of.

> "Patience is waiting. Not passively waiting. That is laziness. But to keep going when the going is hard and slow – that is patience."
>
> Unknown

Passion

It is much easier to stick to the task if you are passionate, interested and enthusiastic about what you are doing. A passionate person is fully engaged, deeply involved and totally dedicated to whatever they undertake. A strong passion points out the means and thus ensures success. When you have a passion to do something you begin to see resources all around to help you achieve your purpose. Passion provides you with the purpose, energy, drive, persistence and enthusiasm to pursue what you want to do. Sometimes it may even prevent you from sleeping at night because of the excitement, enthusiasm and anticipation of what you want to do the following morning. Those with a passion for their work look forward to getting up in the morning while those without a passion dread going into work.

Tanya Streeter is passionate about her free-diving, the sport of plunging deep into the water without tanks or other breathing equipment. She is a world champion free-diver and has set nine world records. She was inducted into the Women Diver's Hall of Fame in March 2000. For a while she held the overall "no limits" free-diving record with a depth of 525 feet or 160 metres, greater than the men's record. An average person can hold her breath for one minute while Streeter can do it for six minutes. After giving birth in August 2008, Tanya Streeter officially retired from free-diving.

Charles Atlas (1892-1972) born Angelo Sicilano, through passion and determination built up his body from a 97 pound weakling to became known as "The World's Most Perfectly Developed Man" and founded a multi-million dollar business exploiting his famous brand. He claimed that he was bullied and harassed incessantly when he was an underweight youth. His famous cartoon advertisement featured on the back page of numerous comics and magazines over many years. It depicted a bully kicking sand in his face at the beach in front of his girlfriend. Of course, he goes home ashamed and dejected but determined to do something about it and sometime after returns to the beach as a well developed muscleman and confronts his tormentor to win the admiration and respect of his girlfriend. Whether true or not, this story inspired many a male teenager to take up bodybuilding. Atlas trained himself to develop his body from that of a scrawny thin person to eventually becoming the most famous muscleman of his time. Even today the company he founded continues to market fitness programmes. Charles Atlas became a role model for other skinny and underdeveloped men and an inspiration for later bodybuilders including Arnold Schwarzenegger who went on to become a famous Hollywood actor and US governor.

> "Nothing great in the world has ever been accomplished without passion."
>
> Hebbel

Willpower

Willpower is a combination of determination and self-discipline that enables you to do something extraordinary despite the difficulties involved. People bring much unhappiness and distress to themselves because of their failure to control unhealthy urges and impulses such as smoking, drug taking and excessive eating and drinking. Some people have more willpower than others and thus are better at doing the good things and avoiding the bad things. People develop willpower from practise. Willpower is like a muscle; the more you exercise it the stronger it becomes. If people want to develop their willpower, they must practise self-denial. If an athlete wants to build up strength they must eat a healthy diet, avoid alcohol, go to the gym regularly and exercise with weights. If you want to lose weight you must exercise more and eat less. If you want to avoid drug taking you must have the discipline to say no.

There is a downside to willpower in that we may stick to a project longer than is desirable. Some business people fail to disengage from a pet project because they feel that they will lose face even when the signs are evident that it will not succeed. Instead they throw good money after bad and increase their losses. Others are reluctant to move away from a successful project even when it is finished. Some managers are reluctant to delegate the tasks that won them the recognition and promotion in the first instance.

> "Strength does not come from physical capacity. It comes from an indomitable will."
>
> Mahatma Gandhi

Resilience in the Face of Adversity

Resilience is the ability to recover quickly and bounce back, survive and flourish from the trials, tribulations and frustrations of life. Resilient people pick themselves up and start all over again. They consider difficulties, setbacks and stress as a normal part of life. Those without resilience become helpless, adopt a victim mentality or plunge into depression. We all experience the vicissitudes of life from our favourite football team losing a match, becoming ill, suffering bereavement or divorce and being made redundant. Every day we read news reports of people experiencing and overcoming cancer, heart attacks, house fires, plane crashes, car crashes and vicious assaults. In parts of the world people who courageously deal with natural disasters such as tsunamis, hurricanes, tornados, earthquakes or floods are not unusual. Many business people who go bankrupt reinvent themselves and against all the odds start afresh and go on to build a successful business all over again.

The difference that makes the difference is the way that people respond to these events. People who survive adapt successfully to the challenging or threatening circumstances and manage to grow and develop. They become stronger, more resilient and able to deal with more difficult problems. They begin to appreciate the important things in life such as family and friends and that life is too short not to follow your dreams. What doesn't kill you makes you stronger and often wiser. Some children from dysfunctional families who suffered appalling abuse go on to live successful and productive lives despite their backgrounds while others become alcoholics and drug abusers.

Bill Clinton, the charismatic former President of the United States (1993-20001) is an example of someone who rose above adversity; some of his problems were outside his control while others were self-inflicted. He bounced back from growing up in an alcoholic home and won the presidency after losing big elections earlier in his career. He survived the self-induced character assassination brought on by his sexual indiscretions during his term of office and endured repeated questions about his morality.

Brian Keenan, who emerged from captivity with resilience and strength after four and a half years, has become an inspiration for many people. On the morning of the 11 April, 1986 Keenan was kidnapped by Islamic Jihad. After spending two months in isolation, he was moved to a cell shared with the British Journalist John McCarthy. He was blindfolded throughout most of his ordeal, and was chained hand and feet when he was taken out of solitary confinement. Keenan recounts his experiences in a book titled An Evil Cradling. His example suggests that each of us have a reserve of resilience that can be called upon when we need it most.

In his book titled Man's Search for Meaning, Victor E. Frankl tells how he developed the resilience to survive the concentration camps set up by the Nazi regime during the Second World War by imagining a future for himself. He realised to survive the terrible conditions experienced in the concentration camps he had to find hope for the future and a purpose for living. He imagined himself giving a lecture after the war on the psychology of the concentration camps so that outsiders could understand what he and others had suffered and been through. By creating some goals for himself and occupying his mind with an imagined future he was able to rise above the terrible sufferings experienced on a daily basis. Freud maintained that a critical difference between ordinary grief and acute depression is that people experiencing ordinary grief anticipate a future meaningful life where they will again be happy, whereas those with acute depression are preoccupied with a grim and hopeless future.

J.K. Rowling is the author of the Harry Potter fantasy series. The books have sold in excess of 400 million copies and are the basis for a series of popular films. She is renowned for her resilience in overcoming a series of setbacks such as a broken marriage, disapproval from her parents and as a single mother struggling to raise her daughter, to becoming a best-selling author and multi-millionaire. She went back to her first dream of writing because she had nothing left to lose and something to gain. She is one of the richest women in Britain as well as being one of the most admired. She was once the recipient of welfare payments but is now estimated to be richer than the Queen of England. In October 2010 she was named the most influential woman in Britain by leading magazine editors. She is living proof that people who follow their dreams despite adversity can become successful provided they work hard and have the talent and willpower to do so.

"I have missed more than 9,000 shots in my career. I have lost almost 300 games. On 26 occasions I have been entrusted to take the game winning shot......and I missed. I have failed over and over again in my life. And that's precisely why I succeed."

Michael Jordan

Resilience and Success

Resilience is probably one of the most important characteristics for success in life. George Washington (1732-1799), the founding father and first president of the United States defeated Great Britain, the world's most powerful military nation, against all the odds. His army suffered from a shortage of food, supplies and ammunition and he personally served without pay. At times he even used his own money to pay his troops. He overcame political in-fighting, betrayal, and threat of mutiny from his own troops. He endured more losses than victories but nevertheless had the resilience to keep going against all the odds. He realised that defeats are only temporary setbacks and something you can learn from, while continually keeping focused on his long-term goal of independence from Britain. You may lose the battle but win the war and he certainly lost more battles than he won. He persevered through eight years of setbacks, extremely cold winters, suffering and defeats to ultimately win independence for the United States of America. He is remembered for his patriotism, principled leadership, integrity, honesty and selfless devotion to public service. He became the automatic and unanimous choice for the first president of the United States and served two terms. He then retired quietly and modestly to his Mount Vernon estate in Virginia.

Andrew Wiles spent more than thirty years trying to solve Fermat's Last Theorem, a problem that had defeated mathematicians for 350 years. He was only 10 years old when he came across and became fascinated with this problem. In 1993, after 7 years of intense work and more than 15,000 hours study, Wiles presented his proof to a conference of fellow mathematicians in England. However, some of his peers found several small errors. Nevertheless he didn't get frustrated or discouraged and after a further year of hard work, Wiles answered his critics. The Princeton professor attributes his success not to his brains but to his persistence. It is passion and commitment that will help you endure and deal successfully with the setbacks that inevitably occur in any long-term project. Committed people are curious, passionate about learning, willing to challenge the status quo and prepared to experiment with new approaches to solve a problem until they are eventually successful.

Genius alone does not guarantee success. Wolfgang Amadeus Mozart (1756-1791) in his diaries claims that an entire symphony appeared intact in his head. This particular passage is often quoted but the next paragraph where he says he spent months refining and perfecting his work is usually ignored. Just like anybody else famous composers spend many years of training and practise perfecting their craft often from a very young age. There is a ten year rule which states that on average it requires 10 years of hard work and constant practice before people become expert in a particular area. This is an average t only and many people have spent 15 years or more perfe their art before they become proficient and well-known. We only hear about them when they are successful not realising all the hard work and persistent application over many years that lies behind their success.

The ability to persist in the face of obstacles is an essential ingredient to this success. Thomas Edison the famous inventor is said to have made 10,000 attempts before he successfully made a functional light bulb. When confronted by reporters about how he felt about failing 10,000 times, he retorted that he didn't fail but merely discovered 10,000 ways that wouldn't work and so was becoming closer to a successful outcome.

Some people believe intelligence is fixed while others believe it is malleable and a work in progress. Those who accept that intelligence is fixed are less resilient as they don't believe that they can learn from their mistakes and thus don't see the point in trying again when they fail. They fear failure and take it personally. Those who accept that their intelligence is a work in progress are more resilient and have no fear of failure because they see it as a learning opportunity. They believe that hard work will be rewarded and is just as important to success as intelligence.

Even dyslexia is not a handicap to many people and does not prevent them from reaching their potential. Research shows that entrepreneurs are five time more likely to suffer from dyslexia than the average person. Richard Branson of Virgin Atlantic has dyslexia as does John Chambers the CEO of Cisco Systems who allegedly can't even read his own email. Nevertheless, these people went on to become highly successful and did not let dyslexia limit their potential.

"Nothing in this world can take the place of persistence. Talent will not; nothing is more common than unsuccessful people with talent. Genius will not; unrewarded genius is almost a proverb. Education will not; the world is full of educated derelicts. Persistence and determination alone are omnipotent. The slogan 'press on' has solved and always will solve the problems of the human race."

Calvin Coolidge

Resilience & Mental Discipline

Gary Player (born 1935) a South African is one of the greatest golfers of all time. He came from a poor background and his mother died from cancer when he was only eight years old. Player has won over 165 tournaments on six continents over six decades. He was elected to the World Golf Hall of Fame in 1974. He is renowned for his mental discipline, integrity, sound family values and devotion to keeping healthy and fit. When he travelled to England in 1955 he was advised that he was unsuitable to become a professional golfer and should take up some other career instead. At 5 feet 7 inches and 150 pounds he was considered too small for a professional golfer. Despite this and against all the odds he returned to England the following year and won the Dunlop Masters the first of his 13 South African Opens. Together with Jack Nicklaus and Arnold Palmer he dominated world golf during the 1960s and 1970s earning them the title "The Modern Triumvirate."

As a teenager he read and was inspired by Norman Vincent Peale's book The Power of Positive Thinking and Maxell Maltz's book Psycho Cybernetics and went on to apply the psychological principles to his game of golf such as visualising and mentally rehearsing each shot in his head before he took them. In addition to his dedication to physical fitness he believed that mental discipline such as patience, resilience, focus and determination were of prime importance to success in golf. He agrees that the real barrier to success is often in the mind. In 2000, he was voted the 8th greatest golfer of all time by Golf Digest magazine. He retired at the age of 73 on the 23 July 2009 having competed in the Senior British Open Championship at Sunningdale.

Sports psychologists maintain that mental rehearsal confers almost the same benefits as an actual workout. People who combine physical with mental imagery training do better than those who just do physical training. Imagery can help people achieve peak performance by mentally rehearsing successful strategies and potential pitfalls before the actual event. A diver might mentally perform a double somersault with a half twist one final time as he prepares himself on the diving board. Duncan Goodhew who won an Olympic gold medal for Britain in 1980 would visualise each stroke in detail before he actually swam. A surgeon might run through a difficult procedure in his mind before he actually performs the operation. Arthur Schnabel, the famous Austrian concert pianist, claims that he spent more time practising in his head than on the actual keyboard.

"The harder you practice the luckier you get."

Gary Player

Visualisation

The techniques of visualisation and mental rehearsal are widely used in gymnastics, ice skating, tennis and golf and were popularised in the books named The Inner Game of Golf and The Inner Game of Tennis by W.Timothy Gallwey. Ben Hogan who was one of the greatest golfers in the history of the game claims that he mentally rehearsed each shot before taking it. He depended on what he called "muscle memory" to carry out the shot as he visualised it. These techniques are part of autogenic conditioning created by a German psychiatrist Jonannes Schultz in 1932. For many years, in the 1940s and 1950s, German athletes dominated the Olympic Games, winning most of the medals. Many years later their secret was discovered and their success was attributed to the autogenic exercises they had been doing.

Dick Fosbury won the gold medal for the high jump at the 1968 Olympics in Mexico City. He is creator of the famous "Fosbury Flop," which is now the most popular high jumping technique. He attributes his success to the use of visualisation strategies. He describes the effects such practices had on his performance as follows: "I began to develop my new style during high school competition, when my body seemed to react to the challenge of the bar. I became charged by the desire and will to achieve success. Then I developed a thought process in order to repeat a successful jump: I would psyche myself up; create a picture; 'feel' a successful jump; and develop a positive attitude to make the jump. My success came from the visualisation and imaging process."

Muhammad Ali gained a mental edge over his opponents by psyching them out and psychologically undermining them before contests and became the greatest boxer of the 20th century. Before the Thriller in Manila (1975) Ali taunted Frazier with various slurs and poems. Frazier threw in the towel after 14 hard rounds. He famously claimed that he could float like a butterfly and sting like a bee. He showed how a positive attitude can boost an athlete's performance and how psychological mastery can destroy opponents. He always talked positive and proclaimed to the entire world that he was the greatest.

> "The strongest oak of the forest is not the one that is protected from the storm and hidden from the sun. It's the one that stands in the open where it is compelled to struggle for its existence against the winds and rains and the scorching sun."
>
> Napoleon Hill

Seven Learnable Skills of Resilience

The following is based on the work of Dr Karen Reivich who has highlighted the seven learnable skills of resilience.

- Self-efficacy. This is the self-confidence that you possess the ability to solve problems. It's about self-awareness, self-belief and knowing what your strengths and weaknesses are. You know what you are good at and this gives the strengths to draw on in order to cope in times of difficulty.

- Impulse control. Resilient people are disciplined. Self-discipline is the ability to refrain from doing something detrimental to health such as smoking, drinking, eating to excess or wasting too much time on trivial pursuits. Resilient people consider problems in a thoughtful and rational way before they act. They remain calm even when provoked. They think before they react because they know that inappropriate words will only add fuel to the fire and create enemies.

- Optimism. Resilient people are realistically optimistic. They have their feet on the ground and consider the facts before they make up their minds. They are realistic optimists and avoid catastrophic thinking which may trigger panic, and impulsive behaviour. Unrealistic optimists ignore the scientific based advice on the prevention of disease from unprotected sex, excessive eating, drinking alcohol and smoking. They believe bad things only happen to other people and not to them. When Hurricane Iniki battered Hawaii in 1993 those who survived best were those who took the advice of weather forecasters and took preventative action by boarding up their properties and taking out adequate insurance. Similarly, it was resilience, passion, hard work and self-belief that kept Chester Carlson (1906-1968) the inventor of photocopying going. Twenty companies and the National Inventors Council rejected his work before his invention was finally accepted and became a worldwide phenomenon.

- Causal analysis. Resilient people solve their problems by applying a systematic problem solving approach. They have the capacity for abstract thought, reflection and adopt a flexible approach to problem solving. They know that for every effect there is a cause and for every action there is an outcome. They know if they want things to happen in their lives they must make them happen. They define the problem, consider the facts, look at alternatives, pick the best alternative and then implement their solution. Resilient people are able to improvise when confronted with unusual situations.

- Emotional awareness. Resilient people are aware of their feelings and know how to control them. Losing your temper only hurts you and spreads like a contagious disease to infect the attitude of the people around you.

- Risk. Resilient people are prepared to take appropriate risks. They try out new things, accept that failure is part of life and are willing to learn from their mistakes.

- Empathy. Resilient people are good at reading and understanding the emotions of others. They have the ability to get inside the minds of others and see things from their point of view. This ability is essential for building up social relationships with others. For good mental health we need a support network in the form of family, friends and colleagues.

"In order to succeed, people need a sense of self-efficacy, to struggle together with resilience to meet the inevitable obstacles and inequities of life."

Albert Bandura

Summary

The quality of persistence enables you to stick to a task despite obstacles and setbacks. People fail because they give up even after one attempt. Many people are on the threshold of success when they quit. We know that quitters are not winners. The deeds of many famous people from many walks of life suggest that hard work and persistence pays off in the end. Patience is the ability to endure waiting or delay without getting frustrated or upset. Passion is about being fully engaged, deeply involved and totally dedicated to a meaningful pursuit. Willpower is having the determination and self-discipline to do what you want to do. Willpower is like a muscle; the more you exercise it the stronger it becomes. Resilience is the ability to bounce back from disappointment and failure to start all over again with hope and optimism. Those without resilience become hopeless and helpless, adopt a victim attitude, become despondent or plunge into depression.

Five Activities to Improve Your Persistence and Resilience Skills

1. Think about previous successes that you have enjoyed reminding you how you have overcome adversity in the past. Make a list of these to inspire you in the future.

2. Believe in yourself and recognise your strengths. See adversity as something that makes you mentally stronger and more determined rather than something that brings you down.

3. You can't control what happens to you in life but you can control how you respond to it. Resilient people adopt a positive attitude to pick up the pieces and start all over again.

4. Study the lives of famous people to see how they triumphed over setbacks and failures and adopt them as role models.

5. Believe that in every obstacle lies an opportunity. It just requires thought and an action plan to exploit it.

7

Motivation

- *What is motivation?*
- *How can we stay motivated?*
- *What is the link between success and motivation?*
- *What are the modal operators?*

Introduction

Motivation is a positive attitude of mind that you are going to succeed despite setbacks and obstacles encountered on the journey to your goals. Motivation is more important than ability in determining success. Motivated people are purposeful and passionate about their lives as they realise that life is not a dress rehearsal, that they only pass through it once, and that they must make the best of it. There are two types of motivation: internal and external. Internal is where you want to do things because you really want to do them and you find them inherently interesting and satisfying. External is where you are meeting the wishes of others such as family or want to abide by the rules of an organisation. Abraham Maslow said that self-actualisation, where people became what they are capable of becoming, is the highest form of motivation. The key factors of motivation are courage, optimism, purpose and energy. Tips for staying motivated include being grateful for what you have and keeping things in perspective. Successful people like their jobs and enjoy taking on new challenges. You can motivate yourself by changing the words of your internal dialogue and free yourself from self-imposed limitations.

What Is Motivation?

The word motivation comes from motive, and is derived from the Latin 'movere', which means to move. Thus motivation means taking action to move you towards your goals. Motivation is a can do attitude of mind that you will be successful despite setbacks and obstacles encountered on the way to your goal. It is a persistent drive while maintaining enthusiasm, interest and commitment to achieve a desired outcome. Motivation is a strong desire or force that energises you and propels you forward to achieve your aims and reach your goal. Motivated people are purposeful and passionate about their lives as they realise that it is the only one that they have and so they are determined to make the best of it. They know who they are and what they really want to do with their lives. They don't hesitate to put their own needs first as they realise that they are not responsible for other people's lives. Discovering your purpose is ongoing throughout your life. It changes in line with your life stages and requires self-questioning and reflection to discover what it is. You must be ready to take the necessary risks, undertake the hard work and perform the actions necessary to achieve your purpose.

There are two types of motivation: internal (intrinsic) and external (extrinsic). Internal motivation is where you do things because you want to do them for your own reasons, satisfaction and enjoyment rather than meeting the wishes of others. It means that you are motivated by personal goals, ability, and a robust sense of self-worth. We are intrinsically motivated to learn, grow and succeed. Internal motivation is the strongest source of motivation in our lives and isn't just more effective than external motivation but the two are often inversely related. The more we are rewarded for something, the more we tend to lose interest in it. At work internally motivated people actually enjoy their work and derive great satisfaction from it irrespective of the monetary rewards. Explorers, inventors, humanitarians and writers are internally motivated to innovate and achieve things that have never been achieved before. Making money is only a secondary consideration. Children are intrinsically motivated to explore and engage in the fantasy of play and by the joy of learning.

External motivation is meeting the wishes of your family or abiding by the rules of an organisation and can be a big influence on our lives. However it can backfire if it is contrary to your own interests, beliefs, values and needs. Ultimately we can only motivate ourselves although others can help and inspire us on the journey to achievement by giving us encouragement and giving us the resources to achieve what we want to do provided that their wishes do not clash with our own. Obviously your motivation will be optimised if you are lucky enough to be motivated by a combination of internal and external sources.

141

"Stop acting as if life is a rehearsal. Live this day as if it were your last. The past is over and gone. The future is not guaranteed."

Wayne Dyer

Motivating Others

When considering motivators, rewards are more effective than punishments. You should keep this in mind when trying to motivate other people. Reward positive behaviour and punish negative behaviour; lean heavily towards rewards and go sparingly when dishing out punishments. Try to encourage people to set themselves standards as they tend to live up to their own expectations and the expectations of others. Sincere support and encouragement acts like a tonic giving people a lift to keep going despite the difficulties. Learn from sport where it is more difficult to defeat teams playing on their home ground as supporters raise their spirits and drive them on to overcome the most testing and fierce-some opposition. Help people develop their own goals, as goals they develop and choose themselves are inherently rewarding to accomplish. People are more likely to be highly motivated if they have a passionate interest in what they want to achieve. Nevertheless people can also be motivated by trying to avoid failure or to move away from poverty experienced when they were growing up.

Toddlers are naturally inquisitive and thus inherently motivated. They teach themselves to walk, talk, explore their surroundings and are strongly motivated by the sense of novelty involved in doing new things. They are determined, curious, energetic, and engaged with an amazing sense of wonder. They are unaware of danger and risk in their attempt to learn as much as they can as quickly as they can. As adults we must balance our security and safety needs with an acceptable level of risk. However if we can rekindle those feelings of childhood wonderment we will be highly motivated in whatever undertaking we choose to do.

"People who are unable to motivate themselves must be content with mediocrity, no matter how impressive their other talents."

Andrew Carnegie

142

Toward/Away From Motivation

People move towards what they want or away from what they don't want. Toward people are goal-oriented because they are motivated by rewards or achievements. They see achievement providing the status and recognition that they want and see money as a means of providing the resources to get what they want. In contrast, away from people see what can go wrong and are motivated to avoid what they don't want such as failure, punishment or pain and this compels them to take action to prevent it from happening. They speak of "preventing problems," "evading disasters," or "avoiding difficulties." Away from people typically see money as a source of security which keeps them debt free and helps them to avoid poverty.

In business there are two types of manager: the toward manager who is successful because he is aggressive, goal and achievement oriented, and the away from manager who is successful because of the fear of being unsuccessful. However, the toward manager in achieving his objectives has no guarantee that he will be happy. If his identity and self-esteem is exclusively tied up in achievement then he will often lack an internal sense of worth. Contrary to expectation getting the top job doesn't always guarantee a healthy sense of self. He will now measure himself against people in other top jobs who may have bigger salaries and bonuses than he does. In addition he may feel threatened and insecure as there are always younger, brighter and more talented people than him on the way up.

The away from manager may be motivated to avoid being like his father who lost his job when the manager was a child, and stayed at home and struggled to support his family and fill his time. Psychologists claim that a negative source of motivation generates anxiety and stress. Under such circumstances people feel drained and experience little job satisfaction.

The Hierarchy of Needs

Abraham Maslow (1908-1970) was keenly interested in human potential and how people become self-actualised. Maslow's theory of motivation is based on what motivates people to take action to meet their needs. His model of motivation though not empirically proven is hugely popular and widely accepted as being reasonable, comprehensive and logical. The theory is intuitively appealing and makes sense to many people. It is probably the most quoted motivation theory in existence and is still popular in training and corporate circles. There are five basic assumptions in Maslow's theory:

1. It considers the total person both physiological and psychological.
2. Motivation can be complex as several sources can contribute to behaviour. In addition motivations can be unconscious or operating without awareness, as well as being conscious or operating with full awareness.
3. People are motivated by various needs. As one need is satisfied another one takes its place.
4. People are motivated by the same basic needs.
5. Basic needs can be arranged in a hierarchy.

Certain needs are more basic than others and these must be satisfied first before the higher needs are met. The basic needs are physiological and safety while the higher needs are love, esteem, and self-actualisation.

1. Physiological needs. This is the most basic need and consists of air, food, shelter and clothing. These needs are easily met in developed countries but often are a challenge in third world countries where the need for food and shelter may dominate every minute of people's lives. Physiological needs are the only needs which can be completely satisfied or indeed over satisfied as in Western countries where obesity is a health issue. They are recurring so that we need to satisfy them on an ongoing basis if we want to stay healthy and alive.

2. Safety needs. This is the need to feel safe and secure and to be protected from harm. Countries provide this through, social mores, the legal framework, policing and the army. Organisations provide this through secure employment, health insurance and pension schemes. Safety needs can never be over satisfied. If children's safety needs are not met they become anxious and may develop into neurotic adults. In stable peaceful societies safety needs are easily met and taken for granted. However in politically unstable societies they may be continually under threat through

violent protest, insurrection and sabotage. Safety needs become a priority during natural disasters such as floods, extreme wintry conditions, hurricanes and earthquakes and when fires, accidents and other life threatening events arise. When our basic needs are met we can then concentrate on meeting our higher needs.

3.   Love and belongingness needs. This is the level that most of us stay at. People desire friendship, a mate and to be part of a family. A child who has experienced love and closeness will grow up to be a mentally healthy adult who will be able to handle the normal ups and downs of life and not feel devastated by the occasional setback or rejection. When people satisfy their need for relationships then they can progress to the next level.

4.   Esteem needs. This is the need for self-respect, self-belief, confidence, competence, and the respect of others. The reputation a person holds amongst their peers will influence their sense of self-esteem and feelings of self-worth. In the corporate world recognition and promotion brings feelings of status and enhanced self-esteem and thus acts as a strong motivator and incentive to work hard in the hope that it will be rewarded. When esteem needs are met people are then ready to progress to the highest level of needs, namely self-actualisation.

5.   Self-actualisation needs. This is reaching your true potential by achieving long-term goals or becoming what you are capable of being. Maslow maintained that only people who reach this level are 'fully human' and he estimated that only 2 per cent of the general population reach this stage. People who arrive at this stage have adopted values such as truth, goodness, justice, fairness, humour and autonomy. Without these values you are unlikely to become self-actualised. The process of trying to become self-actualised may be the ultimate motivation and driving force for most people rather than actually attaining it. Self-actualisation needs can be met by lifelong learning and continuous self-improvement.

"When people say to me: 'How do you do so many things?' I

> often answer them, without meaning to be cruel: 'How do you do so little?' It seems to me that people have vast potential. Most people can do extraordinary things if they have the confidence or take the risks. Yet most people don't. They sit in front of the telly and treat life as if it goes on forever."
>
> Philip Adams

Other Needs

In addition to the Hierarchy of Needs, Maslow mentioned other needs that people should also satisfy:

- Cognitive needs. These are the needs of the mind. They are the desire for knowledge, to be challenged, curious and to solve problems. These needs must be satisfied before any other needs are satisfied. We need knowledge to satisfy our basic needs and we need problem solving skills to satisfy our higher needs. Reading and research are a way of meeting cognitive needs.
- Aesthetic needs. This does not apply to everybody but some people are motivated by the need for beauty and order. Artists such as painters, sculptors, poets and writers may be motivated by aesthetic needs. In the professions, engineers, architects, town planners and designers are often motivated by aesthetic needs or the need to create beautiful and functional streetscapes, buildings and bridges.
- Neurotic needs. These are non-productive compulsive needs which create an unhealthy lifestyle. These act as compensations when a person fails to meet one or more basic needs. For example, if safety needs are not satisfied as a child, then a person might develop an obsession to hoard material possessions. If you don't experience love as a child you may become overly aggressive and hostile to others as an adult.

Self-Actualised People

Self-actualised people have a meaningful philosophy of life and are often driven by a need to serve and help others. They are very much in touch with reality and have a clear sense of right and wrong. They are natural and spontaneous and accept themselves and the rights of others. They are independent minded and autonomous and may express views contrary to the conventional wisdom. They are considerate to others irrespective of age, gender, race or social status and are more likely to have deep and lasting relationships.

According to Maslow becoming self-actualised is the strongest source of motivation. It means different things to different people with different drivers, although many people who are self-actualised are innovators and pioneers in their fields. Self-actualised people come from all walks of life. Some are politicians, philosophers, writers, visionaries, social reformers, humanitarians and activists for human rights who often led unconventional lives but left a lasting legacy for mankind. Famous people Maslow considered inspirational and self-actualised included the following:

- US President Thomas Jefferson (1743-1826) was a politician, lawyer and champion of liberty. He was motivated by an unselfish and patriotic desire to serve his country. He became the third President of the United States and is the original Renaissance man. His energy, creativity and writing skills were extraordinary. He was instrumental in putting through legislation for religious freedom, separating church from state, which lies at the heart of American democracy. He believed in the individual's right to life, liberty and the pursuit of happiness. His marvellous writing skills are contained in the American Declaration of Independence. In addition to English he knew French, Italian, Spanish, Latin and Greek. He was an archaeologist and architect and a wine expert who promoted the establishment of American vineyards. He was keenly interested in Native American culture. He was an inventor who invented a swivel chair and an early type of automatic door. He founded the University of Virginia which he considered among his greatest achievements and he left his library to the American nation which became the Library of Congress.

"We hold these truths to be self-evident: that all men are created equal; that they are endowed by their Creator with certain unalienable rights; that among these are life, liberty, and the pursuit of happiness."   Thomas Jefferson

- William James (1842-1910) was an American author, philosopher and psychologist. He came from an affluent family, receiving the best education and was immersed in culture, literature and art. He studied first to be a painter before qualifying as a medical doctor, although he never practised. Around this time he suffered from poor health and depression which didn't seem to hold him back but instead spurred him on to become a great original thinker. He was fluent in both German and French. After some time in Germany he eventually realised that his true interests were in philosophy and psychology and decided that he would make his mark in that field. Sometime after graduating from Harvard Medical School he was offered a job as a lecturer and spent the next 35 years there. He set up the first experimental psychology laboratories in the US. He later decided that he wasn't interested in experimental psychology and abandoned it for the broader scope of observation, reflection and speculation which philosophy allowed. Many of his students became famous in their own right including Edward Thorndike and John Dewey. He went on to become one of the most important figures in the new discipline of psychology. In 1902 he wrote "I originally studied medicine in order to be a physiologist, but I drifted into psychology and philosophy from a sort of fatality. I never had any philosophic instruction, the first lecture on psychology I ever heard being the first I ever gave." He wrote influential books on psychology including the classic textbook The Principles of Psychology (1890). It influenced generations of thinkers throughout the world including Bertrand Russell, John Dewey and Ludwig Wittgenstein. He was the brother of the more famous novelist and playwright Henry James. He was the first president of the American branch of the Society for Psychical Research. He made some of the most important contributions to philosophy in the last decade of his life. He was a pioneer of and laid the foundations for the modern science of psychology. When Sigmund Freud and Carl Jung went to the US in 1909, the man they most wanted to meet was William James.

"The greatest discovery of my generation is that a human being can alter his life by altering his attitude of mind."

William James

- Aldous Huxley (1894-1963) came from an intellectual family and was a novelist and critic and was best known for his novel Brave New World (1931) dealing with the dehumanising aspects of technological progress such as mass production and psychological conditioning. He also wrote short stories, poetry, travel articles and film scripts. He spent the later part of his life in the USA, living in Los Angeles from 1937 until his death in 1963. At 16 he suffered an eye disease and was totally blind for about 18 months. He learned Braille and despite near blindness he graduated with a BA in English from Oxford in 1916. Some people think his blindness was a blessing in disguise because it put a stop to his idea of pursuing medicine as a career and instead gave the world a legacy of unique and wonderful novels. He was a humanist and a pacifist and in later years developed an interest in parapsychology and philosophical mysticism. During this time he began experimenting with psychedelic drugs and wrote about his experiences in his essays titled Doors of Perception and Heaven and Hell. He is reputed to have taken LSD on his deathbed but despite this he was opposed to the indiscriminate taking of drugs during his lifetime. He died on the 22 November 1963, the same day as US President John F. Kennedy was assassinated and the same day that the writer C.S. Lewis died

> "There is only one corner of the universe you can be certain of improving, and that's your own self."
>
> Aldous Huxley

- Jane Addams (1860-1935) was a sociologist, public philosopher, author, and leader in women's suffrage and world peace. She won worldwide recognition as a pioneer social worker and feminist and became a role model for middle class women who wanted to improve the social conditions in their communities. She lived at a time when women had no vote and were not encouraged to better themselves through education or the professions. Their role was considered to become a stay at home housewife and rear a family. In contrast, she believed women should have the same rights as men and be able to vote and pursue a career. She had ambitions to become a medical doctor in order to help people but was forced to discontinue her medical education because of ill health and chronic back pain due to curvature of the spine, which was later corrected by an operation. Though disappointed she realised that there were other ways in which she could achieve her ambitions of helping the less well off in society and this became the prime motivator for the rest of her life. In 1889 she and her friend Ellen Gates Starr co-founded a settlement house in Chicago. The settlement house was a way of helping the poor in urban areas by living among them and meeting their social and educational needs. They offered food, shelter and education to the needy. Settlement house workers encouraged social policy initiatives and pioneered the profession of social work. The adult classes were the forerunner of the continuing education classes offered by many contemporary third level colleges. Their free legal aid system for the poor pioneered the free aid legal system offered in many countries today. Jane Addams was a passionate campaigner for better housing, social welfare improvements, factory inspections, rights of immigrants, stricter child-labour laws, the protection of working women and an eight hour day. She highlighted and fought against political and corporate corruption where officialdom turned a blind eye to health and safety codes. In 1910 she received the first honorary degree ever awarded to a woman by Yale University. In 1915 she became national chairman of the Women's Peace Party and was also elected President of the Women's International League for Peace and Freedom. She made a speech on pacifism at Carnegie Hall and was branded unpatriotic by the New York Times, and in 1917 she opposed the US entry to the war and was harshly criticised as a pacifist. Her efforts were finally recognised in 1931 when she was awarded the Nobel Peace Prize: the first US woman to win such a prize.

"Nothing could be worse than the fear that one had given up too soon, and left one unexpended effort that might have saved the world."

Jane Addams

- Albert Schweitzer (1875-1965) was a philosopher, theologian, physician, author, organist and humanitarian. He has been called the greatest Christian of all time for his unselfish devotion to improving the circumstances of the poor and needy. He based his personal philosophy on reverence for life and was motivated by a deep commitment to serve humanity. He wanted to repay the world for the privileges and happiness that it had given him and to serve humanity using Jesus as his role model. He abandoned a promising career as a musician and theologian to fulfil his ambition to serve the needs of others. In 1912 as a qualified medical doctor he went to work without pay in the Paris Missionary Society's mission at Lambarene on the Ogowe River in Gabon (then a French colony). Schweitzer was inspired and motivated to become a medical missionary after reading an evangelical paper about the needs of medical missions and to do something practical to help those with the direst needs. He built a hospital in French Equatorial Africa (Gabon) serving thousands of Africans. He used his $33,000 Nobel Prize money, royalties from books and fees earned for personal appearances to expand the hospital and to build a leper colony. From 1952 he campaigned against nuclear tests and nuclear weapons with Albert Einstein, Otto Hahn and Bertrand Russell. In 1955 Queen Elizabeth 11 awarded him the 'Order of Merit', Britain's highest civilian honour. For his many years of humanitarian efforts he was awarded the Nobel Peace Prize in 1962. His "The Problem of Peace" lecture is considered one of the best speeches ever given. He died on the 4th September 1965 and his grave, on the banks of the Ogowe River, is marked by a cross he made himself. His legacy still lives on in the form of the Albert Schweitzer Fellowship which sponsors the training of medical staff to help the needy and his hospital in Lambarene is still functioning.

"Constant kindness can accomplish much. As the sun makes ice melt, kindness causes misunderstanding, mistrust and hostility to evaporate."

Albert Schweitzer

- Eleanor Roosevelt (1884-1962) was the wife of President Delano Roosevelt and campaigned tirelessly on behalf of the disadvantaged right up to her death in 1962. She stood by her husband when he was unfaithful and when he was stricken with a paralytic illness in 1921 which resulted in permanent paralysis of his legs. She encouraged her husband to return to public life and made public appearances on his behalf after he became paralysed. She became active in the Women's Trade Union League supporting their goals for a 48 hour week, minimum wage and the abolition of child labour. She also supported the African-American civil rights movement. In 1943 she visited thousands of wounded servicemen in the South Pacific winning the admiration of many. During her time as First Lady (1933-1945) she held weekly press conferences and also wrote a newspaper column. She wrote about issues affecting American women such as unemployment, poverty, education and the role of women in society. In 1946 she became the first chairperson of the new United Nations Commission on Human Rights. She played an important role in the drafting of the Universal Declaration of Human Rights. President Truman in praising her work called her the "First Lady of the World." She supported John F. Kennedy for president against Richard Nixon and he appointed her to the United Nations from 1961 to 1962. Throughout the 1950s she made countless national and international speeches and made radio broadcasts and appeared on television. During her lifetime she received 48 honorary degrees including many doctorates. At her memorial service UN Ambassador Adlai Stevenson said: "What other single human being has touched and transformed the existence of so many?" As a child she considered herself plain and craved affections but transcended these feelings to become one of the most admired people of the 20th century. She became self-actualised at a time when women's place was considered to be in the home.

"You gain strength, courage and confidence by every experience in which you really stop to look fear in the face. You must do the thing which you think you cannot do."

Eleanor Roosevelt

Key Factors of Motivation

These can be quickly recalled by the acronym COPE:

C   Courage. We must have the initiative to persevere in the face of difficulties and setbacks. Re-motivate yourself after setbacks and when the goal seems too difficult and far away. Recall the benefits and rewards of being successful. Great explorers and mountaineers show great courage and determination in the face of hardship and danger.

O   Optimism. We must engender positive expectations of success. Visualise a successful outcome and the positive things that await you as anticipated success is highly motivational. Work back from the outcome and consider the resources you'll need to achieve it, the journey you need to take, and the likely obstacles that you will encounter. Preparation is the best form of defence against anticipated obstacles.

P   Purpose. We must have a vision, sense of mission and purpose to achieve whatever we want to do. Most people know what they don't want. Few know what they want. Always think of what you want rather than what you don't want as this will motivate you to move forward. Generally we all want to be happy, to grow as human beings, to achieve success in whatever we wish to do in life, and to be remembered for the legacy we leave after we are gone. Throughout our lives we crave acceptance in the form of respect, recognition, friendship and validation

E   Energy. We must have the energy to take appropriate actions and the resilience to come back from setbacks. Few worthwhile things in life are achieved without commitment and hard work. On the journey to your success reward yourself for achieving progress points and for not giving up when everything seems to be going against you.

"Be miserable. Or motivate yourself. Whatever has to be done, it's always your choice."

Wayne Dyer

Tips for Staying Motivated

- Stay connected with your family and friends as you will need their encouragement and support in difficult times to stay motivated.

- Create a buddy system. Find people who share your interests and want to achieve what you want to do so that you can learn from them.

- Create a mission statement for inspiration and revisit it often. Nothing remains the same so that you will need to revise it frequently.

- Decide that you want to be happy and nurture your sense of humour. Mix with positive and happy people as happiness is contagious.

- Find a mentor to encourage you and be a mentor to someone who needs your guidance. Mentoring others will give you a fresh perspective and help you develop new skills. Most successful people admit to being mentored at some stage in their lives.

- Develop a sense of self-awareness by focusing on what you consider important in your life. Stay in touch with your thoughts and feelings by keeping a morning diary.

- Be grateful for what you have. Focus on the good things in your life rather than what you lack. Create a list of things that you are grateful for and read it now and then to remind yourself what you should be thankful for. We often take things for granted and never miss them until they are gone.

- Keep things in perspective. Things are seldom as bad as they seem and most things work out well in the end. Our worst fears are seldom realised. Learn from the present and the past and think about future possibilities.

- Do something practical or different. Take up an interesting hobby or go on a foreign holiday.

"Don't wait until everything is just right. It will never be perfect. There will always be challenges, obstacles and less than perfect conditions. So what! Get started now! With each step you take, you will grow stronger and stronger, more and more skilled, more and more self-confident and more and more successful."

Mark Victor Hansen

Success and Motivation

- Successful people are motivated and self-starters. They are enthusiastic and enjoy achieving goals and the recognition and status they receive for their achievements. They seek out and welcome new opportunities.

- Successful people like their work and enjoy taking on more responsibility. They like to grow and develop and seek out challenges and opportunities to learn. They seek out things that give their lives meaning and satisfaction. They know that predictability can breed boredom.

- They set new goals as others are achieved. The journey towards success never ends. They know that the process towards the goal is more enjoyable than achieving the goal. It is important to celebrate small successes on the way as these will act as motivators for greater achievements.

Success means different things to different people. Some people are successful in sport and this is the source of their happiness and pride. Nothing makes some people happier than helping others. Others crave to be rich and famous often at the cost of matrimonial harmony, family and friendships. Some people see success as making a difference to the world while others are happiest when they are creating something unique.

Sometimes you have to be very courageous, take considerable risk and do the unusual to achieve fame and recognition. Over a thousand people have climbed Mount Everest, the highest peak in the World. Apart from fulfilling a personal ambition it is not now unusual to achieve this goal. However Stephen Venables is someone special. When he set foot in 1988 on the 8,850m summit he became the first Englishman to do so without the use of bottled oxygen. He now writes and gives inspirational motivational talks to business managers about his exploits. Because of his achievements in the world of exploration and adventure he is seen as a role model, as someone who has survived against the odds and achieved very difficult things. To do what Venables did requires a special kind of motivation with a very high level of physical fitness, dedication, mental stamina and sheer willpower to survive in the most trying circumstances. Above 8000m you operate on the edge of what is physiologically possible and are in constant danger of death from lack of oxygen. He was in a team of four but he alone decided to press on to reach the top of the world despite the strong possibility of not surviving. He has written several books about his exploits and appeared on BBC documentaries and in the IMAX film Shackleton's Antarctic Adventure.

"Reach high, for stars lie hidden in your soul. Dream deep, for every dream precedes the goal."

Pamela Vaull Starr

Modal Operators

Modal operators are part of the language of motivation and will influence your feelings and thinking on your journey to success. Modal operators are rules of conduct that you believe you must comply with and set limits to what you are capable of doing. You can motivate yourself by changing the words of your internal dialogue or modal operators and free yourself from self-imposed limitations. Being aware of modal operators may help you free yourself from the mental barriers that may be holding you back from achieving what you want. There are different types of modal operators.

- Modal operators of necessity. These motivate you by making you feel that what you have to do is mandatory and suggest that you have no choice. They can motivate us to get important things done or alternatively waste our time doing trivial things. They consist of words like, have to, should, need to and must; words imprinted on our minds from an early age. Ask yourself what would happen if you did or did not do this? Once you consider and evaluate the consequences of doing so then you can make a more informed judgement as to what you should do. Some rules help us live a sensible life but others may hold you back and limit the possibilities open to you.

- Modal operators of possibility. These define what is considered possible and empower you to do something. They consist of words like can, could, might, possibly and maybe. You are more likely to accomplish something if you believe you can. A can do attitude is encouraged by tasks that are stretching but achievable rather than ones that are too difficult or insurmountable. People become engaged and energised when they can use their creativity, explain their reasoning and defend their views and conclusions. Great discoveries and advancement in thinking have often come about as a result of answering the question: "What would happen if?" or "why does it have to be this way?"

- Modal operators of impossibility. These limit your ability to do something. They consist of cannot, will not and must not. If people say they can't swim it just means that they haven't learnt to swim yet. The mindset of impossibility creates a defeatist attitude even before you try. With this attitude people have little motivation and give up when life gets too difficult for them. They feel hopeless and helpless thinking that they should win at all costs and tend to generalise that all is lost. Instead you should accept it as a temporary setback while refocusing on your long term goal. In life there is no guarantee of a positive outcome each and every time. There is always a solution to a problem even if it seems to be very difficult. Even changing the words "I can't" to "I won't" reframes them to a possibility of choice. Saying you can't make a presentation to a large group of people is different than saying you won't which means that you have a valid choice of whether you want to or not. Many assumed limitations are based on an erroneous belief and it should always be remembered that beliefs can be questioned and changed.

"You are the embodiment of the information you choose to accept and act upon. To change your circumstances you need to change your thinking and subsequent actions."

Adlin Sinclair

Summary

Motivation is a strong desire or force that propels people forward to achieve goals. Motivated people put their own needs first as they realise that they are not responsible for other people's lives. Internal motivation is the strongest source of motivation in our lives. Internally motivated people enjoy their work and derive great satisfaction from it. When considering motivators rewards are more effective than punishments. Abraham Maslow maintained there was a hierarchy of needs which motivated people ranging from basic needs through to self-actualisation. Self-actualisation means reaching your potential by becoming the best you can be. Famous people Maslow considered self-actualised included Thomas Jefferson and Albert Schweitzer. Key factors of motivation include courage, optimism, purpose and energy. Tips for staying motivated include putting variety into your life and finding a mentor to guide and encourage you. Successful people seek out motivational things that give them meaning and satisfaction in their lives. Some people find success in sport while others are happy to help others. Modal operators such as words of necessity, possibility and impossibility can influence your feelings and thinking in a positive or negative way facilitating or hindering your endeavours to find success.

Five Activities to Improve Your Motivation Skills

1. Stay motivated throughout your life by finding a job or a hobby that really interests you.

2. Start each day by reflecting on five things that you are grateful for in your life.

3. Rekindle the feelings of curiosity and novelty you had as a toddler.

4. Study the lives of people Maslow claimed became self-actualised to see how they became self-actualised and use them as inspirational role models.

5. When engaged in self-talk use words of possibility like can, could, and might, possibly and maybe. Great discoveries and new ways of thinking often come about as a result of posing the question: "What would happen if?

8

Lifelong Learning & Continuous Improvement

- *What is lifelong learning?*
- *What are the benefits of lifelong learning?*
- *How can I become a lifelong learner?*
- *What are the 8 intelligences?*
- *What is a growth mindset?*

Introduction

Lifelong learning is a philosophy that people should continue learning throughout their lives rather than stopping at 16, 18 or 21 years of age. Lifelong learning can be undertaken as a serious leisure time pursuit, as a way of self-improvement or as a way of upgrading work related knowledge and skills in order to retain employment or improve employment prospects. There are many benefits of lifelong learning including filling your time productively, providing structure for your day and social contact with other people. It is also a source of self-actualisation or becoming the person you are capable of becoming. There are barriers to lifelong learning such as lack of interest and ambition. There may also be physical and mental barriers to accessing learning facilities. To become a lifelong learner you must adopt a positive attitude towards learning, develop a questioning mind and adopt a style of learning that suits you.

If you don't change throughout your life you will stagnate and your skills will become peripheral or outdated. Lifelong learners adapt to change enabling them to prosper and grow. We have a range of natural abilities that we can develop. People become successful when they exploit what they are particularly good at. Successful people continually learn from their mistakes and make sure not to repeat them. People with a growth mindset believe that they can improve their intelligence through lifelong learning and new experiences.

Commitment to Lifelong Learning

Lifelong learning is learning activities undertaken throughout one's lifespan, in different environments and in different ways to improve knowledge and skills and equip you for the challenges of life. The learner is solely responsible for their lifelong learning as nobody can force you to learn. Learners choose what, when, where and how to learn and the pace in which learning takes place. Successful people know the importance of continuing learning throughout their lives. Lifelong learners are passionate about research and inquiry and motivated by the thrill and novelty of discovering new information. They are proactive in searching out new and creative solutions to problems. They are motivated by a love of learning rather than mere career advancement or financial gain. They may be keenly interested in an absorbing hobby such as astronomy, photography, painting, sculpture, gardening, amateur dramatics or philately. Others get involved in a volunteer activity which provides them with a substitute vocational, intellectual and social outlet. These provide them with a sense of challenge and self-actualisation often absent from their full time jobs. In some instances they may also be the source of future employment opportunities.

Learning is a light load to carry; nobody can take it away from you and is an appreciating asset. In a competitive world it is important to keep up to date generally and in your specific subject of expertise as otherwise your knowledge will become out of date and redundant. The ability to engage in lifelong learning presumes good literacy skills such as the ability to locate, read, mentally digest, comprehend, question, analyse and evaluate information. These literacy skills should be developed, practised and maintained at the highest level during your lifetime to facilitate lifelong learning. All human knowledge has doubled in the last 10 years and the trend is likely to accelerate. It is essential that you try out new things as everything you do provides learning and valuable experience for the future. Getting stuck in a rut and doing nothing worthwhile is no formula for a successful life. To counteract the tendency to stay within your comfort zone challenge the conventional wisdom and adopt new ways of questioning, thinking, approaching problems and behaving. Get rid of the things that are holding you back such as limiting beliefs, emotional blocks, self-destructive behaviour and negative attitudes and habits.

Improve your mind by increasing your knowledge. Build up a home library in the subjects that you are interested in. Improve your ability to assimilate and recall by acquiring learning to learn skills. These skills include learning to read faster and more effectively so that you can read and understand more in the same time, and acquiring the skill of mind mapping to improve your ability to synopsise information and focus your concentration. These skills also include critical thinking, analysis, problem solving, decision making, questioning, research, time management and planning. Improve your skills by applying what you learn as knowledge is turned into skill and becomes your own by judicial practise and application. Increase your earning capacity through further education and training and by acquiring appropriate experience and skills. Decrease the time you watch television and turn it into learning time by improving your mind through reading and research in your chosen subject. Set yourself the target of reading for at least one hour per day. Remember that great leaders are great readers. The margin between greatness and being average is small. In athletics the difference between winners and losers is often only a fraction of a second. In life the difference between winners and losers is often a matter of attitude, dedication, commitment and hard work.

> "You cannot teach a man anything – you can only help him find it within himself."
>
> Galileo Galilee

Classical Facilitators of Lifelong Learning

The greatest facilitator of lifelong learning was the invention of printing which meant that books could be easily and inexpensively produced. This facilitated the spread of libraries which were no longer dependent on original texts and precious handmade copies that were time consuming to do and could only be produced at exorbitant cost. Johannes Gutenberg (1398-1468) was the inventor of printing from movable metal type although strangely none of the books printed by him survive. Printing in a primitive form already existed but Gutenberg refined and revolutionised the process and made books universally available. They say that there is nothing new under the sun and the printing press was developed from similar screw-type presses used for manufacturing wine in the Rhine valley. Many historians regard his invention as one of the most important of all time because of the impact it had on enabling education, learning and the spread of knowledge. He brought learning to the masses by making books cheap and widely available and so made possible the spread of information and lifelong learning which up to that time was confined to those in seats of power, universities, monasteries and the very rich. Provided people were able to read they could now independently educate themselves and pursue interests by engaging in lifelong learning. He helped the spread of knowledge through the mass production of books and ideas and so transformed the world and changed the course of history.

The first printed Bible in 1455 is attributed to Guttenberg. This opened up the famous holy book to interested readers and undermined the monopoly power of the clergy, democratised Christianity and eventually led to the Protestant Reformation. The creation of mass printed books opened up learning and inquiry to anybody interested and allowed the spread of scientific, philosophical, artistic, historical and cultural ideas which lead to the European Renaissance. The dissemination of information led to an explosion in new ideas, scientific inquiry, creativity and invention. It took another five hundred years before his method of printing was superseded by the development of lithographic printing, phototypesetting, word-processing and computer technology. A vast resource of information is now available on the internet at the touch of a button.

Plato (429-347 BC) one of the Greek philosophers, could be credited for being one of the first to suggest the importance of learning and education to the development of a person. His theories on knowledge, religion, politics, and ethics, shaped Western thought for a thousand years, and still exert a profound influence today. He was a student of Socrates and taught Aristotle. His teacher Socrates was executed because of his ideas and on the pretext of corrupting the young. Unlike his mentor Socrates who was a teacher, talker, thinker and debater rather than a writer, Plato left a substantial body of writing and his most famous is The Republic. Written around 380 The Republic contains the first reference to the concept of utopia and remains one of the foundations of political philosophy. He wrote about the lost city of Atlantis and scholars to this day debate whether it was fact or fiction as it has never been found. He attached the utmost importance to education and founded the Academy around 387, which stood for 1000 years and was the first institution of learning in the Western World. However some of Socrates ideas are preserved by Plato in the form of dialogues. Some people think he adopted this style because he was afraid he would suffer the same fate as Socrates. He originated the idea that humans have a soul separate from the body and that this soul survives death. This idea was adopted and developed by Christian theologians and forms an important part of Christian belief.

Confucius (551-479 BC) was a Chinese teacher, thinker and philosopher whose influence is still felt not only in China, Japan, Korea, Vietnam and other countries of East Asia but also in the countries of Western Europe. His influence on Chinese history has been compared to that of Socrates on the West. He believed that study and lifelong learning was the true path to enlightenment and self-improvement. He argued that the only real understanding of a subject comes from long careful study and reflection. He particularly emphasised the value of reflection and said: "He who learns and does not think is lost. He who thinks but does not learn is in great danger." He believed that moral education was the way to restore values to society. He encouraged people to think deeply and to study the outside world. He believed people were responsible for their own actions and for the way they treated others. He felt that the length of our lives was predetermined but we could determine what we accomplished in life and what we will be remembered for. By the age of 15 Confucius was an avid and dedicated learner. He was particularly noted as an incessant questioner of his teachers. He married at 19 and spent most of his twenties devoted to learning and education. He had a great knowledge of history, poetry and music and in his thirties he began a teaching career. He said: "It is by poetry that one's mind is aroused; it is by ceremony that one's character is regulated; it is by music that one becomes accomplished."

Confucius believed in education for all as a means of preparing pupils for a role in society. He believed that leaders should be educated so that they could disseminate their learning to their subjects and improve society as a whole. He saw himself as a mere conduit of learning that invented nothing but simply passed on received wisdom and knowledge and promulgated the benefits of self-inquiry. He believed that the family unit played an important role in society and that children should have respect for their elders. His sayings were collected after his death and in the West his philosophy is known as Confucianism. His most famous saying: "do not to others what you do not want done to yourself" has become known as the golden rule and is mirrored in Christian moral systems. The concept of reciprocity, honesty, humanity and concern for others runs through the ethics of Confucius. He believed leaders should be chosen on the basis of merit rather than family connections and should win the respect of their subjects by governing by example. His influence has endured for 2500 years and is likely to do so for many more.

"Man is a tame or civilised animal; nevertheless he requires proper instruction and a fortunate nature, and then of all animals he becomes the most divine and most civilised; but if he is insufficiently or ill-educated he is the most savage of earthly creatures."

Plato

Modern Practitioners of Lifelong Learning

Teachers, lecturers and research academics are examples of modern lifelong learners. Research academics spend their lives formulating novel questions in their area of interest and seeking solutions through research. Their academic status and worth is determined by the number of research papers they get accepted by their peers and published in academic journals. They work in a profession where "publish or perish" is the motto. They are usually internally motivated as proven by the fact that many continue with their research into retirement despite the absence of external motivators such as monetary reward. They are motivated by; an inherent interest in the subject matter, innate curiosity, enthusiasm, the need for recognition, sheer enjoyment and a passion for lifelong learning. There is now an acceptance that knowledge goes out of date and needs to be constantly updated. Medical doctors, consultants, pharmacists, engineers, accountants, lawyers, architects and other professions now have to undertake continuing professional education during their careers if they want their licences to practice to be renewed. Lifelong learning and keeping up to date is now a formal part of their training.

Those who get to the top of their organisations and become chief executives usually spend many years learning about the various aspects of the business such as finance, operations, marketing, human relations and management. They usually amass experience in these areas before they get to the top. The basics may be learned in college but there is no substitute for hands on experience and the challenge involved in operating at a senior managerial level in a business, making decisions and learning from feedback on their successes and failures. Their key to development is to acquire a broad experience and to take on more complex responsibilities as they progress through their careers. Many chief executives praise the role that mentors played in their development and success.

In reality most of us will not become chief executives but will have to settle for something much less. Nevertheless we should aspire to become the best in whatever job we choose. Knowledge becomes out of date within 5 to 10 years so that it is imperative to upgrade our knowledge and skills continuously. The old idea that college prepared you for life, and you didn't need to undertake any more formal learning when you graduated is redundant,. and is now replaced by the concept of lifelong learning through continuous education and training. Regardless of how up to date educational programmes are the content knowledge and technical skills acquired by students will inevitably go out of date with the passage of time. In addition many students leave college despite having gone through an assessment system with a poor grasp of fundamental concepts. It seems that learning a traditional discipline is a gradual process of discovery and development rather than end stage mastery when the degree programme finishes.

People in fulltime employment can undertake part-time studies at degree and post graduate level to upgrade their knowledge and more importantly to acquire research, critical thinking, problem solving and decision making skills which they can apply to work processes and business problems. They can even pursue degrees by distance learning or over the internet if they feel that commuting to and from a college will take up too much time. Organisations also provide opportunities for lifelong learning through learning centres, seminars, workshops, sponsored degrees and training courses.

> "Learning is an active process. We learn by doing. Only knowledge that is used sticks in your mind."
>
> Dale Carnegie

Famous Lifelong Learners

Famous lifelong learners include entrepreneurs, philosophers, scientists, inventors, writers and politicians. These people did not stop learning when they finished school or college. Instead they were infused by a passion, interest and enthusiasm for their chosen subject, project or hobby and continued to go on learning for the rest of their lives. They supplemented their formal learning by further study, research and experimentation and worked long hours in the pursuit of their goals. Many of them overcame setbacks, discrimination and personal trauma on their road to success. Most of them were driven by a love of learning and an innate curiosity rather than the prospect of becoming rich and famous. These outcomes are often a by-product of learning rather than a prime consideration.

Richard Branson (born 1950) in his early days is an example of someone who showed great entrepreneurial flair from an early age and learned from experience. He successfully set up a magazine called Student when only 16. In 1970 he set up a record mail-order business and in 1972 he opened a chain of record stores. Branson's Virgin brand grew rapidly during the 1980's with Virgin Atlantic Airways and expansion of the Virgin Records music label. Branson had ideas, worked hard, studied the competition, took action and learned from his successes and failures. Branson is now a billionaire despite the fact that he has dyslexia, did poorly at his academic studies and left school at 16.

Thomas J. Watson was the president of IBM who oversaw its growth into a major company from 1914 to 1956. He was a firm believer in corporate training and leadership development and set up a formal training organisation in IBM. Engraved in the granite of the training department's lobby were the words: "think," "observe," "discuss," "listen," and "read," which shows how passionate Watson was about learning. He died in 1956, one of the richest men of his time and was known as the world's greatest salesman.

Gregor Mendel (1822-1884) had a lifelong interest in botany and discovered the basic principles of genetics now known as "Mendel's Laws of Inheritance" after concentrated study, hard work and dedication. He is an example of a lifelong learner with a passion and enthusiasm for his subject, who showed determination and perseverance in the pursuit of his ground-breaking ideas. His discoveries have revolutionised the cultivation of plants and the selective breeding of domestic animals for desirable traits. He trained as a science teacher and became a monk, entering the Abbey of St Thomas at Brunn in 1843. He studied botany, chemistry, physics and zoology at the University of Vienna in 1841 and pursued this lifelong interest when he entered the monastery by studying and experimenting with plants. The abbey was a teaching order and supported scientific inquiry. He applied the scientific approach to his studies using quantified measurements and applied statistics to support and prove his theories. He grew pea plants in the garden of the monastery and in a series of experiments over many years found that traits such as tallness in pea plants were determined equally by both parents and were inherited by the offspring. He published his findings in 1865 but they aroused very little interest. His groundbreaking research and findings were not understood or appreciated during his lifetime much to his frustration and disappointment. Like many other great people his work was not recognised until after his death in 1900 when it was rediscovered and its greatness acknowledged by other biologists working in the same area.

Benjamin Franklin (1706-1790) was a printer, scientist, diplomat, publisher, politician and writer and was one of the Founding Fathers of the American Republic having helped in the drafting of the Declaration of Independence. He was a man of innate curiosity with an insatiable thirst for knowledge. He is regarded as one of the most famous and influential Americans of the 18th century. In his early career he was a successful printer and journalist making sufficient money to support his interest in science and politics. He was a lifelong learner and successful researcher in electricity and is well known for his experiment with a kite in a thunderstorm which established the link between lightening and electricity. Equally important he invented a battery to store electricity and made a unique contributed to the vocabulary of electricity. He invented the lightening rod, bifocal spectacles and discovered the course of the Gulf Stream. His contribution to the science of electricity was recognised when he was elected to the prestigious Royal Society in London. He published his findings in a book titled Experiments and Observations in Electricity in 1751. He spent 18 years in England campaigning on the rights of the colonists to determine and manage their own tax affairs. In 1775 on his return to America he was an active participant in drawing up the Declaration of Independence that launched the Revolutionary War in 1775 which lasted until 1781. In 1783 he was made ambassador to Paris making the case for the colonists in the American War of Independence, and on his return to Philadelphia was elected president of the state of Pennsylvania, serving for two terms.

"An investment in knowledge pays the best interest."
Benjamin Franklin

Marie Curie (1867-1934) was a famous chemist and physicist who formulated the theory of radioactivity and was the winner of two Nobel prizes. Her achievements were all the more remarkable because of the prejudice and discrimination as a woman she had to endure and overcome to study at the highest levels in a male dominated scientific profession. She showed remarkable intellectual abilities from an early age but could not pursue her dream of becoming a scientist at 18 because of limited family financial circumstances. She worked as a governess for two years to support her sister's medical education on the understanding that she would do likewise for her. In 1891 she started studying in the Sorbonne and graduated with a degree in mathematics in 1894. She intended to pursue further studies but was denied a place in Krakow University because she was a woman. She married her teacher and fellow scientist Pierre Curie in 1895 and specialised in the electrical and magnetic properties of crystals; the area of study which first drew the Curies together. In 1898 they discovered two new elements which they named polonium, after her native land Poland, and radium because of its intense radioactivity. Despite the tragic and sudden death of her husband in a traffic accident Marie continued her research and was appointed to his professorship a month after his death and became the first female professor at the Sorbonne. For many years she worked extremely hard in cold ill-equipped laboratories and with substances that were to prove lethal. To this day, her notebooks are so radioactive that they are stored in lead lined boxes. From 1922 she concentrated on finding practical medical applications for her radioactivity which today is used to treat cancers. She died in 1934 almost certainly from the effects of radioactivity exposure endured over a dedicated working lifetime.

> "The most successful men in the end are those whose success is the result of steady accretion. It is the man, who carefully advances step by step, with his mind becoming wider and wider – and progressively better able to grasp any theme or situation."
>
> Alexander Graham Bell

Alexander Graham Bell (1847-1922) was the inventor of the telephone and was a teacher of elocution. He was born in Scotland and immigrated to Canada in 1870. He developed a method of teaching speech to the deaf and was appointed professor of vocal physiology at Boston University in 1873. Bell's telephone was one of the inventions that transformed the 20th century and eventually spawned further inventions such as fax machines, email and the internet. On the 10 March 1877 he gave his historic demonstration of his newly invented telephone by ringing his assistant Thomas Watson, and a few weeks later made his first long-distance telephone call from New York to Boston, also to the same assistant. He formed the Bell Telephone Company in 1877 to commercially exploit his invention. Throughout his life he had a passion for identifying practical problems and inventing devices to solve them. His family background prompted him to develop an interest in communication, speaking and listening devices. He invented the photophone a device that could transmit sound and was the forerunner of fibre optic cables. His scientific interests were wide ranging and he explored heredity, invented an air conditioner, a prototype iron lung, a metal detector, an audiometer and explored the possibility of alternative fuel sources. However, he is best remembered for his invention of the telephone that opened up communications between people, countries and continents all over the world. People now take devices like the mobile phone for granted.

Henry Ford (1863-1947) was a US motor-car manufacturer and was the first to make cars for the mass market and was the first to develop continuous production lines reaping huge economies of scale. Despite what many people think, Ford did not invent the internal combustion engine. The first practical internal combustion engines were made by Belgian engineer Etienne Lenoir in 1859 and in 1876 this was improved by the German inventor Nikolaus Otto. Ford was a mechanic by training who set up the Ford Motor Company in 1903 and from 1908 to 1927 the famous Model T was sold all over the world. By the time the last Model T had rolled off the production line in 1927, Ford had sold more than 15 million. As a twelve year old child Henry Ford saw his first steam engine and so began a lifelong fascination and passion for engines. He started a workshop on his father's farm, studied to be a mechanic, read everything relevant he could lay his hands on about the emerging field of automobiles, and built his own prototypes from scratch. Through continuous learning Ford acquired a unique and vast knowledge of the developing science of motor mechanics. This knowledge was the foundation for the success of the Ford Motor Company. Ford showed great perseverance when pursuing his goals and did not give up when confronted by obstacles and setbacks. Ford also believed in learning from his competitors. During the early days of the Ford Motor Company he would buy competitor's new cars and take them apart to see if he could learn anything new from them. This approach is now known as reverse engineering.

Benefits of Lifelong Learning

The benefits of lifelong learning include the following:

* Structure.
  People who are unemployed or retired often find the day very long and miss the challenge, structure and social contacts that paid employment provides. Having something to do and to look forward to, can be a key aspect of

171

maintaining mental health. Taking up a lifelong interest as a hobby or going to adult education classes can fill the void.

- Social contact.
  A person who takes up amateur astronomy or public speaking and joins a local club for amateur enthusiasts will have a social outlet and an opportunity for collaborative learning and friendships with others based on shared interests. Attending adult classes in your subject of interest will provide the same opportunities.

- Goals.
  A serious leisure pursuit such as a hobby is like a second career or an only career to those who are unemployed, home carers or retired. Lifelong learning as leisure will provide this through setting personal learning goals or working towards more formal educational qualifications such as certificates, diplomas or degrees. It provides the same benefits for those stuck in jobs or careers that don't challenge them mentally or utilise all their talents.

- Social status.
  Becoming a lifelong learner and expert in a subject that interests you will provide you with a sense of identity, self-worth and social status amongst your peers. You may be employed during the day in a routine soul destroying job which you must do to support your family and pay the bills but have a part-time hobby that provides challenge. For example a factory worker on an assembly line may develop an interest in local history and become an expert in this field achieving status as a local celebrity among neighbours that otherwise would not be available to them. They may be interviewed by local radio and newspapers about unique aspects of local history of interest to listeners or readers. It also provides a sense of excitement as an antidote to a soulless occupation. For others it may be a means of providing relief for a boring or stress filled fulltime job.

- Self-actualisation.
  People become self-actualised by doing something which give them self-expression and becoming what they are capable of becoming in an area that they are keenly interested in. An accountant may find an outlet in sculpture,

painting or writing in their spare time while a factory worker may get involved in trade union politics, sport or charity work as an alternative outlet for hidden talents and self-expression.

- Social capital.
  People involved in amateur activities and volunteering, network with others and thus create community spirit and a sense of citizenship and social awareness. Great satisfaction can be derived by making a contribution to society and helping others less well-off than you.

- Improved Mental Health
  Lifelong learning may prevent Alzheimer's as research has found that vigorous mental activity may hold the key to how well we age. Sophisticated mental activity increases the neural connections in the brain and may prevent or at least delay the onset of the disease. It is also possible that people who are mentally active create a brain "reserve" through education and continuous learning that slows up the progress of Alzheimer's. It seems that better educated or more intellectually engaged people seem more equipped to fight the disease. So people who have challenging hobbies, regularly read, solve crossword puzzles, play cards, chess or draughts, or visit museums are less likely to experience mental decline that those who do not.

- Corporate competiveness.
  Employees need to keep up to date and upgrade their skills so that the company can compete, survive and thrive in a highly competitive world. The only sustainable advantage for an organisation in the future may be the ability to learn faster than competitors and come up with smarter and more innovative solutions to problems.

"One of the things that may get in the way of people being lifelong learners is that they're not in touch with their passion. If you're passionate about what it is you do, then you're going to be looking for everything you can do to get better at it."

Jack Canfield

Barriers to Lifelong Learning

There are barriers to lifelong learning. Some people have little ambition, are content with their present job or circumstances and so don't see the point in undertaking any learning activity. They feel they already possess sufficient skills and knowledge and that they have been doing their existing job so long that nobody knows more about it than them. Some people have a negative connotation of what being a learner means. They do not like being viewed as learners or novices because it assumes that they are deficient in some way such as being inexperienced and lacking competence and expertise. They see this as a stigma giving rise to feelings of inferiority and inadequacy, undermining their sense of power and self-esteem. It's similar to the "L plate syndrome" that learner drivers experience. They are often treated with contempt and insensitivity on the road by experienced and qualified drivers, and so want to graduate from the role of learner driver as quickly as possible.

Many contemporary work arrangements discourage learning, let alone lifelong learning. Some organisations lack a culture of learning and do not organise work in an interesting way to stimulate and maximise learning effects. Workers feel alienated from their work and thus do not view it as a learning opportunity. They don't realise that a person with an outside perspective will often see improvements that they can't because they lack a questioning approach and are too close to the job. Some people may lack confidence and fear that their abilities are not up to the challenge of learning anything new.

Some people are so busy balancing family commitments with the demands of their job feel that they haven't the time to commit to lifelong learning in any form or shape. Some people work in organisations where there is little commitment to personal growth, training and development and thus no incentive for continuing learning. Mid-career managers who have reached a plateau in their career are often reluctant to undertake any form of further education or training. There may be cultural barriers as well, as research shows that people with a third level education and from a professional background are more likely to become lifelong learners than others without this advantage. In addition managers and professional staff are more likely to get further training and development than operatives. People who are mentally or physically challenged may find it difficult to access and make use of lifelong learning opportunities as their specific needs may not be catered for. Those who are located far away from educational and training facilities may find access difficult although the internet is now making lifelong learning facilities universally available. Refugees and asylum seekers may experience language and cultural barriers to accessing learning opportunities.

"If you have the desire, passion and enthusiasm to do something, nothing in the world will stop you."

Luke Poyner

Becoming a Lifelong Learner

To become a lifelong learner you should practise the following (use the acronym PRACTICED to recall the key points):

P Priority. Make lifelong learning a habit and a priority in your life. Adopt a philosophy that lifelong learning should be integrated into your life and become a way of life. Learning should be viewed as a work in process rather than a finished product. A process assumes that it is continuous while a product assumes that it is finished. The first step is to assess your learning needs by making an inventory of your current knowledge and skills. Compare this with your desired level of knowledge and skills and then draw up an action plan to fill the gap. Part of the solution to fill this gap is to set aside one hour each day to learn. Draw up a daily schedule and stick to it. Many organisations now expect employees to draw up personal development plans outlining the knowledge and skills they need to do their jobs more effectively, and learning activities they should undertake to enhance their career prospects and personal development. These personal development plans are reviewed, analysed and revised each year taking account of corporate and personal development needs. Lifelong learning means that you are constantly researching and investigating the subjects you are interested in, and continually broadening your horizons by seeking out opportunities for personal development. To aid this approach adopt an inquisitive, enquiring and broad minded view of the world.

R   Reflect. Reflect on how subjects are inter-related and how one subject may have applications in another. It is by actively making links and associations from one subject to another that we learn. People make discoveries by building on the knowledge of others and applying it in new and unique ways. Try to ascertain how new knowledge and perspectives may be applied to solving issues and problems in other areas of your life. Learning should be guided by feedback about successes and failures so that we build on prior learning and abandon inappropriate approaches and assumptions to become more effective learners.

A   Active in your professional body. Take an active part in your professional body. Attend meetings and seminars. You can use the opportunity to network, make friends, share ideas, interact and learn from others at these meetings and events. Many professional bodies such as accountancy make it mandatory that members undertake continuous professional development a type of lifelong learning ensuring that they keep up to date.

C   Curiosity. Be curious about subjects outside your core interest. Develop a broad base of general knowledge in such fields as history, science, politics, psychology, sociology, business and economics. Use the internet to research your favourite subject. Develop a questioning approach to life. The question "Why" should be a constant part of your vocabulary. The ability to be able to ask questions and seek answers is more important than knowledge. Learning new topics will increase the number of brain cells in your brain and the links between them, and make you more intelligent and increase your capacity for learning.

T   Teach. Teaching a subject leads to a deeper understanding of it. Try to get a part-time job teaching your favourite subject at a college near you. There is no better way of learning a subject than researching and preparing it for a presentation. You will help others and also help yourself to gain mastery of the topic. We should also assist others to acquire the learning skills that we are proficient in. In a work context it is a good idea if employees take turns in mentoring and coaching each other thereby transferring unique personal knowledge and skills. There is saying that two heads are better than one and there is no doubt that collaborative learning can be very effective and beneficial.

I   Insight. Develop the insight that novelty brings to people who can see things as if for the first time. People with strong fixed convictions are often not open to new ideas. Seek out contrary viewpoints that challenge your firmly held beliefs. If you foster this skill it will help you understand and value the benefit of different viewpoints.

C   Childlike wonder. Develop a sense of childlike wonder and the freshness and enthusiasm which accompanies it. Everything to a young child is new so that their interest and enthusiasm is unbounded. Enthusiasm is like the chicken pox, highly contagious. Being enthusiastic about your subject will also further engage the minds and arouse the interest of others.

E   Exercise. You will need to take physical exercise in order to relax and boost your sense of well-being. A brisk walk for about an hour each day should do the job. Exercise helps prevent heart disease, obesity and diabetes as well as keeping the brain oxygenated. The brain needs oxygen to thrive and survive; so get out in the fresh air. Exercise boosts circulation, including blood flow to the brain, which uses 25 per cent of the oxygen that enters our lungs. It also protects the brain from stress which damages the brain. In addition, the brain needs a proper diet. A diet rich in vegetables, whole grains, olive oil, fruit and fish will help you keep a healthy brain in a healthy body. If you are overweight, losing weight is the most important thing you can do to improve your health and quality of life. Research shows that losing just 5 to 10 per cent of your weight can lower blood pressure and cholesterol, thus cutting the risk of heart disease, joint disease, diabetes and cancer. The brain also need 7 to 8 hours sleep a night to keep it in tip top shape. Sleep is vital to brain development in children and essential for effective learning, emotion and memory in adults.

D   Different ways. Vary the way you learn to optimise your learning. People learn through their visual, auditory and kinaesthetic senses. In other words, they see, hear and feel. The more of the senses you engage while learning the more effective and memorable the learning will be. We should strive to become deep learners rather than surface learners. Deep learning is trying to get an understanding of what you are learning by thoughtful reflection so that you can apply it to new practical situations. Surface learning is rote learning where information is memorised for exams without necessarily understanding it. We all have different learning styles and the more variety we adopt in our approaches to learning the better. View DVDs on topics that interest you. Listen to CDs and use mind maps to synopsise and capture the essential points of what you want to learn. Use the internet to get access to an unlimited amount of information. Read widely. Observe others, work with challenging and interesting teams and undertake stretching projects. One of the best ways of learning is to learn by doing.

"They know enough who know how to learn."

Henry Adams

Focus and Concentration

Reading is the method we use to gather ideas and information outside our direct experience. Good readers have good powers of concentration to help them learn and absorb what they want to know. Concentration is the ability to cope with, manage and eliminate distractions. Successful learners follow a plan and concentrate and focus on one task at a time to the exclusion of everything else. When our minds are focused our thoughts are not dissipated on irrelevant matters. Learning is impossible without good powers of concentration and focused attention. The person who does not concentrate will either be a mediocrity or a complete failure. Nothing will focus your concentration better than the actual process of beginning the learning task. There are many benefits of concentration. It helps you learn and comprehend more effectively, improves your memory and helps you achieve tasks more easily and efficiently. It gives you the ability to choose and control your thoughts. Focused concentration will also help you meditate and calm your mind. You can improve your concentration by developing a sense of mindfulness or being fully in the present moment. Most of us are rushing around the place trying to get things done quickly and on time. We need to slow down, to relax and meditate in order to refresh our minds and bodies.

Newton's most famous work, the Principia Mathematica (1687), is often said to be the single most important book published in science. When he was asked how he made the astonishing discoveries in the book, he replied "by thinking on it continually." The difference that makes the difference seems to be hard work, focused attention and reflection.

Michelangelo (1475-1564) was a sculptor, painter and architect. He was a man of genius comparable to the great Leonardo da Vinci. Michelangelo had a remarkable ability to concentrate his thoughts and energy on the task at hand. Often while working, he would eat very little, would sleep on the floor beside his unfinished painting or statue, and was so absorbed in his work that he continued to wear the same clothes until his work was finished. Reading, studying and paying attention to what you do, will improve your powers of concentration.

Improving Your Concentration

Concentration is like any other acquired skills and can be improved through practise. The following CONSENT acronym will help you develop good powers of concentration:

C   **C**hunk. Live by the principle of divide and conquer. Imagine perfect execution and then do it. The prospect of reading a book can be overwhelming. Instead concentrate on the first chapter, within the first chapter concentrate on sections, within sections concentrate on paragraphs and within paragraphs concentrate on individual sentences. This chunking has the psychological effect of making the task more manageable and less daunting. Your span of attention is about 20 minutes, so you should chunk your time in blocks of 20 minutes, taking mini breaks in between.

O   **O**ngoing recall. For serious reading spend up to 50 per cent of your time recalling mentally the information you want to learn. Build up notes, preferably in mind map or summary form, at the recall stage and use these to recall the information you want to learn. Having a fixed routine can help improve concentration. So apply the well known SQ3R approach to reading demanding material. This stands for survey, question, read, recall and review. Survey provides you with the big picture. Question prepares your mind for learning as we learn better if we are seeking answers to questions. Reading helps you come to grips with the detail. Recall helps you to learn the key concepts and review helps you consolidate the learning. As you read convert key words into images, as visual memory lasts longer and is more permanent than verbal memory.

N   **N**eeds. Identify how the reading meets your needs and purpose. What benefits will accrue to you as a result of reading and learning the key concepts in this book? Focusing on how the reading will meet your learning needs and thinking about how you can use the information will create interest and motivation during the process of reading.

S   **S**elf-talk. Positive attitude and self-perception is an important aspect of good concentration. We are what we think we are. The more you believe that your concentration is good, the better it becomes. Affirm to yourself, "My concentration is focused;" "I am totally concentrated;" "My powers of concentration are excellent." Feed these statements into your mind over a period of time so that it becomes part of your subconscious. Relax and use repetition each day to imprint affirmations and images into your subconscious. Self-talk is a way of psyching yourself up so that you achieve your best.

E   **E**liminate internal and external distractions. You can choose to be distracted or not distracted and you can choose how you will react to distractions when they occur. If you get distracted it is important that you get back on track quickly.

To eliminate internal distractions, relax, know your optimum time of day for learning and plan your reading schedule accordingly, verbalise and visualise what you want to achieve, set specific realistic goals and break your goals into manageable sub-goals. To eliminate external distractions create a learner friendly work environment, read in a familiar quiet place or with suitable classical music in the background, organise your workspace, use good lighting and sit in a comfortable chair.

N **N**ow. Do it now! Procrastination is the thief of time. Procrastination has been defined as the automatic postponement of an unpleasant task, for no good reason. Stay in the moment by thinking about what you have to do right now. You want to get in the zone and be totally absorbed. Getting in the zone is the trance-like "flow" state that many athletes, footballers, musicians, writers and other people report experiencing when they are intensely engaged in an activity. Take a point of view or perspective as you read to focus your attention and enhance your recall.

T **T**argets. Read with a purpose. Specify your learning objectives in advance of each chapter and self-test at the end of the reading session. Reading with specific chapter objectives in mind directs attention and facilitates comprehension of relevant information, so that the positive feedback involved in achieving one goal helps to propel you forward to the next. Have start and finish times for your reading session so that you maintain a sense of urgency. "That which can be done at any time, rarely gets done at all."

"Concentrate all your thoughts upon the work at hand. The sun's rays do not burn until brought to a focus."
Alexander Graham Bell

Continuous Improvement and Cyclical Change

If you don't change throughout your life you will stagnate and your skills will become redundant. Lifelong learners must adopt and adapt to change if they want to prosper and grow.

181

Continuous improvement by updating your skills and knowledge will help you become the best you can be and is necessary to survive in a competitive world. There is always a better, smarter, faster, more efficient and less costly way of doing something. Even in a routine job you can continually challenge yourself by asking yourself: "Is there a better and more efficient way of doing your existing job?" Processes can be eliminated, improved, rearranged, simplified, standardised and combined.

Change is inevitable and the only constant is change. Nothing lasts forever. The British Empire came and went. Even civilisations that lasted for thousands of years such as the Pharaohs in Egypt, the Aztecs in South America came and went, to be replaced by others. Hitler thought the third Reich would last a thousand years, but it lasted not much longer than a decade. Relationships wax and wane, babies grow up and every one of us will eventually fade away and die. Some change is predictable while other change is unpredictable. The biological stages of the human life cycle are predictable in that we are born, grow up, mature, grow old and die. As mature adults we are more likely to experience the death of a parent or the death of a partner. As we grow old we will experience the deterioration of the senses such as eyesight, hearing, mobility and a decline in fitness and stamina. We will also experience the death of family and friends. The seasons are predictable. We know when winter, spring, summer and autumn will happen. Stock markets, commodity markets and economies are predictable to the extent that we know they operate in cycles of prosperity and decline but we don't know how long each cycle will last and when each cycle will begin and end.

The economic recession of 2008 came without warning and spread from the USA to the western world like a contagion. Many countries including Ireland went from boom to bust in a very short space of time brought on by inappropriate economic policies, imprudent banking lending policies and lack of financial regulation. Some change can be anticipated and planned for such as going to college, annual holidays, getting married, family planning, changing a job, moving house or preparing for retirement while other change is unpredictable. Life is transitory and even things that seem to stay the same like our skin replenishes itself over and over again and not one of our skin cells is more than a few years old. Even we ourselves change as we interact with and experience the world.

Unpredictable change when it happens can be traumatic. The death of a parent, sibling, spouse, or child is something that we will all experience in our lifetimes but a sudden death is often very difficult to come to grips with. Similarly being suddenly made redundant is very hard to accept. Sickness and incapacity may be trust upon us without warning and have a devastating effect on our lives. There are new developments all the time in technology, manufacturing processes, information and communications technology and in management organisation and business procedures. Generally political, economic, social and medical developments are happening at an ever increasing rate. You will find that similar changes are taking place in your own area of skill and expertise. Business is changing at an accelerating rate. New legislation in the areas of environmental protection, health and safety, product quality and employee protection, compels those with responsibilities in these areas to keep up to date.

> "The young man who has the combination of the learning of books with the learning which comes of doing things with the hands need not worry about getting along in the world today, or at any time."
>
> William S. Knudsen

Embrace Change

Embrace change as an opportunity for growth. Change presents new challenges, experiences and new possibilities for learning and development. Approach change with a sense of excitement, wonder, anticipation and optimism. Old skills and knowledge will not suffice in the future. New skills and knowledge must be acquired if you want to progress and do well in life. Continuous improvement is best done by small incremental steps. Set your immediate goals in small manageable easily mastered steps. This prevents you from feeling overwhelmed and reinforces your belief that you can improve surely, steadily and gradually. Trying to achieve too much too soon is a recipe for disappointment, discouragement and disillusionment.

Knowledge and skill are acquired by going through a gradual systematic process. You can't skip steps by trying to accelerate the learning. The acquisition of knowledge and skill takes time. You will go through many stages of learning on your journey to competence. At the start of undertaking a new task you will go through a rapid period of learning and then arrive at a plateau where learning obstacles and difficulties are encountered. It is during these plateaus that many people get discouraged and give up not having the endurance to stick with the task. To overcome these barriers will take persistence and determination until you enter a new phase of rapid progress. More plateaus will be encountered until finally a high level of expertise is acquired. Even then learning never stops as you will need to practise your skills and update your knowledge and expertise. Learning and continuous improvement will increase your self-esteem, self-confidence and earning power.

Decide what areas you want to improve on. To improve your career prospects you will need excellent interpersonal relationships skills, be able to communicate effectively, negotiate and assert your rights as appropriate. On the technical side you will need all the skill you can acquire in your area of expertise, general computer skills and good financial knowledge. Many people find themselves in financial trouble through lack of financial expertise and discipline by overspending on their credit cards and then being unable to pay back the debt incurred. As a parent you will need parenting skills, budgeting skills, communication skills, cooking skills, do-it-yourself skills, and problem solving skills. You will need health and fitness skills so that you diet, exercise, and control your weight as appropriate.

Change can involve major things such as changing careers, returning to college, starting your own business or minor things such as going on a diet or giving up smoking. A person might forego a career in business to take up a lifelong interest in writing. A person who is many years out of formal learning may decide to go back to college and pursue a lifelong interest in a subject that they love. A person with an entrepreneurial spirit may decide to leave their permanent well paid job and set up a new business to do something they always craved to do. A person may decide to quit smoking because they want to become healthier and fitter and are concerned about dying from emphysema, heart disease or lung cancer.

Tips for Handling Personal Change Successfully

Just like intelligence, behaviour is not fixed and can be changed. Even without any intention on our part behaviour changes naturally over time in line with age and major life changes such as starting work, marriage, becoming a parent with increased responsibility, and coping successfully with retirement. We are not surprised if teenagers are rude and disagreeable, but we expect older people to be agreeable and more emotionally stable. Your thoughts influence your behaviour; change your thoughts to change your behaviour. If you believe you can change your behaviour you are more likely to do so. The following are some tips for coping with change:

- If you want to change behaviour, break it down into parts and learn each part thoroughly. Tackle the most difficult parts first. Ignorance or fear of the unknown is the major barrier to change. Reward yourself when you successfully implement one part as achieving a series of small successes will gradually build up your self-esteem and help you reach your ultimate goal.

- Change is more effective when it is gradual, allowing behaviours to become automatic. Practise makes perfect. It takes up to 21 days or more to change a habit. New behaviour will fade and disappear if not continually used and reinforced.

- Prepare people that you interact with frequently for the change so that they are not surprised and give you support.

- Make sure your goals are realistic as unrealistic goals create fear, disappointment and frustration when you fail to accomplish them.

- The consequences of change should be beneficial, based on the principle of reward rather than punishment. People will not continue activities that are more painful than rewarding.

- Anticipate problems and have a contingency plan in place to deal with them.

- Enjoy the journey, as the process should be as enjoyable as reaching the goal. Design the journey with this principle in mind so that it is smooth, uncomplicated and rewarding. Examine your environment to see what is helping and hindering your progress. Eliminate the obstacles and increase the supports. The more familiar you are with the process the greater the probability of success.

- Give a genuine and trusted friend permission to give you feedback and support regarding the progress you are making as this will help you keep on track and learn from your shortcomings.

- Revisit your plan frequently as review and repetition increases the probability of success.

- Some behaviour can be difficult to change, so you may need to call on the moral support of a trusted friend.

- Our memory is fragile, so use memory aids such as mnemonics, mind maps or a list to remind you what to do.

"To think of learning as a preparation for something beyond learning is a defeat of the process. The most important attitude that can be formed is that of a desire to go on learning."

Daniel Bell

Learning to Break Habits

A habit is an action or behaviour pattern that is regular, repetitive, and often unconscious. About 90 per cent of our behaviour is habitual such as drinking and eating and this is the reason why it is very difficult to cut back in these areas. Habits free up the mind while the body is on automatic pilot making us highly productive saving us from reinventing the wheel at every turn. An experienced driver can converse and drive at the same time and will know how to react in unusual and emergency situations. The danger is that we may become locked into familiar ways of doing things and become blind to more efficient and effective methods. Psychologists call this the Einstellung effect which states that after learning to solve a problem one way we become impervious to better ways and so we are inclined to stick rigidly to the tried and trusted ways of doing things rather than exploring alternatives. Einstellung literally means "attitude" in German. Sometimes experience has a negative value when solutions which worked in the past are no longer appropriate to a new situation. We may need to redefine the problem, consider alternatives or consult someone with a different perspective.

It is important that you break the negative habits that are holding you back. Negative habits such as smoking, excessive drinking and eating always have negative consequences such as damage to our fitness and health. On the other hand positive habits such as saving produce positive results such as creating a contingency financial fund for emergencies. You'll keep on doing the same old thing unless you purposefully take action to stop and get rid of the negative habit. We don't realise the strength of habits until we try to change them and then discover how difficult it is to do so. When formed habits are involuntary and unconscious and happen without effort or thought on our part. Good or bad habits always deliver results and determine our future for good or for bad.

Substitute productive habits for unproductive ones. As previously mentioned, it takes at least 21 days of dedicated effort, patience and perseverance to get rid of an existing habit or develop a new one. Don't quit as it takes determination to succeed despite repeated failure. Firstly change your thoughts as you become what you think most about. You should start thinking positive thoughts that will help you achieve desirable results. Habits are like Newton's first law of motion: a body at rest and a body in motion tend to stay in motion unless it is acted upon by an outside force. Similarly you'll keep on doing the same old thing unless you purposefully decide to take action to get rid of the negative habit. All habits are learned and can be unlearned. What you are today is as a result of conditioning through repetitive action. You can change if you really want to.

Take action by:

- Making a list of your negative habits. These might include gambling, hoarding, compulsive spending, not keeping your promises, not paying your debts on time, not being punctual, and being indecisive. These become self-fulfilling prophecies if you fail to take action to counteract them. For example compulsive gambling can bring financial ruin and kleptomania (an uncontrollable desire to steal) can land you in jail. If you suffer from an obsessive compulsive disorder, you should seek psychological or medical advice.

- Choose positive success habits and develop systems to support them. These might include reading personal development books, keeping your promises, paying your debts on time, spring cleaning, being punctual and being decisive.

To change a habit you must sincerely want to change, you must be willing to change and be prepared to put in the effort to change. It often means substituting delayed gratification for instant gratification. For example if you want to adopt a healthy diet and exercise regularly you should focus on the long term benefit of a normal weight, fitness and health, rather than the immediate discomfort of foregoing your favourite junk food or soft drink. Draw up a plan of actions and stick to it. It is best if you only try to change one bad habit at a time and treat occasional lapses as temporary setbacks. Break your goal into smaller steps and reward yourself each time you accomplish one of these. Tell friends about your goal; focus on the benefits of success and keep a diary of your progress.

> "Habit is habit, and not to be flung out of the window by any man, but coaxed downstairs a step at a time."
>
> Mark Twain

You Have More Ability Than You Think

Many people who lack intelligence in the traditional sense have gone on to live very fruitful and successful lives by developing their natural talents and unique intelligences. The world is full of people who did relatively badly at examinations but yet went on to become successful business people or make a major contribution to their chosen careers. Albert Einstein failed his German polytechnic entrance examinations twice and only managed to scrape through on his third attempt, yet went on to become the most famous scientist of all time. Isaac Newton got the lowest BA degree at Cambridge where he was seen by his contemporaries as a failure, yet went on to discover the laws of gravity and become Chancellor of the Exchequer. Michael Faraday left school at 14 but yet went on to discover the fundamental laws of electricity. George Boole, who invented Boolean Logic which is the basis of modern computer science, was a self-educated mathematician.

Howard Gardner has made a strong case that we have many intelligences, rather than the traditional way of looking at intelligence as being good at maths and language. For most occupations we need a combination of intelligences to be successful. A lawyer needs language, logical and interpersonal intelligences. An airline pilot needs map reading and spatial awareness while an artist requires sensitivity to aesthetic design, colour and form. The eight intelligences according to Gardner are:

1.   Spatial. This is the ability to picture things or see images in your imagination. Albert Einstein maintained that one of the keys to his intelligence was his ability to visualise problems and then translate them into mathematical formulae. It is claimed that he developed his theory of relativity by imagining he was on a sunbeam travelling at the speed of light. People with this ability have very strong powers of visualisation and are very good at recognising shapes and symbols and reading maps and visualising journey routes in their heads. They like to use charts, graphs, flowcharts, mind maps, cause-and-effect diagrams, pictures, plans and demonstrations to help them understand things. Men are thought to have an advantage over women in spatial intelligence and this might be the reason why they do so well in professions using spatial skills. People with this intelligence make good architects, airplane pilots, sculptors, engineers, landscapers and designers. Walt Disney and Calvin Klein are examples of people with this intelligence.

2.   Interpersonal. This is the ability to get along well with others and people with this intelligence have a strong emotional

facility to quickly and sensitively read and respond to the moods, temperaments, motivations and desires of others. They are tuned-in to voice inflexions, facial expressions and body language generally. They like to socialise, cooperate and collaborate with others. They are good at resolving disputes, negotiating, persuasion and teamwork. While emotional intelligence may not get you hired for a particular job it is very likely to get you promoted. Being able to listen, compromise and collaborate are essential to getting along with others. Learners with this intelligence like to learn in social settings cooperating with others. They like collaborative learning, experiencing and explaining things to others and exchanging information and expertise. People with this intelligence make good teachers, social workers, politicians, sociologists, psychologists and salespeople. Tony Blair, Bill Clinton, Barack Obama and Martin Luther King are examples of people with this intelligence.

3.   Musical. People with this ability remember tunes, lyrics and poems easily and have a natural sense of rhythm. Most of us are not over-endowed with this intelligence but just like to listen to and enjoy music or sing along to a tune. This is often an innate intelligence as evidenced by the story of Louis Armstrong the famous jazz musician. He grew up in an orphanage in New Orleans and by 12 years of age had his own band and was able to play the trumpet without any formal instruction in music. Some autistic children display a high musical ability or posses a phenomenal memory while at the same time being unable to talk, interact, look after themselves and socialise with other people. There is a known positive correlation between musical and mathematical ability. When people listen to music the right or creative side of the brain is engaged and when people are learning to read music the left or logical side of the brain is engaged. Learners with musical ability may like to put key ideas they want to remember to the tune of a favourite song or to the rhyme of a made up poem. Advertisers are aware of this phenomenon and so like to put their message into rhyme and song so that they are easily imprinted and recalled. People with musical intelligence make good musicians, song writers, and composers. Mozart, Beethoven, and Andrew Lloyd Webber are examples of people with this intelligence.

4.   Intrapersonal. This is the ability to be thoughtful, reflective, introspective and philosophical and people with this facility have a high degree of self-awareness. They like to meditate, reflect and understand their own thoughts and feelings and are aware of their strengths and weaknesses. They like to keep diaries to enable them to review and reflect on issues. They tend to be introverted and make good   psychoanalysts,   philosophers,   academics, researchers and creative writers. This facility has a long historical legacy and started in ancient Greece with the philosophers Socrates, Plato and Aristotle. Sigmund Freud and Anne Frank are examples of people with this intelligence as are Christian and Buddhist monks and nuns.

5.   Linguistic. People with this ability are good at languages and literature. They have an extensive vocabulary, understand the meaning of words and can articulate ideas in writing or verbally. They are good at explaining things to others and like to tell stories, make jokes, use puns and invent rhymes and poems. Learners with this ability have no problem listening to lectures or reading books. Linguistic skills are highly valued in the workplace as they are needed to complete forms, write memos, letters, emails and reports and to prepare presentations. We also need linguistic skills to communicate with colleagues, customers, suppliers and other stakeholders. Learners with linguistic intelligence use cue cards, mnemonics, acronyms and rhymes to help them memorise and recall information. People with this ability make good journalists, poets, public relations officers, writers, talk show hosts and public speakers. James Joyce, Oscar Wilde, Stephen King, J.K. Rowling and Terry Wogan are examples of people with this intelligence.

6.   Logical. People with this ability are analytical and good at solving problems with a keen facility to see patterns and relationships between things. Logical intelligence is highly sought after for many jobs in the workplace. Managers need to be able to plan, schedule, co-ordinate and control. On a daily basis they solve problems and make decisions. As they progress in their jobs they become responsible for budgets, monthly accounts, interpreting management information, agreeing prices and drawing up estimates and

invoices. They need to become financially literate and be able to read and understand monthly accounts such as cash budgets, profit and loss accounts and balance sheets. Leonardo da Vinci had not only a great mathematical brain but was the original Renaissance man displaying a wide range of intelligences including superb scientific and artistic talents. People with logical intelligence make good accountants, economists, engineers, scientists, mathematicians, barristers, detectives, programmers and system analysts. Bill Gates and Albert Einstein are examples of people with this intelligence.

7.   Physical. People with this ability have good control over physical movements and are able to handle tasks skilfully. They learn best by doing and are usually mechanically minded being good at repairing things or taking things apart and putting them back together again. They like to move while learning and are generally bored and feel confined by formal classroom instruction. We need physical dexterity to manipulate tools, drive a car, operate machines, perform do it yourself tasks around the house, and work a computer keyboard. People with this ability usually have pastimes requiring manual skills such as DIY, gardening and woodwork. They make good athletes, footballers, surgeons, dancers and craftspeople. Michael Jordan, Tiger Woods, Michael Jackson, Fred Astaire and Madonna are famous people with this intelligence.

8.   Naturalistic. People with this ability understand the natural world environment. They are good at classifying and categorising information. It goes back to the time of the hunter/gatherer, when it was important for survival to be able to differentiate between the various forms of flora and fauna, so that you knew what was edible and what was poisonous. Employees with naturalistic intelligence are very observant of the work environment and will notice small changes that the rest of us would not see. They like to learn outdoors in practical situations. Charles Darwin is a well-known example of a person with a strong naturalistic intelligence which enabled him to formulate the theory of evolution one of the greatest intellectual contributions of the 19th century. This was facilitated by his keen interest in nature and his ability to identify and classify insects, birds,

fish and mammals. People with this ability make good farmers, park rangers, gardeners, botanists, geologists, archaeologists and Green Party politicians. Similarly Mendel, the famous botanist who discovered the laws of genetics had this intelligence.

"I don't divide the world into the weak and the strong, or the successes and the failures, those who make it or those who don't. I divide the world into learners and non-learners."

Benjamin Barber

Using Our Many Intelligences

The average person uses all these intelligences to a lesser or greater extent every day when going about their business. In fact it would be difficult to live effectively and survive without these eight intelligences. People can develop an exceptional ability by concentrating on what they are particularly good at. We need spatial skills to drive and find our way around. We need interpersonal relationships skills to relate to family, friends and work colleagues and create respect and trust when interacting with others. Irrespective of technical abilities those with social skills are often the highest paid. We need intrapersonal skills when reflecting on issues, making self-assessments and learning from our mistakes and the mistakes of others. We need logical skills to schedule tasks, identify and solve problems, make effective decisions, budget our personal finances and compile our tax returns. We need linguistic skills when communicating with others, filling up forms, sending texts or emails, completing returns and writing reports. We need physical skills for do-it-yourself jobs around the house and gardening, and to work skilfully and effectively. We need naturalistic skills to observe what is going on around us in the environment. We need musical skills to appreciate classical music, jazz, pop music or just to sing alone to a tune.

You don't have to be brilliant to be successful in life. Edison is reputed to have said that genius was 1 per cent inspiration and 99 per cent perspiration highlighting the fact that irrespective of intelligence and special aptitudes there is no substitute for enthusiasm, dedication and hard work. Considering the eight intelligences will help you determine where your strengths lie. Focus on the intelligences where your special talents lie and try to develop those further that you are not so good at. Everybody is talented at something. Develop and give your strengths the recognition they deserve. Use them to do what you love to do. Some people with natural talent fail to exploit it and consequently never become as successful as they should. Talent alone is insufficient and must be developed through application and hard work.

> "If you want to earn more – learn more. If you want to get more out of the world you must put more into the world. For, after all, men will get no more out of life than they put into it."
> William J.H. Boetcker

Learning from Mistakes

Successful people learn from their mistakes and make sure they don't repeat them. This is a great way of acquiring new knowledge and understanding of why things go wrong and how we can learn from these events. There is an old saying that an ounce of prevention is worth a pound of cure. This suggests that learning from mistakes can be an expensive way of learning and that preventative action when successful costs less in the long term and is the ideal approach. This is particularly true in health and safety situations where a mistake may have fatal consequences. Successful organisations learn from their mistakes by building the lessons into their systems and procedures so that they become a part of the culture and fabric of the organisation. However, you should remember that you learn better if you focus more often on your successes than on your mistakes. Similarly, organisations that place too much emphasis on mistakes may create a dysfunctional atmosphere adversely affecting the morale, self-esteem, energy, performance and initiative of employees.

The lessons learnt should be brought forward and implemented into action plans so that the same costly errors do not take place again. The railway companies are a case in point. Consider national disasters such as the Hatfield rail crash in England in 2000, where following investigation and recommendations, rail companies insisted that lessons had been learned. Despite this similar disasters occurred at Potters Bar in 2002 and Grayrigg in 2007. Ideally mistakes should only happen once with preventative plans in place to ensure that they won't happen again. Unfortunately this is not the case as witnessed by the same medical errors that seem to happen over and over again.

Medical errors and hospital mistakes often hit the headlines when they become legal issues. Instead of accepting responsibility many hospitals fight the issue to the bitter end and many cases are settled out of court for huge sums of money without any admission of liability. They seem to follow rigidly the usual legal advice of "say nothing, do nothing, admit nothing," rather than doing the right and ethical thing. Typical errors reported include sponges or implements left inside patients after surgery, giving the wrong type of blood, and medication errors such as drug name mix-ups. Hospital acquired infections which can be life threatening are also common. More serious errors such as removing a healthy kidney instead of the diseased one have been reported in the press. Typically patients are billed for the additional care they need to recover from hospital mistakes. This only adds insult to injury. It would be more equitable if hospitals had to suffer the cost of their own mistakes. In fact this would be an incentive for them not to make them and to put adequate control procedures in place to prevent them.

They should take a leaf from the book of Willie Walsh, chief executive of British Airways who took responsibility after the Heathrow's Terminal 5 fiasco. He won the admiration of many at a time when so many people just pass the buck by admitting a mistake had been made and that he was taking responsibility. Henry Kissinger famously said "a crisis ignored is a crisis ensured." Typically people try to cover-up their mistakes or blame somebody else because they are afraid of being singled out or fired. Humans are prone to error and even the best of leaders with the best of information and intentions can make mistakes from time to time. Some of these mistakes can have disastrous consequences.

Brigadier General Matthew Broderick, chief of the Homeland Security Operation Centre was responsible for the disaster which happened in New Orleans on 29 August 2005 when Hurricane Katrina breeched the levees. He went home after reporting that they seemed to be holding, despite multiple reports of breaches. He had experience of dealing with previous hurricanes but had no experience of a hurricane hitting a city built below sea level. There are times when experience proves to be more a handicap than a help particularly when the unique circumstances of a problem are not taken into consideration.

After the Bay of Pigs fiasco and the criticism it attracted, President Kennedy determined to learn from the failure, split his team of advisors into a blue team and a red team. The blue team would brainstorm all the reasons why a particular decision would succeed while the red team would give all the reasons why it could fail. This approach is credited with the success of the stand-off with Russia during the missile crisis of October 1962 when the world was on the brink of a nuclear war. Common sense prevailed, the Russians backed off and a catastrophe was avoided. Most people think they apply a logical process when making decisions. In fact they are often unduly influenced by their emotions and intuition. They are ruled by their heart rather than their head. Intuition works well in some areas but requires checks and balances in others. Science is full of stories why we should not rely too much on intuition. Until Galileo's scientific observations proved otherwise, people for thousands of years believed the sun revolved around the earth because it was intuitively appealing. Our brains may leap to conclusions without establishing the facts and exploring alternatives.

"Many people would learn from their mistakes if they weren't so busy denying them."

J. Harold Smith

Before Action and After Action Reviews

The US Army uses before action reviews (BARs) to minimise risk; and uses after action reviews (AARs) to maximise learning. The before action reviews involve four questions:
1. What are the intended outcomes and how can we measure these?
2. What problems and challenges should we expect?
3. What did we learn or others learn in similar situations?
4. What do we think will make the biggest difference this time?

The after action reviews ask the following questions:
1. What did we expect to achieve?
2. What did we actually achieve?
3. What was the reason for our results?
4. What will we keep or improve?

An airline pilot will tell you that a plane is off course 99 per cent of the time so that the crew is constantly correcting and aligning the plane on the flight plan in line with prevailing conditions. When an accident happens airlines carry out a thorough investigation after each accident in order to establish the facts and learn lessons for the future. Recommendations are made and corrective action taken so that the same mistake will not occur in the future. That is the reason why there has been such a spectacular improvement in airline safety. Before take-off a checklist is used to ensure that all systems are working satisfactorily.

In sports a good manager will take corrective action as the game progresses based on players' performance and the performance of the opposing team. If these adjustments and corrections are taken too late the team will lose. Mistakes are not always bad and can lead to great discoveries as when Columbus was trying to find a quick route to India and by chance discovered America. In creative problem solving, a mistake is an experiment to learn from and discover what not to do. If you live a very cautious life, take no chances and make no mistakes you will fail to learn and come up with anything unusual or innovative.

Many novel ideas, famous discoveries and inventions in science and medicine were inspired by serendipity or chance. However, when this happens, the significance of the chance event should be realised and investigated further. Alexander Fleming did not achieve fame until the chance discovery of a mould in his laboratory in 1928 which led to the development of penicillin. Similarly, if Charles Goodyear who invented vulcanised rubber and Wilhelm Rontgen who discovered X-rays had not recognised the significance of a chance event that led up to these discoveries then the happy accidents would have been dismissed as inconsequential.

In business when a mistake is made affecting a customer it should be put right as quickly as possible. It is always easier and less expensive to keep a customer than to find a new one. Don't be defensive, but do apologise to the customer for any inconvenience the error may have caused. Ask the customer what you can do to make amends and rectify the problem. Handling a mistake in customer service and putting it right to the satisfaction of the customer will provide you with an opportunity to improve the service and the relationship with customers. A satisfied customer will recommend other people to use your service. An unhappy customer will tell all their friends and acquaintances about how shoddy they were treated and lose you potential customers in the future.

Types of Learning

Apart from learning from mistakes there are three ways that we learn: formal, informal and incidental. Formal learning takes place in a class room, lecture room or training room often leading to official certificates and diplomas. Informal is self-directed learning which we acquire through personal experience, the experience of others or through experimentation. The main source of informal learning is on the job experience or learning from a more experienced employee. Incidental learning we acquire unconsciously without being aware of when it happens. Incidental learning is unstructured and happens by chance as a by-product of interacting with others or working in a team. Ongoing learning happens when we reflect on what we can improve, draw out important lessons, and evaluate what we learn and then apply it to new situations.

Every time you learn something your brain improves because the number of brain cells and pathways between them increases. People with a growth mindset believe failure is an opportunity for learning and not a source of shame. They tend to flourish and thrive because they believe that hard work is the way to achieve success in life rather than relying solely on innate ability and that practise is the road to mastery. IQ can be improved through new learning, new challenges and new experiences. Success is about doing your best and not about being better than others. They like being challenged by difficult problems and believe that ability must be combined with effort, study and learning if you want to succeed in life. Even the most talented people must work hard if they want to be successful in whatever they undertake. They feel happy when they are making progress towards their objectives.

On the other hand, people with a fixed mindset believe that IQ is God-given, intrinsic and fixed for all time and can't be improved. Consequently, they avoid challenges and give up too easily when faced with an obstacle and don't believe that hard work will make a difference. They tend to ignore useful feedback because they view it as criticism and resent the success of others. They rely too much on their natural talents, don't believe in the need to practise, work hard and thus tend to stagnate.

It is useful to know the difference between deep learning and surface learning. Deep learning is about getting the big picture by understanding key concepts. Surface learning is often about the rote memorisation of disconnected facts without any real or deep understanding of the subject matter. It's the sort of learning we did in school as infants when learning multiplication tables by rote. Even surface learning can be improved if you engage all your senses such as writing, seeing, touching, talking, listening and even smelling. The more of these senses you stimulate when memorising the better your ability to recall. Deep learners think about the significance of what they are learning. Deep learning affects the learner's fundamental values and beliefs and may transform a person's outlook and the way a person behaves. A deep learner makes the knowledge their own through reflection and practical application. They think about their thinking processes, learning styles, critically examine their assumptions and try to make their thinking as objective as possible. They use questions to trigger off their curiosity and to discover areas for further study and research.

"The development of general ability for independent thinking and judgement should always be placed foremost, not the acquisition of special knowledge."

Albert Einstein

Learning versus Wisdom

The ancient Greeks valued wisdom, sound judgement and debate as the highest form of learning, and believed this was only acquired through age and learning from experience, and the mistakes of life. Wisdom may also be acquired from listening to wise people and following their advice. Older people have experienced the peaks and valleys of life and may have developed unique insights into the human condition. They have been there and done that. In some cultures such as Chinese, the wisdom of older people is highly valued and respected. Leaders from antiquity surrounded themselves with wise older people and sought their advice before they took important decisions. People with wisdom have the knowledge, experience and insight needed to make sensible decisions and judgements. Wise people know what is important, meaningful and ethical in life. They are guided by values such as truth, honesty, justice, fairness and goodness. They are able to step back from experience and gain a broader perspective of things. They are not easily influenced by superficiality, sensationalism or celebrity. They are unlikely to be caught up in materialism and consumerism.

Wisdom and self-discipline go hand in hand. Wise people keep a calm and composed demeanour and do not let their emotional states oscillate widely in response to the moods of others or the vicissitudes of life. People without self-discipline are prone to anger, make hurtful remarks, drink to excess, abuse drugs and indulge in immature and morally unacceptable behaviour. The rich and famous often lack the wisdom to conduct their lives in a sensible and sober way. Those who achieve celebrity too quickly often lack the skills to handle the problems and pressure that come with success. There can be no real success in life without wisdom. Wisdom has nothing to do with IQ as some people with a high IQ are often irresponsible, emotionally immature and unable to sustain lasting relationships, and live selfish and dissolute lives. There are many clever and educated failures in the world.

Knowledge only becomes wisdom when it is tempered by reflection, learning from experience and common sense. Wisdom has nothing to do with age. Unlike wine many people do not become wise with age because they fail to learn from their mistakes and life experiences. There are exceptions to this rule as we do come across young people who are wise beyond their years. Wise people manage their lives effectively and instinctively and know the right thing to do when confronted by moral dilemmas. They are good at managing their money, getting along with others and avoiding trouble. They know how to choose the right partner and make the right friends. They live their lives according to good values and principles. There is a strong link between wisdom and both happiness and mental health.

Wise people replace guesswork with research and due diligence. Accept with caution but check and verify should be your motto. Due diligence is where you establish that things are what they purport to be. Accountants are often employed to carry out a due diligence of a company that is about to be taken over to establish its financial viability. Successful people know where to get the information they need and possess the investigative skills to check it out. It is more important to know where you can find the information you want rather than knowing it yourself. Genius has been defined as common sense intensified. Don't waste your time reinventing the wheel but find out the existing state of knowledge in the area that you want to know through research and talking to knowledgeable and experienced others and build from there. The purpose of knowledge is to make you a better person. Learning needs to be applied to be useful. Theory without practice is of limited use. Learning acquired through experience is superior and more memorable to learning acquired through studying books.

> "A single conversation across the table with a wise man is worth a month's study of books."
>
> Chinese Proverb

Summary

Successful people know the importance of continuing to learn throughout their lives. They are motivated by a love of learning and a natural curiosity rather than career advancement or financial gain. The benefits of lifelong learning include having a meaningful structure for your day and making social contact with others. People become self-actualised by doing something they are challenged by and innately interested in. Some people find this in serious leisure activities or volunteering. Lack of ambition, motivation, interest and curiosity will act as barriers to lifelong learning. Many routine contemporary jobs and work arrangements discourage any form of learning, not to mind lifelong learning. Learning needs a supportive context and culture if it is to thrive. To become a lifelong learner you must make it a priority and develop study, questioning, critical thinking and reflective skills. Continuous improvement by updating your skills and knowledge will help you become the best you can be and is necessary to survive and thrive in a competitive world.

Embrace change as an opportunity for growth with the challenges and new possibilities for learning and development. We have more abilities than was conventionally thought. It is up to us to develop our special abilities and make our mark on the world. Successful people learn from their mistakes and make sure they don't repeat them. It is more important to know where to find information than knowing it yourself. People with a growth mentality believe that they can improve their intelligence through continuous learning and novel experiences. They believe that success is achieved more through hard work than innate ability. Wisdom is the highest form of learning and is acquired through experience and applying the lessons derived from failure.

Five Activities to Improve Your Lifelong Learning Skills

1. Improve your ability to assimilate and recall information by acquiring learning to learn skills. These skills include research, speed-reading, writing, memory, time management, concentration and mind mapping.
2. Assess your learning needs by making an inventory of your current level of knowledge and skills. Compare this with your desired level of knowledge and skills and then draw up an action plan to bridge the gap. To support this draw up a schedule of start and completion times for each activity.
3. Reflect on how one subject may have applications in another area by actively making links and associations between them. Mind maps can be used for this purpose. This will make your learning and research more memorable, purposeful and relevant.
4. Take up a part-time teaching job in a subject that interests you. The best way to learn a subject is to research, prepare and teach it. Preparing handouts for students will develop your writing and presentation skills.

5. In whatever you do consider if there is a better, faster or smarter way of doing it. This will provide challenge and make you a more efficient person.

9

Personal Values

- *What are personal values?*
- *How are values formed?*
- *Why is self-discipline so important?*
- *Why is a code of personal values important?*

Introduction

Values are rules that guide you safely and ethically through life. The values you adopt determine your character and the way you are going to conduct and live your life. Core values might include honesty, integrity, loyalty, fairness, truthfulness, kindness and being trustworthy. Principles are ethical standards that help you make decisions in harmony with your values. Our values and principles are formed through our family and childhood experiences. They are also influenced by religion, education, life stages and ethical training.

Values change as we intellectually mature and absorb the experiences and influences of the world around us. It is important for your psychological health that your personal values are congruent with the values of the company that you work for. Enron was a company that espoused high values but then failed to live up to them. Some people with great talent and potential have gone from hero to zero because of a lack of guiding values, principles and self-discipline to keep them on the straight and narrow. A code of personal values will help you live a meaningful, principled and successful life.

Personal Values

Values are rules around which you construct and live your life. The values you adopt determine who you are, what's important to you and how you are going to behave as you pass through this life. Values are deeply held convictions guiding decent behaviour and sound decisions. Core values might include honesty, integrity, loyalty, fairness, truthfulness, kindness and being trustworthy. People with character and integrity inspire confidence in others because they can be trusted to do what they say they are going to do. When people show concern for others by putting their needs and interests first, this demonstrates empathy and elicits trust. People who show respect, loyalty, concern and appreciation for others will always have friends. People who are kind to others reap many benefits such as increased feelings of well-being. In addition the people you are kind to may appreciate it greatly and might even reciprocate.

If one of your values is that all people are created equal and worthy of respect then you will treat everyone with equal consideration and deference regardless of sex, race, religion, age, education, wealth or status. On the other hand, if you believe that all people are not created equal then you are likely to adopt racist, sexist, sectarian and discriminatory values, attitudes and behaviours. Hitler's belief that the Germans were the master race and that Jews were inferior led to the abomination of the concentration camps and the mass murder of the Jews and other minority groups. The belief that blacks were inferior to whites led directly to the slavery trade and the disfranchisement, denigration and maltreatment of generations of black people. This belief led directly to the American Civil War and hundreds of thousands of confederate deaths trying to defend the indefensible. It also led to the mistreatment of the black community as second class citizens in the southern states right up to the 1960s, and the creation of the sectarian and racist Klu Klux Klan who believed in white supremacy, and were prepared to kill and maim those they considered inferior such as blacks, Jews and Catholics. The belief that women were inferior to men held back their intellectual development and deprived them of their vote and legitimate contribution to society for hundreds of years.

The most resilient and successful organisations and people have sound value systems. The Catholic Church has survived and bounced back despite the protestant reformation, wars, corruption, paedophile priests, and schism for more than 2000 years, thanks largely to its immutable set of values.

A few years ago I was deceitfully sold a personal computer as new that was in fact a reconditioned old computer. I had given my computer in for repairs with a local self-employed computer technician and he told me that it was not worth repairing and that I should buy a new one. He went on to suggest that he had a new computer in stock that would meet my needs. He assured me that the computer he was giving me was new, and as I was eager to resume my work I took up the offer. I subsequently found out that the computer was not new when I brought it to my local computer store some time later to sort out a virus problem. They asked me how old my computer was and I said it was only a few months old. They informed me that it was at least 4 years old and I then realised that I was the subject of a scam as the computer I had given in for repair was a newer and more powerful machine and worth more than the one he gave me which I paid for as if new. He kept the old one which he said was not worth repairing and so had no value. He obviously repaired it and sold it on at a profit. I haven't done business with that person since and won't do so ever again. In addition I have alerted others to his scam. It takes a long time for trust to be built but only an instance for it to be destroyed.

Obviously my self-employed computer technician lacked certain values such as character, fair play and integrity. If you value honesty you will respect individuals, believe in fairness, always tell the truth, keep your promises, never claim more expenses than you are entitled to and refrain from engaging in dishonest practices such as refurbishing old computers and selling them as new!

Principles are similar to values and are ethical standards and rules that you live by that help you make decisions in harmony with your values. Some people buy recyclable products as a matter of principle because they are environmentally conscious and want to keep the world pollution free and safe for future generations. Others feel a patriotic duty to buy local produce because it keeps money circulating in the local economy and provides local employment. Unconscious choices put you at the mercy of the dice roll, leaving things to fate rather than making principled choices.

"Real success requires respect for and faithfulness to the highest human values – honesty, integrity, self-discipline, dignity, compassion, humility, courage, personal responsibility, courtesy, and human service."

Michael DeBakey

Formation

Our values and principles are formed and nurtured by our family and childhood experiences. They are also influenced by religion, education, life stages and ethical training. Children absorb their parent's personal, religious and political values through osmosis and personal example. They are strongly influenced if their parents believe in the work ethic, take pride in their work and demonstrate a belief in fair play. They are more influenced by parents who give good example and do what they say rather than make empty statements. Parents complain that television, movies, and pop stars have more influence on the values of their children than they do. We can counteract this by our personal example as parents. Individuals with strong values tend to behave more ethically than those with weak ones. Our values play a role in interpersonal relationships and affect our problem solving and decision making approaches. They influence the way we behave, treat other people, and how we communicate and interact with each other.

Values change as we intellectually mature and absorb the experiences and influences of the world. As small children we just follow rules without question in order to be praised, get a reward or avoid punishment. Some children just like adults will ignore the rules if they think they'll get away with it and won't get caught. Our sense of right and wrong and good and bad is got from our parents. As we mature as children we develop the basics of a conscience while at the same time becoming more concerned with our own selfish interests and personal satisfaction. We do things for others on the understanding that they will return the favour. As young adults we identify with our peers and often adopt their attitudes and standards of moral behaviour. We like to be seen as one of the crowd and win the approval of our group. This is the stage when many young people are most impressionable and go astray particularly if the values espoused by their peers are anti-social and even criminal. Adults may adopt the prevailing ethos of a company like the infamous Enron even though it is not congruent with their personal values and they know in their heart that it is wrong.

As we move from our teenage years into our twenties we begin to take a wider interest in the society in which we live and even in the world. We begin to see the need for obeying the law and observing rules that are for the common good. If we settle down and get married we become aware of the importance of paying our bills, meeting our tax obligations, playing our part in the local community, obeying the law and serving on juries, helping family and friends and supporting charitable causes. At a more advanced stage of personal values we may question the suitability of laws and realise that they need to be repealed or changed because they are unjust or inappropriate to the needs of certain segments of society. A small minority will even take up legitimate forms of protest and agitation to change things if they feel strong enough about the perceived injustice.

At the most advanced stage of personal values we may realise that life is complex and that there are moral and ethical dilemmas with no easy answers. Nevertheless the answers to these should be guided by conscience and principles of fair play and natural justice. These are the stages of values that many people go through. Only a tiny minority have a highly developed sense of good values. However there are many who never develop any worthwhile values and others who never go beyond the primitive stages as they lack empathy for other people. This is the reason we have criminals, murderers, paedophiles, sex offenders, drug dealers, and fraudsters in the world and also why we have patriots, philanthropists, humanitarians, and inspirational leaders. If those who inflicted grief and pain on others felt it themselves they would be unlikely to perpetuate it on others. However this is not so and we have sociopaths, sadists and masochists who enjoy inflicting pain on others and on themselves.

Values may also change depending on context, culture and convention. What is unacceptable today may be quite acceptable to-morrow. Cohabitation or living together outside of marriage was once considered a grievous sin but is now almost the norm. Changing values and norms and the arrival of contraception means that premarital sex is not seen in the same light and does not pose the same risks as previously. At one time marriage was considered for life but now divorce is acceptable. Times change and in most Western countries sex outside marriage is now considered the norm. Similarly unmarried mothers were looked down on, victimised and discriminated against whereas now it is accepted, and single parent families are acknowledged and supported through social welfare payments by the state.

Marriage between people of the same gender is now legal in many countries but is considered an abomination by Muslims and not acceptable to the Catholic Church. Even surrogacy is legal in some societies. This is an arrangement where a woman agrees to become pregnant and deliver a child for another couple or person. The most famous surrogate arrangement was that which made gay couple, Elton John and David Furnish parents for the first time with the birth of their son through a Californian surrogacy arrangement announced to the world on the 29 December 2010. Women priests are now ordained in the Anglican Church. The death penalty for murder is no longer acceptable in many countries throughout the world. One of the last taboos – abortion is now legal in most European countries but can still arouse passionate emotions on either side of the argument.

"We cannot define God or any of the real values of life. What is the vague thing called forth that is worth having and dying for? Beauty, truth, friendship, love, creation – these are the great values of life. We can't prove them, or explain them, yet they are the most stable things in our lives."

Jesse Herman Holmes

Corporate Values

It is important that your personal values are compatible with the values of the company for which you work. Work requirements may clash with personal values and be a source of psychological stress. If you have a core value of truthfulness and you are required to tell a lie to make a sale to a customer then you have a conflict of values that can only be resolved by telling the truth. Misleading advertising is commonplace and that is why we have an Advertising Standards Body to make sure that advertisements are reasonably factual and not downright lies.

Many companies are two faced; saying one thing and doing the opposite. A company may promulgate a belief that employees should adopt a balanced lifestyle and yet expect them to put in long hours of overtime or work unsocial hours at very short notice. Some companies with a risk-averse culture may claim that they encourage employees to be creative and learn from their mistakes, yet penalise them for making mistakes, using their initiative and being innovative. Some companies may substitute poor quality materials in the manufacture of a quality product while others may exaggerate the curative powers of a medicine. When company values are not in harmony with personal values this could have a detrimental effect on your psychological health and prompt you to find another company more in tune with your mores.

Enron's espoused values were communication, respect, integrity and excellence. This didn't prevent Enron from sowing a culture of fraud, greed and corruption in the company that eventually reaped corporate death and destruction in 2002, bringing financial ruin and misery to stakeholders such as managers, employees, shareholders, creditors and lenders. Pharmaceutical giant Johnson & Johnson, calls its value system the Credo which is given to every new employee at induction. The Credo is integrated into everyday decision- making and so becomes a living document for its employees rather than a mere aspiration. In 1982 seven customers died after being poisoned by Tylenol. Some capsules had been interfered with and contaminated with cyanide. Adhering to its Credo the company openly admitted the problem and ordered that every bottle of Tylenol should be removed from the shelves at enormous cost to the company. The company was not prepared to put its profits before people and instilled the right values in their employees through example. It pays to have values because 25 years later Johnson & Johnson is rated the top company for corporate ethics among large companies. The difference between Johnson & Johnson and other companies is that they practise what they preach.

In 2002 we were bombarded on the news with corporate scandals. At the time we thought these were aberrations. Eight years later the situation has worsened and we find even the corporate policemen such as government departments, central banks, regulators, business people and auditors were not doing their jobs. The developed economies seem to be in a mess with the burden of recovery falling on the taxpayer. The press is still full of stories about paedophile priests, fraudulent bankers, reckless developers, dishonest business people, ineffective auditors and solicitors misappropriating client funds. In addition we have dishonest overpaid politicians claiming inappropriate excessive expenses and greedy bank managers and employees claiming bonuses even thought the companies they work for are insolvent. They are in fact being bailed out by the government and the European Central Bank and ultimately the taxpayer.

People currently have very little trust in companies, banks, politicians, business people and the church because they seem to lie so frequently. Politicians make promises at election time that they have no intention of keeping. As soon as they get into power the promises are quietly forgotten about. This is not surprising as a trademark quality for a politician is to be economical with the truth. Even bishops tell lies when it suits their agenda and they want to cover up the sexual abuses of their paedophile clergy by transferring them around different parishes. Corporate values are just a reflection of personal values and if managers and staff lack the personal values of honesty and integrity then the company lacks them as well. At the end of the day it is people who have values rather than soulless corporate entities.

It is people who have the courage often at enormous personal cost to become whistle blowers highlighting corporate fraudulent malpractices and cover-ups. Instead of being rewarded and winning respect for their integrity, whistle blowers are often treated like pariahs by their work colleagues and employers because they are seen as traitors and troublemakers. They are made feel unwelcome and forced to seek alternative employment or in many cases just fired. Companies are like families and like to keep their secrets within the confines of the family, and resent it when employees go outside the family, even when they feel they have no other option.

"We must all suffer one of two pains, the pain of discipline or the pain of regret....discipline weighs ounces while regret weighs tons".   Jim Rohn

Self-Discipline

Self-discipline is the ability to do what is necessary or sensible even if you are reluctant to do so without needing to be urged or compelled by someone else. People with self-discipline have a positive sense of self and minds of their own and feel less compelled to follow the crowd. They stay on course, do their own thing and think for themselves. They are self-disciplined and responsible, not because they have to but because they want to. When out socialising they confine themselves to three alcoholic drinks rather than indulging in binge drinking because they know that it is the responsible thing to do and they won't be damaging their health or suffering a hangover in the morning. Weight control is all about having the self-discipline to avoid fattening foods and sticking to the healthy options such as vegetables and fruit because you want to avoid obesity and keep your heart healthy and waistline slim. The best way of reducing weight and keeping it off is through exercise, a calorie controlled diet and eating smaller portions at meal times. Researchers have found that those with an "Internal Locus of Control," who take responsibility for their lives, are more successful, cope better with stress, and are happier.

People with self-discipline can mobilise their energies with motivation, conviction, commitment and concentration to do what is right and achieve what they want to do. They know that success is achieved through discipline and hard work. They are able to manage their own lives and they are not subject to uncontrolled impulses, tantrums, desires or emotion. You can only control yourself and you are not responsible for other people's behaviour. You are in control of your feelings, thoughts and willpower. We are the sum total of our thoughts: either you shape your thought or your thoughts will shape you. Thoughts come before actions and they should be positive and focused.

Success is how we think and thus we become what we think about. Self-discipline will bring you success and happiness. Your attitudes are totally under your control and you can't have a positive attitude and be miserable at the same time. Getting on with other people requires sensitivity, self-control and mastery of your emotions. You can control yourself and you can control the way you respond to others. Programme your mind to remain calm, relaxed and objective even in the face of provocation rather than losing your temper and becoming angry. Don't get upset over unimportant matters and over events you cannot control. You can often influence events in a positive way but you can't control events and you have little control on how people behave and react.

> "Life can only be understood backwards, but it must be lived forwards."
>
> Soren Kirkegaard

Instant and Delayed Gratification

Some people are able to postpone instant gratification for future good because they realise that sacrifices have to be made now for future gain. People give up smoking in order to live healthier, fitter and longer lives. People control what they eat and skip dessert and tea and biscuits in order to lose weight. People pay into a retirement fund because they realise that in the future they will need a sufficient income to live an independent, comfortable and secure life when they get old. They postpone buying things on credit and instead save up and wait until they have sufficient money to pay for it and save interest charges. This is more prudent than buying first and paying later so that the monthly payments keep on accumulating until eventually you are unable to meet them.

Prudent people save for their holidays rather than getting loans to pay for them. It should be a principle to live by that you will not fund consumption items with loans but only spend what you can afford. Employees will work hard for months with the prospect of earning a bonus dangling in front of them like a carrot and thus have no problem delaying gratification. People who control their spending to what they can afford and live within their means live happier and less stressful lives. The ability to delay gratification is also a better predictor of academic success than I.Q.

There is a downside to delayed gratification. Sometimes we should just enjoy the moment and avoid postponing what we really want to do. People who unnecessarily delay gratification say to themselves that they will do such and such a thing, when they are married, as soon as the children are grown up, when they have more time or when they are retired. They are always postponing things into the future with the result that they never actually do them. Such people are always waiting to experience life and enjoy themselves but are continually postponing the event. Eventually they come to the end of their lives and regret doing what they always wanted to do but now it is unfortunately too late. Some women postpone having children because of career commitments until it is too late and their biological clock has run out. I know people who saved all their working lives so that they could travel and enjoy themselves when they reached 65. Sadly they were struck down by a debilitating illness, some with Alzheimer's so that they never got to enjoy their golden years.

People realise that where they are now is as a result of choices made in the past. They know that they are responsible for their own lives and that most outcomes are caused by actions taken by them in the past. Life is a do it yourself project and you should shape your own destiny rather than leaving it to luck, fate or chance. Life is not a dress rehearsal so you won't get a second chance at it. Life is like a game of cards in that you should make the best of the hand given to you. In other words you should exploit your unique talents to the utmost rather than wasting them and regretting the talents you do not possess. Some people are born with few talents and make the most of them. Others are born with many natural gifts but fritter them away. Undertake lifelong learning so that you systematically reach your potential and become what you are capable of becoming.

> "It is a funny thing about life; if you refuse to accept anything but the best, you very often get it."
>
> Somerset Maugham

Hero to Zero

A lack of sound values and self-discipline is often the cause of people's downfall. Living according to a personal code of ethics and living a more measured, moderate and sober lifestyle would have prevented their fall into the gutter. Lack of integrity, dishonesty, unrestrained greed, alcoholism, selfishness, hedonism and common sense brought about the downfall of sporting legends George Best and Jack Doyle. They hadn't the self-discipline or sense to take control of their lives, capitalise on their skills and take care of themselves. At the end some were abandoned by their supposed friends and died penniless. Greed and fraudulent behaviour ruined the lives of the US financier Bernard Madoff and the Russian scientist Trofim Lysenko. When this was exposed they spent the remainder of their lives in ignominy and disgrace.

George Best (1946-2005) was a famous Northern Ireland footballer who played for Manchester United in his heyday. He is renowned more for the unique talent and potential he wasted rather than what he achieved during his short football career. It will never be known if he could have been greater still. He squandered one of the most precious football talents to ever grace a football pitch in favour of a life of hedonism, drunkenness and reckless living. His time at the top of football only lasted six years before his decline into alcoholism, self-indulgence, womanising, bankruptcy and even a short spell in jail. It was the alcoholism and the inability to control his drinking which eventually led to his death. His celebrity status and good looks attracted some of the most beautiful and desirable women in the world. He lacked the wisdom, self-discipline, sobriety and personal values needed to live a sensible life. His temperament was completely unsuited to handle the world of fame and celebrity that was thrust upon him. He wasn't the first and won't be the last to crumble under the weight and scrutiny of the media spotlight.

At one stage he was receiving 1,000 fan mail letters a week. He was called 'the fifth Beatle' because his hair style was similar to the famous pop group. He became distracted by the celebrity lifestyle of modelling assignments and personal appearances and his football prowess was beginning to suffer. In 1981 while in the United States he stole money from the handbag of a woman to fund a drinking session. In 1984 he was imprisoned for three months for drunk driving and assaulting a police officer. In September of the same year he appeared while drunk on the Terry Wogan chat show. Despite having a liver transplant in August 2002, Best continued to recklessly drink alcohol contrary to medical advice and did so right up to his death. In 2004 his second wife Alex Best alleged that he was violent and abusive towards her during their marriage. He punched her in the face on more than one occasion, something he didn't deny. However people only remember the charismatic and charming side of him and almost 25 years after his heyday he was voted the greatest British sportsman of all time by a panel of 1,000 journalists and sports personalities. The airport in Belfast is named after him.

> "I spent a lot of money on booze, birds and fast cars. The rest I just squandered."
>
> George Best

Jack Doyle (1913-1978) was a famous Irish boxer, actor and tenor. Lack of self-discipline and personal values, alcoholism, womanising, poor financial decisions, debauchery and immaturity all played a part in the downfall of Jack Doyle. He was born in Cobh in county Cork, Ireland. He could have been a contender for the world heavyweight championship but he threw it all away and instead chose a dissolute, destructive and irresponsible lifestyle. In his day he was known as "The Gorgeous Gael "and the "Rudolph Valentino" of the ring because of his rugged good looks and at 6 feet 4 inches he had the physique to go with the looks. Everything seemed to come too easy to Jack. He was charming and irresistible to women but was not one for loyalty, commitment or long-term relationships. The fun was in the chase and the conquest and as soon as he bedded women he lost interest in them and quickly moved on to the next conquest. In 1929 and at the age of 16 he joined the Irish Guards in Wales and quickly excelled at boxing, being famed for his deadly strong hooks that won him the British Army Championship.

He was only 18 when he came to the attention of boxing promoter Dan Sullivan and turned professional quickly winning 10 victories making him the hottest property in sport. His parents were in Cobh so that he had no parental guidance at hand on how to handle the fame with a level head that was so quickly thrust upon him. He was winning fights so easily by just relying on his natural strength and ability that he thought there was no need to train in the gym like other professional boxers had to do. Success and wealth was coming too quickly and too easily and this proved to be his ultimate downfall. In July 1933 he fought for the British Heavyweight title and was disqualified for punching low. He was banned from the ring for six months and his prize money of £3,000 was confiscated. It was rumoured that he was drinking before the fight and decided to take the easy way out by intentionally punching low when he realised that he wasn't going to win. Reckless, excessive and compulsive drinking became a feature of his life and he was frequently inebriated when he went into the ring. His singing voice was discovered by Dr. Vincent O'Brien and was compared to that of the famous Irish tenor, Count John McCormack, and so began a singing career with appearances in the London Palladium and the Royal in Dublin. He was signed up for the Decca label and made several 78 inch records.

He went to America in 1934 and continued with his high living of gambling, drinking and womanising. He made two movies and mixed with the glitterati of Hollywood such as Errol Flynn and Clark Gable, and married his second wife the starlet and Mexican aristocrat Movita. He married her in Dublin and they toured both sides of the Irish Sea, selling out concert venues. His first wife the actress Judith Allen had left him because of his womanising, and this set a pattern for the rest of his life. Movita also left him because of his drinking and violence towards her and she subsequently married Marlon Brando. Jack Doyle made plenty of money in his heyday but threw it all away on an irresponsible lifestyle of gambling and drink and finished up bankrupt. He admitted himself that he wasted his money on slow horses and fast women. He eventually hit rock bottom and couldn't afford the rent on his flat and slept instead in the homes of friends. In addition it is thought that his generous nature was exploited and that he was swindled by several people. In his later years he was reduced to bumming drinks in pubs and he died penniless in a London Hospital in 1978. His body was brought back to his native Cobh in County Cork for burial by his former boxing club where his legend lives on.

"In today's regulatory environment, it's virtually impossible to violate rules."

Bernard Madoff

Bernard Madoff (born 1938) was a stock broker, investment advisor to the rich and famous, and non-executive chairman of the NASDAQ stock market. He promised returns of 10 to 12 per cent which sounded too good to be true and turned out to be so. He was a sociopath motivated by greed and avarice, and supported a lavish lifestyle with his wife and children mixing with the elite of society by fraudulently using other people's money. He lied, cheated and defrauded during his time as an investor and showed little empathy for the suffering he brought on his clients. He eventually pleaded guilty to laundering, securities fraud and perjury. He was a man completely devoid of ethics, values and principles. He is the admitted operator of the largest Ponzi scheme in history. A Ponzi scheme is one where early investors are paid a return with money from new ones so that the early investors are kept happy. He was never caught but asked his sons to report his crimes to the FBI when he knew the game was up. The fraud lasted for over 20 years. He was sentenced to 150 years for this crime, and will spend the rest of his life behind bars, after admitting 11 charges of fraud, perjury and false reporting relating to the $65 billion scam.

He defrauded investors out of billions of dollars leaving many of them in penury after losing their life savings. Some had lost their retirement fund and even at seventy years of age had to return to work in order to survive. Some were forced to sell their homes while others were reduced to surviving on social security. His clients included the rich elite of Palm Beach Florida, Swiss Bankers, French aristocrats, charities, local government pension funds, big investment firms and ordinary men and women saving for retirement. He has gone from a life of unimaginable luxury and mixing with the rich and famous to being incarcerated in a federal prison. He has traded his dark smart business suit, white shirt and dark tie for the ignominious regular prison uniform. From earning millions of dollars a year he will now work within the prison system for a few cents a day. His $7 million Manhattan penthouse apartment and its valuable contents have been sold to compensate defrauded investors. He has brought humiliation and disgrace to himself and his wife and family. His wife Ruth, has not been charged with any crimes but has been vilified by defrauded investors, shunned by people she once knew well, and hounded by the New York press. The fallout from Madoff's downfall is already happening when on 13 December his son Mark was found dead in his New York apartment from an apparent suicide. He was being investigated in the same fraud that saw his father jailed. The moral of this story is that crime does not pay and its ramifications eventually catch up with you.

Trofim Lysenko (1898-1976) a soviet scientist who became famous more for his political contacts, ruthlessness, lack of integrity and intrigue than for his scientific ability. He was driven by a Machiavellian ambition for fame and power. He rejected the views of Mendel, the famous 19th century biologist and geneticist, as capitalistic propaganda. He led the study of genetics and agricultural sciences down many dead ends, while numerous scientists who contradicted his erroneous ideas had their careers and reputations malevolently cut short and ruined. He came to prominence in 1929 when he managed to grow a winter crop of peas in Azerbaijan and came to the attention of Stalin. This meant that livestock could be fed in the winter when fodder was scarce. However, nobody was able to repeat his success and suspicions grew that the results may have been faked. He successfully persuaded the Soviet leaders to accept collectivisation promising them huge new harvests. By 1932 he was in charge of all Soviet agricultural science and research. He controlled the publishing of works in his subject and suppressed any work that disagreed with his theories.

In 1935 Stalin gave Lysenko practically unlimited power in the field of agricultural science which he used to hound, persecute, condemn and destroy other scientists with different views. These were dismissed from their posts and sent to the gulag labour camps. He used lies, fabrications and intrigue to malign, destroy and undermine his opponents. More than 3,000 biologists were fired, arrested, or executed. A prominent Soviet scientist, Nikolai Vavilov was unfairly dismissed from the presidency of the Agricultural Academy in 1938 and died in prison in 1940. When Stalin died in 1953 Lysenko lost his patron and found he had little influence over the new leader, Khrushchev who initiated an inquiry into his work. The investigation found that Lysenko's work was false and fraudulent and he was dismissed from all his posts. He had promised spectacular advances in breeding and agriculture, which never came to fruition. He used incomplete statistical data to support his ideas and tampered with data to match his expectations and fraudulent claims. He blamed his failures on the sabotage of others. The progress of genetic science in Russia was effectively hindered and set back during his time in charge in Russia and it took many years for it to recover. Lysenko's work was officially discredited in 1964 and the ideas of Mendel reinstituted.

"He is responsible for the shameful backwardness of Soviet biology and of genetics in particular, for the dissemination of pseudo-scientific views, for adventurism, for the degradation of learning, and for the defamation, firing, arrest, even death, of many genuine scientists."

Andrei Sakharov Physicist

Zero to Hero

Mother Teresa displayed values such as courage, care, compassion, charity, humility, unselfishness, spirituality and great humanity throughout her life. She had no interest in personal wealth and aggrandisement but devoted her life to improving the lives of the most destitute in Indian society. Nelson Mandela overcame racial prejudice, injustice and almost 26 years in jail and won the admiration of the world for his attitude of love, tolerance, forbearance, forgiveness and reconciliation to his white fellow South African countrymen. Barack Obama has brought inspiration and hope to the people of the USA and to the world in general. All three of these people have won the Nobel Peace Prize in recognition of their work. Oprah Winfrey is an inspiration to many women throughout the world having overcome a very deprived and difficult childhood to become the most successful and richest black woman in history. Charlie Chaplin emerged from a childhood of extreme poverty to become the most famous comedian and film star of the silent era.

Mother Teresa (1910-1997) who was born in Albania was a Roman Catholic nun and missionary. In 1928 she left her home and joined the Sisters of Loreto, an Irish Catholic order of nuns in Rathfarnham, Dublin and after a year she was sent to India as a teacher. She took her final vows in 1937. In 1946 she had a calling from God who told her to leave the convent and minister to the poor while living amongst them. She left the Sisters of Loreto to work on her own and help the homeless, destitute and the starving on the streets of Calcutta. In 1950 she received papal approval to set up her own order with an initial congregation of just 13 nuns. Her mission in life was to help the blind, diseased and dying among the poor of Calcutta in India which she did with an unshakable sense of commitment and purpose.

She exemplified the values of charity, care and compassion during her lifetime. She treated all equally and her homes were open to all regardless of faith. She helped those who no one else would touch; the desperately poor, illiterate, diseased, sick and undervalued people of the slums. In 1948 she founded the Order of Missionaries of Charity and opened the Shanti Nagar leper colony near Asono in 1964. Her order now runs schools, clinics, children's homes, and hospices in cities throughout India and in other developing countries. In 1979 she was awarded the Nobel Peace Prize for her humanitarian work amongst the poor, orphaned, lepers, sick and dying. In 1983 she suffered one of a number of heart attacks but continued working unselfishly amongst the needy for the rest of her life despite her ill-health. There are moves to make her a saint and she was beatified in 2003 gaining the title of Blessed Teresa of Calcutta. When she died in 1997, the Missionaries of Charity numbered 4,000 nuns, an associated order of 300 monks, and around 100,000 lay members operating in a total of 610 missions in 123 countries.

"Our Lord wants me to be a 'free nun', covered with the poverty of the cross."

Mother Teresa
(in her diary in 1949)

Many people such as Nicolaus Copernicus, the 16th century astronomer who received little recognition in his lifetime have gone from zero to hero by living principled and disciplined lives and are now admired for the contribution they've made to science and the betterment of humanity. Copernicus was a church canon and doctor and spent years labouring in his free time to prove his theory that the earth revolved around the sun and so helped usher in the modern scientific age. His theory was condemned as heresy by the Church because the conventional wisdom at the time suggested the opposite. His reputation has now been restored by the Church and he was reburied with full

Church pomp almost 500 years after he was laid to rest in an unmarked grave.

Nelson Mandela (born 1918) is renowned for his determined fight against apartheid in South Africa. He became the first black president of his country in 1994 displaying amazing patience, resilience, tolerance and dedication to purpose on his journey to the presidency. He was the son of a tribal chief and a qualified lawyer. Initially he advocated peaceful protest in the form of strikes, boycotts and civil disobedience but in 1961 he realised this was getting him nowhere and he renounced his commitment to peaceful agitation and adopted violence as a legitimate form of protest. In 1964 he was sentenced to life imprisonment for treason and spent the next 26 years in jail. On more than one occasion he refused to be released on the basis that it would compromise his principles.

Despite his long incarceration, on release he showed no hatred towards the white minority who had imprisoned him, and did not seek revenge for the years of apartheid, but instead held out the hand of reconciliation, friendship and forgiveness to those who had persecuted him. His attitude has helped heal the divisions in South Africa's society and has encouraged it on the road to a multiracial democracy. This gesture won the respect and admiration of the entire world. In 1993 he was awarded the Nobel Peace Prize jointly with de Klerk. In 1994 he led the ANC to an overwhelming victory in the country's first multiracial elections. During his lifetime he has displayed values of integrity, equality, benevolence and honesty and these have won him the respect and admiration of people throughout the world. He is now seen as an iconic figure and a man of great influence and stature. He retired from political life in 1999 and is still a sought out figure in international politics.

"I have fought against white domination, and I have fought against black domination. I have cherished the idea of a democratic and free society in which all persons live together in harmony and with equal opportunities. It is an ideal which I hope to live for and to achieve. But if needs be it is an ideal for which I am prepared to die."

Nelson Mandela,
(defending himself at the Rivonia Trial 1964)

Barack Obama (born 1961) became the first African American President of the United States in November 2008. It was seen by many as the culmination of years of civil rights agitation in the USA. He came from humble beginnings and had to work hard to get where he is today. He came from a background which understood the contribution that education and learning can make to a successful life. His mother earned a masters degree, his father a PhD and his mother's parents instilled in him the value of learning. He espouses strong family values and values of integrity, loyalty, tolerance, equality and hope with a conviction that life should be led in service to others. He was born in Hawaii and raised by his mother and by his grandparents. His mother is white and from Kansas and his father is a black Kenyan. They married in 1961 but divorced three years later. His father left when he was very young and remarried in Kenya and his mother married again to an Indonesian. He only saw his father once when he visited Hawaii in 1971. His father was killed in a car accident in 1982 so that Barack never really knew him. Barack spent a large part of his childhood in Indonesia where he lived with his mother from the ages of 6 to 10 attending local schools. His mother died of ovarian cancer in 1994. He chose the name Barack to emphasise his black heritage even though his mother is of English, German and Irish ancestry. He acknowledged his Irish roots on his mother's side of the family during a visit in May 2011 to his ancestral homestead in Moneygall, Co Offaly in Ireland. With such a varied family he obviously comes from a multicultural background with a tolerance for religious, cultural and racial diversity.

He attended law school and became the first African-American to become president of the Harvard Law Review and it was this post that first brought him to public attention. On graduation he returned to Chicago to help lead a voter registration drive, teach constitutional law at the University of Chicago and remain active in his community. Obama served three terms in the Illinois Senate from 1997 to 2004. He was successful in gaining support to reform health and ethics laws. He announced that he would be a candidate for the Presidency of the USA on 10 February 2007. He beat the favourite Hilary Clinton to win the nomination of the Democratic Party which she graciously supported. His acceptance speech was before an attendance of 75,000 people and was watched by a further 40 million television viewers. He used the internet as much as the traditional political campaigning methods when seeking election. He is a devoted family man and is married to Michelle and has two daughters. In 2009 Obama won the Nobel Peace Prize.

"Focusing your life solely on making a buck shows a certain poverty of ambition. It asks too little of yourself. Because it's only when you hitch your wagon to something larger than yourself that you realise your true potential."

Barack Obama

Oprah Winfrey (born 1954) is a black American woman from poor origins who has become one of the most iconic, influential and admired women in the world becoming America's first black female billionaire and most famous television personality. Gender, race, poverty and sexual abuse did not hold her back but seemed to provide her with the steely determination to overcome adversity and succeed. During her life she has exemplified values such as self-belief, resilience, determination, diligence, generosity, empathy, sensitivity, honesty, charity, activism and concern for others. She is a famous television personality, actress, author and philanthropist and has become a role model not only for women in the USA but also for women throughout the world.

Born to a single mother in 1954 Winfrey experienced an unstable, abusive and traumatic childhood. She spent her first six years living in rural poverty with her grandmother. Her grandmother taught her to read before the age of three and brought her to the local church where she learned to recite Bible verses. She gives her grandmother credit for encouraging her to speak in public and for instilling her with self-belief. At six Oprah moved with her mother to an inner-city part of Milwaukee, Wisconsin. Oprah says her mother was less supportive to her than her grandmother mainly because of the long hours she had to work as a maid to support them. From nine years old she was sexually abused by relatives and friends. At 13 she ran away from home and at 14 she was pregnant but the baby boy died shortly after birth. Her frustrated mother sent her to live with her father who was strict but encouraged her education. At college her innate acting ability, outgoing personality and excellent public speaking skills soon came to light. On the basis of this she won a scholarship to Tennessee State University to study communications and graduated with a degree in speech and communications. The rest as they say is history.

"Though I am grateful for the blessings of wealth, it hasn't changed who I am. My feet are still on the ground. I'm just wearing better shoes."

Oprah Winfrey

She gained her experience in local media before becoming a national television celebrity highlighting controversial issues such as gay and lesbian rights, transgender issues and aids. She is a woman of many talents and has co-authored five books. In 1985 she co-starred in Steven Spielberg's The Color Purple for which she was nominated for an Academy Award for Best Supporting Actress. In 1993 she interviewed Michael Jackson on prime-time television and attracted an audience of 36.5 million viewers becoming one of the most watched events in American television history. She is now one of the richest and also one of the most influential, admired and famous women in the USA. She is the difference that made the difference in getting Barack Obama elected President of the USA with her vote pulling power. For lucky authors her book club endorsement is worth instant recognition and millions of sales.

Charlie Chaplin (1889-1977) was a British film comedian, director, and producer who grew up in very poor circumstances in London. The films that he made are based on the harsh times he experienced growing up as a deprived child. His estranged father was a drunk and died from alcoholism when Charlie was just 12. His mother went insane at 33 and Charlie was sent away to a school for destitute children. His childhood experiences influenced and coloured the films that he made during his acting career. His facility for playing drunks is based on his direct experience of observing his father when drunk. The storyline of rescuing damsels in distress are based on his wish to have saved his beloved mother from her descent into madness. Sigmund Fried wrote of Chaplin: "He always plays only himself as he was in his dismal youth. He cannot get away from those impressions and humiliations of that past period of his life. He is,

225

so to speak, an exceptionally simple and transparent case." Nevertheless he showed great resilience in exploiting his childhood experiences and natural talents to become the most famous comedian and film star of his day. George Bernard Shaw said Chaplin was the only genius to come out of the movie industry. Though his best films were silent they are still popular and enjoyed by thousands today.

A Code of Personal Values

Some values become more important as you grow older such as appreciating your family, keeping your friends and maintaining your health. Thus you may prioritise exercise and a healthy diet as part of your everyday routine. Knowing and prioritising your personal values will help you make decisions congruent with them. For example a person with a priority value of success would have no hesitation in accepting promotion and making the necessary sacrifices to do so. On the other hand a person with family values might be reluctant to accept promotion if it meant spending significantly more time at work and less time with their family. Similarly if you prioritise telling the truth you may be reluctant to even tell a white lie if it means hurting the one you love. Draw up your own list of personal values that you will aspire to based on your own needs, experiences and stage of life. You will need a code of personal values to guide you successfully on the difficult but adventurous journey that is life. The following is a code of personal values that seemed to be appropriate to the author's particular circumstances.

- Keep your promises.
- Show that you are trustworthy by keeping confidences.
- Be honest and truthful in your dealings with others.
- Respect the rights of others and be sensitive to their needs.
- Treat others with care, courtesy, respect and consideration.
- Work hard at your chosen vocation and become the best you can be.
- Show passion and enthusiasm for your work.
- Balance your work with family, play and recreation.
- Always take responsibility for your actions rather than blame others for your shortcomings.
- Become a lifelong learner and learn from your mistakes and successes. Actively research those subjects that interest you.

- Walk the talk. If you condemn the use of anything such as cocaine don't be a hypocrite and take it yourself.
- Encourage others to reach their potential.
- Maintain a sense of wonder and curiosity.
- Be faithful to your wife or partner.
- Keep in touch with your family and friends as they are the most important thing in your life.
- Keep fit and healthy as health is your wealth.
- Become an expert in an area that interests you and that you feel passionate about.
- Be grateful for what you have and count your blessings every day.

Summary

Values are rules that help you live a principled, meaningful and successful life. Values are deeply held convictions guiding sensible, productive behaviour and sound decisions throughout your life. People with integrity inspire confidence in others because they tell the truth and keep their promises. Our values are formed by our family and childhood experiences as we absorb our parent's personal, religious and political values. Values change as we intellectually mature, become more knowledgeable and take on board the experiences and influences of the world.

It is important for your psychological well-being that your personal values are compatible with the values of the company for which you work. A lack of sound values, principles and ethics and self-discipline is often the cause of people's downfall. Many with exceptional talents have finished up in the gutter through living an irresponsible and dissolute lifestyle. Other people have been guided by high principles and become famous and successful winning the admiration of the world. Living in accordance with a code of personal values will help you achieve your dreams and ambitions.

Five Activities to Improve Your Personal Value Skills

1. Set a good example for your children as they are more influenced by your deeds rather than what you say.
2. Work for a company whose values are compatible with

your own.
3. Adopt the core values of honesty, integrity, loyalty, fairness, truthfulness and kindness.
4. Adopt principles in harmony with your values that will help you make principled choices.
5. Draw up a customised code of personal values to help guide you through a principled, meaningful and successful life.

10

Reasons People Fail

- *Why do people fail?*
- *What is procrastination and perfectionism?*
- *Why do we fear failure?*
- *Why do we fear rejection?*
- *What is fear of success?*

Introduction

This chapter is the flipside of why people succeed as set out in the previous chapters. People fail because they don't plan and set objectives. Instead of winning friends and influencing people they antagonise people and make lifelong enemies. Without confidence and self-belief it is difficult to achieve anything worthwhile in life. Pessimistic people expect the worst and so don't do anything to make things better for themselves. Without drive, persistence and determination you are unlikely to succeed. People who refuse to invest in their learning and development throughout their lives will not keep up to date and will be left behind in a very competitive world. Lack of self-discipline and reckless living has seen the demise of many heretofore successful people. Many people with low personal values have seen their careers end up in tatters. Pride, arrogance and hubris has been the ultimate downfall of many celebrities, prominent business people and politicians.

Fear of failure and rejection may prevent people from undertaking activities that might be personally and financially rewarding. A barrier to creativity is fear of looking a fool which discourages people from coming up with alternatives and novel ways of solving problems.

People fear failure because they don't realise that failure is a stepping stone to success, greater maturity and learning. Some people fear success because of the responsibility that comes with it. Procrastination and perfectionism may prevent people from reaching their full potential. The following are some of the common reasons why people fail.

Failure to Plan and Set Objectives

In the absence of a plan we have chaos. There is a well-known saying that failing to plan is planning to fail. A plan is a route map to our goal. We should plan the work and work the plan. Some people are all talk and no action, always telling other people what they intend to do but never actually getting around to doing it. In other words they are not prepared to put their money where their mouth is and to put in the hard work necessary to achieve their goals and realise their dreams.

More specifically, some people fail because they neglect to draw up plans for their finances, careers and retirement. There are many toxic financial behaviours including compulsive spending, excessive frugality, inappropriate financial decisions, serial borrowing and hoarding money. In many instances these could be avoided if people became more informed, educated, sensible and disciplined about their financial affairs. Some fail to plan the steps needed for a successful career. Others fail to plan for retirement and so spend their later years in frugal stressful subsistence living. Even if they do plan they do not have contingency plans to fall back on when things go wrong and when there is a need to put things right. They get to the end of their lives regretting the opportunities they failed to grasp and the things they failed to do.

People without a purpose tend to be reactive, often attending to things at a whim, without much reflection and thought. They are directionless, going around in circles and coming to dead ends. They get bogged down in trivia and get frustrated because they never achieve anything worthwhile. Some people lack the conviction and an intense compelling desire to do something useful with their lives. Some are flippant and immature and haven't taken responsibility for their life and are over-dependent on others. They are unsure what they want to achieve and therefore their needs are often appropriated and sidelined by others. Without goals others will set the agenda for you meeting their needs and fulfilling their interests and goals rather than yours.

Some people with high intelligence and an abundance of talent are unsuccessful because of a lack of purpose, drive, commitment and resilience. Some don't realise the important role that goals play in a happy and successful life. People who aren't successful are not goal oriented. They fail to set a clear goal to pursue and strategies to achieve it. They fail to exploit to the utmost what they are interested in and passionate about. Some have never been formally taught in school or college how to set meaningful goals.

Someone once said that there were three types of people in the world: those who make things happen, those who watch things happen and those who haven't a clue what's happening. Obviously to succeed in life you must make things happen purposefully through goals, plans, sheer hard work and shrewd investment of time, money and resources.

"Let me tell you the secret that has led me to my goal. My strength lies solely in my tenacity."

Louis Pasteur

Poor Interpersonal Relationship Skills

Some people find it difficult to relate to others and lack empathy and other social skills necessary for harmonious living and good interpersonal relationships. Breakdowns in relationships are the major reason for disputes and conflicts between people. Conflicts if left to fester create barriers and hatreds between people and so something should be done to resolve them quickly. You can't prevent all conflicts from arising but you can reduce their frequency through diplomacy. Poor listening skills are one reason why some people don't progress in life as far as they should. Our ears enable us to hear but not necessarily to listen. Listening involves interpretation and understanding the other person's point of view.

Instead of winning friends and influencing people they antagonise people and make lifelong enemies. Bad manners and insensitive behaviour will drive people away from you. Bad manners are a sign of low class no matter what the status or position of the person. If your first serious relationship is a negative experience you could become trapped over and over again in self-destructive behaviours and be primed for a lifetime of disappointments. There are many people with a high IQ and tons of ability who fail to progress in their careers because they have a low EQ. Similarly people who are very technically competent but who lack EQ may not do as well in their careers as they should.

We are all aware of celebrities who cannot cope with their fame because of a lack of EQ. They often have inadequate emotional and social skills indulging in behaviour such as drug and alcohol abuse leading to a downward spiral of self-destruction and misery. Lack of self-control means you are unable to control your emotions and manage your frustration calmly and effectively. You lack the ability to think clearly and stay grounded and composed even in the most provocative situations. If you get angry and enraged at the least provocation, this can prove a severe handicap in social and work situations as people will tend to avoid you. Nobody likes being around people who are temperamental and liable to get angry at any moment. Delays, rejections and disappointments are part of life and you must learn the coping skills necessary to take them in your stride.

> "Kindness in words creates confidence. Kindness in thinking creates profoundness. Kindness in giving creates love."
>
> Lao Tzu

Lack of Confidence and Self-Belief

Without confidence you will lack the self-assurance, competence, judgement, persistence and resources needed to succeed in what you decide to undertake in your life. Without confidence and self-belief in your own abilities it is difficult to achieve anything worthwhile in life. If you think you can you will succeed, and if you think you can't you won't succeed. Many people give up on their dreams because they lack the confidence, self-belief, persistence and determination to pursue them. People who are extremely shy find it difficult to socialise and assert their needs and may be overlooked when promotions are decided.

Confidence is linked to locus of control. Those with an external locus of control lack confidence and initiative, because they believe that external influences such as fate, luck, the government and others determine and control the direction of their lives. They believe that they are not in control of their lives and can't do anything to influence outcomes. Some people are hindered by disempowering beliefs imprinted subconsciously during their childhood which hold them back. Your subconscious doesn't know the difference between what is true and what is untrue. It imposes rules on us and then operates as if they are true.

Some people never learn to challenge themselves and move outside their comfort zone. They stick to the same routine, associate with the same people, live in the same town and do the same job all their lives. They are afraid to move outside their comfort zone because the perceived risk in doing so makes them feel uncomfortable, anxious and insecure. They don't realise that exploiting new opportunities that come your way will energise you to break out of your comfort zone and help you succeed and achieve great things in life.

"Regardless of how you feel inside, always try to look like a winner. Even if you are behind, a sustained look of control and confidence can give you a mental edge that results in victory."

Diane Arbus

Lack of Optimism and Self-Esteem

Psycho-sclerosis has been defined as hardening of the attitudes which causes a person to cease dreaming, seeing, thinking, and leading. If we cease to think, dream and see, we cannot achieve because we have no dreams to pursue or goals to reach for. Pessimists see the glass as half empty rather than half full. Unlike optimists, pessimists have negative expectations and so don't think things will work out well. This becomes a self-fulfilling prophecy as people who expect to be unsuccessful will achieve their wish. Pessimism is likely to decrease motivation and effort so that pessimists are more likely to give up when things get difficult or sometimes not even try initially. They see a negative future and thus don't see the point in expending effort to overcome setbacks. They may thus be consumed with feelings of helplessness and hopelessness because they believe they have no control over the future.

Pessimists tend to be risk averse and thus often lack the initiative to do what needs to be done to be successful. They are less likely to try and solve problems because they feel they won't succeed.

Pessimistic people anticipate the worst in other people and situations and have low self-esteem. They lack the positive thinking to see the good side to people and situations and to hope for the best. Consequently they tend to be moody and depressive and find it difficult to do anything constructive with their lives.

People with low self-esteem feel bad about themselves and are more vulnerable to anxiety and depression. They take negative feedback personally and are thus unable to take corrective action to correct their shortcomings. They are slow to emerge from a bad mood with a sense of melancholy likely to persist. They are reluctant to speak up in groups and so their views are unlikely to be heard or taken seriously. When things go wrong they tend to focus on what could have gone worse rather than what might have gone better. Low self-esteem brings on feelings of shame and humiliation and a negative view of intelligence and competence. Because failure is felt more intensely by people with low self-esteem, they are more risk averse and more likely to be cautious and conformists. When confronted by problems they are inclined to ignore them and hope that they will go away rather than solving them. In the case of health problems eventually it may be too late with the disease too far advanced and out of control to rectify the situation. Denial, postponement and wishful thinking are unlikely to solve anything.

"A pessimist is one who makes difficulties of his opportunities and an optimist is one who makes opportunities of his difficulties."

Harry S Truman

Lack of Motivation

Some people lack the drive and determination to work hard enabling them to achieve worthwhile things in their lives. Instead they get stuck in a comfort zone and achieve very little. They have a negative attitude and fail to keep going to overcome setbacks and obstacles on the journey to their goals. They fail to discover their true purpose or goal in life and so never become self-actualised by doing the things that they really want to do. They lack passion about their lives and don't realise that life is not a dress rehearsal and so they don't make the best of the opportunities that life presents.

They lack an internal source of motivation to do the things that are inherently satisfying. They lack the courage, optimism, purpose and energy to pursue their goals. They put the needs of others first and don't realise that they are not responsible for other people's lives. They spend their lives in a job that neither interests nor motivates them.

Their lives are governed by modal operators of impossibility which consist of self-talk like cannot, will not and must not. These limit their ability to do something worthwhile. This mindset creates a defeatist attitude. With this attitude people have little motivation and give up too easily when things get too difficult for them. Many assumed limitations are based on a belief and it should always be remembered that beliefs can be changed.

"The dictionary is the only place where success comes before work."

Mark Twain

Lack of Persistence and Resilience

Persistence is not about doing the same think over and over again but may involve changing your habits, learning new skills and adopting a different approach to reach your goals. Those without persistence are unable to stick to a task to see it through and get disheartened and disillusioned in the face of obstacles and setbacks. Like everybody else they make mistakes, but fail to learn from them. Many give up after just one attempt while others quit when on the threshold of success. Quitters never become winners.

Those without resilience are incapable of getting up and bouncing back from disappointments and failures to start all over again. They become hopeless and helpless, adopt a victim attitude and never achieve much in life. They are unaware of their strengths and weaknesses and thus are unable to exploit them to their advantage. They don't realise if they want good things to happen in their lives they must make them happen. They are not prepared to take appropriate risk, try out new things and accept that failure is part of life and a means of learning.

Some people lack patience and are unable to put up with waiting or delay without getting annoyed, agitated, angry, frustrated, or upset. They are unable to persevere calmly in the face of obstacles and difficulties. They lack control and over-react to situations. Some lack the enthusiasm and passion to get deeply involved and totally dedicated to a worthwhile pursuit. Some lack the willpower and grit to stay focused on their goal. If people want to develop their willpower, they must practise self-denial. If you want to lose weight you must exercise more and eat less

People without willpower lack the determination to succeed. They lack the determination to stick to the task and pursue their goals. They bring unhappiness and distress to themselves because of their failure to control unhealthy urges and impulses.

> "Opposition is a natural part of life. Just as we develop our physical muscles through overcoming opposition – such as lifting weights – we develop our character muscles by overcoming challenge and adversity."
>
> Stephen R. Covey

Lack of Commitment to Lifelong Learning and Continuous Improvement

People who lack commitment are indifferent towards improving themselves and learning new things, are unwilling to challenge the status quo and are not prepared to experiment with new approaches to solve problems. Those without a philosophy of lifelong learning do not continue learning throughout their lives and therefore never reach their full potential. They fail to exploit their leisure time to upgrade their work related knowledge and skills, and thus are unable to exploit opportunities that come their way, and are often overlooked for promotional positions when they arise. They lack a positive attitude towards learning and adopt a passive rather than a curious or questioning approach to life generally and what's going on around them.

They fail to develop study, critical thinking, problem solving, decision making and reflective skills and make learning a priority. They are unable to learn from their mistakes and so go on to repeat the same errors over and over again. They fail to learn from experience and apply the lessons derived from setbacks and failure. They never become self-actualised by doing something that they are challenged by, enthused about and innately interested in. They fail to realise that continuous improvement by updating their skills and knowledge will help them to become the best they can become and is necessary to survive and thrive in a competitive world.

They have a fixed mindset and so believe that their intelligence is fixed and so can't be improved by undertaking new learning opportunities and challenges. They believe that success is achieved more through innate ability rather than hard work. They do not embrace change as an opportunity for growth with the challenges and new possibilities for learning and development that change presents. They fail to recognise and exploit their special abilities and make a mark on the world. They don't realise that the ability to research, find and access information quickly is better than knowing it yourself.

"To stumble twice against the same stone is a proverbial disgrace."

Cicero

Lack of Life Skills and Self-Discipline

Some people have a difficult time controlling their bad temper, intemperate habits and inappropriate behaviour. They cannot manage themselves but need to be constantly supervised by others. They seek instant gratification and adopt self-destructive unhealthy lifestyle habits involving smoking, drink, and drugs and getting into debt. Some people have poor problem solving and decision making skills and thus make inappropriate choices going through life such as making foolish financial decisions, not getting an education, choosing the wrong job or an unsuitable partner.

Choosing the right partner is probably the most important decision you will ever make, while choosing the wrong partner is the one decision you will regret for the rest of your life. Research shows that people generally marry those from the same religious, social and ethnic background, of approximately the same age, with the same intelligence and level of education, and with a similar sense of humour and level of attractiveness. A poor marriage can adversely affect job performance, health, financial security and even life span.

Some people suffer from the sunk-cost bias, where they continue to foolishly invest in inefficient loss-making projects so as not to forfeit the money they already have sunk or invested in it. They don't realise that it's not a good idea to persist in throwing good money after bad rather than quitting and cutting their loses. Many people lack the initiative and discipline to deal with problems as they arise, so they ignore them hoping that they will go away. Unfortunately most problems don't go away, but they usually get worse and become more expensive and difficult to solve.

> "We all have dreams. But in order to make dreams into reality, it takes an awful lot of determination, dedication, self-discipline and effort."
>
> Jesse Owens

Lack of Personal Values

The general public have lost trust in banks, politicians and the church because they have told lies, made reckless financial decisions and abused their powers. Some politicians who told lies and engaged in cover-up when confronted with proof of their deceit and fraudulent expense claims were forced to resign with their careers and reputation in tatters. People without integrity inspire lack of trust in others because they tell lies and fail to keep their promises.

Lack of honesty and integrity in businesspeople has seen them jailed and disgraced. Some people with great talent and potential have gone from hero to zero because of a lack of guiding values, principles and self-discipline to keep them on the straight and narrow. Lack of integrity, dishonesty, unrestrained greed, alcoholism, selfishness and hedonism brought about their downfall.

They hadn't the self-discipline to take control of their lives, live sensibly, capitalise on their skills and take care of themselves. At the end some were abandoned by their supposed friends and died penniless. Others fraudulent dishonesty was exposed and they spent the remainder of their lives incarcerated or in ignominy. They lacked a code of personal values that would have helped them live meaningful, principled, sensible and successful lives. The values you adopt determine your character and the way you are going to conduct and live your life for good or for bad.

> "People with integrity do what they say they are going to do. Others have excuses."
>
> Dr. Laura Schlessinger

Lack of Humility

Pride and arrogance are the downfall of many prominent people. Arrogant people are obsessed with their own image or how they are perceived by others and are very quick to take offence. They think they know everything, never admit that they are wrong and thus don't realise how much more there is to learn. They are quick to anger, slow to forgive and take criticism personally. Arrogant people are self-conscious and full of a sense of their own importance. They consider themselves to be the centre of the universe and show hubris, affectation and pride. They focus on their own well-being rather than the well-being of others and show lack of concern and respect for other people.

It seems organisations; politicians, hospitals and even the church don't do humility and prefer to cover up their mistakes even when they are obvious to everybody else. True leaders are good at moving the attention away from themselves and acknowledging the contribution of others. Humility is the antithesis of hubris; that excessive pride that often leads to the downfall of people just like the tragic heroes in a Greek drama. Jim Collins, the author of Good to Great found that the best CEOs had the humility to acknowledge that they did not have all the answers. To succeed, they got their best people together to brainstorm possible new strategies. These leaders acted as catalysts rather than decision makers when it came to developing new directions.

Humble people can achieve great things in their lifetime and win the respect and admiration of the world. Generally, modesty is a highly valued trait in society. People who respond modestly to their achievements are better liked that those who are boastful and full of their own importance. Mahatma Gandhi (1869-1948) though one of the humblest, spiritual and gentlest of men, had great conviction, courage and determination which won independence for India from British rule without striking a single blow. He believed social and political progress could be achieved through peaceful means rather than war and conflict.

I was recently watching a television news headline where a mother of a disabled child was awarded over 4.5 million euro in damages by the Irish courts after 17 years of persistent action on her part against a hospital who failed to admit liability even though handing over such a large sum of money is a tacit admission of liability. The hospital failed to administer oxygen to the child at birth which meant that the child is disabled for life. Organisations usually cover up by attributing the blame to systemic errors, rather than saying: "we're human, we made a mistake and we're sorry."

"The arrogant man has no friends."

Moroccan proverb

Procrastination

Procrastination means putting off today what you feel you can do just as well to-morrow. It pervades all parts of the procrastinator's life at home, at work and socially. The problem with this approach is that you never actually accomplish anything worthwhile and are therefore unlikely to be successful. The tendency to procrastinate has probably increased in modern times with the increase in the variety and accessibility of distractions such as television, computer games, mobile phones and the Internet. Tasks may be seen as unpleasant so that you avoid the discomfort through diversion.

Set your priorities right instead of doing the unimportant and unproductive tasks first and leaving the most important tasks to last. Usually the least important tasks are the most fun to do and this is why the more urgent and important tasks are ignored. To overcome this tendency project yourself into the future and try to visualise what it will be like. For example, if you are inclined to postpone saving for retirement you should project into the future how much it will cost to keep you at your present lifestyle plus the extra expense of providing for health care in your old age. This will act as a wake-up call to take action about your retirement fund now!

Procrastination is particularly rampant amongst students who leave it to the last minute to plan and prepare assignments and delay studying until the exam date is right on top of them. Many students believe that they work best under pressure and to tight deadlines, or that they will feel better if they tackle the work later. They claim they enjoy the adrenaline rush and get great satisfaction finishing their assignments just before the deadline. Alas, tomorrow never comes and work done at the last minute is usually rushed and of an inferior standard.

"He slept beneath the moon,
He basked beneath the sun
He lived a life of going to do
And died with nothing done."

Epitaph of James Albert (1838-1889)

Perfectionism

Some psychologists make a distinction between neurotic perfectionism and normal perfectionism. It is the neurotic perfectionists who can cause problems and create much damage to themselves and those around them as they find mistakes unacceptable. Neurotic perfectionism sets people up for failure as achieving perfection consistently is impossible and very time consuming. In the pursuit of the perfect body neurotic perfectionists can develop anorexia and bulimia. In the workplace such perfectionism may cause people to lose time and energy on small irrelevant details of work which adds nothing to value.

They suffer from "all-or-nothing" thinking because they believe that work is either perfect or useless. They are therefore unsuited to work in risky environments such as nuclear reactors where mistakes must be revealed immediately to avoid catastrophe. Neurotic perfectionists can suffer anxiety, depression, low self-esteem and obsessive compulsive disorder. If they are in charge of other people they will frustrate and alienate them causing tension and conflict because they are intolerant of other's mistakes. Unlike neurotic perfectionist, normal perfectionists can accept their mistakes and learn from them.

Normal perfectionists are only satisfied with very high standards whereas neurotic perfectionists believe that only perfection is acceptable. Normal perfectionists possess great drive to achieve quality work and can persevere in the face of setbacks and disappointments. In its normal form perfectionism provides the driving force for great achievement and creativity. Such people want to go beyond the ordinary and what has been achieved before so that great ideas and unique solutions are born.

Perfectionism has its uses as meticulous attention to detail is required in many fields such as accountancy, law, quality control, computer programming, science, engineering, architecture and artistic endeavour. We would not have the electric bulb if Edison had not been so persistent and perfectionist. Great composers would not spend so much time in perfecting their pieces of music. Poets would not spend months in perfecting their poetry often spending weeks finding the right words. Writers would not spend so much time developing great works of literature. Great artists would not have produced masterpieces if they hadn't spent weeks and weeks perfecting the tiniest detail of their work.

Perfectionism drove the English language's three most famous lexicographers – Samuel Johnson, Noah Webster and Peter Roget. After nine year of work, Johnson's Dictionary of the English Language was published in 1755. The dictionary brought Johnson great success during his lifetime. Until the completion of the Oxford English Dictionary 150 years later, Johnson's work was considered the most outstanding English dictionary up to that time. Peter Roget, a British doctor completed his legendary Thesaurus at the age of 73 and had begun compiling copious word lists when he was just 8. The Thesaurus of English Words and Phrases (Roget's Thesaurus) was published in 1852. Noah Webster's dictionary was first published in 1828 as An American Dictionary of the English Language. It had 70,000 entries and at the time it was considered by many to be superior to Johnson's dictionary.

> "Striving for excellence motivates you; striving for perfection is demoralising."
>
> Harriet Braiker

Fear

Fear has been defined as false expectations appearing real. This means that most of our fears are irrational and despite what we think never come to fruition. The fear of something happening can be more damaging to our emotional and physical health than if it actually happens. Rational fears such as fear of injury, death and poverty are part of a survival instinct and stop us from being reckless. They keep us out of trouble and harm's way and thus ensure our safety and well-being. Fear sometimes holds us back from doing what we really want to do and from being successful. Some people have a fear of public speaking, greater than even a fear of death. However, as Franklin D. Roosevelt said: there is nothing to fear but fear itself. We can overcome our fears by confronting and dealing with them.

The more you think about fears the bigger, more exaggerated and unrealistic they get. Irrational fears may become phobias such as a fear of flying, a fear of spiders or fear of socialising. Fearful people continually seek the approval of others and avoid taking risks. Fear robs us of confidence, desire, commitment and hope and can paralyse you in the face of normal challenges. Insecure people have a fear of change and this keeps them stuck in their comfort zone. They like to stick to their everyday routine and find it extremely stressful to deal with anything unusual. If you want to achieve something worthwhile you are going to have to take some risk. People with a positive attitude are less fearful because they are focused on goals and outcomes and have little time to dwell on fears that may pop into their minds.

Focus on the things you want to happen in your life and embrace every opportunity to do them. Life is not a dress rehearsal. You have only one life to live and so make the best of it. The mind like the universe has no limits. The root cause of many fears is childhood conditioning and out of control vivid imagination. Children have innately only three fears: the fear of falling, the fear of abandonment and the fear of loud noises. All other fears are learned. Fear can be caused by ignorance which is called fear of the unknown. The more you know the less you fear as knowledge empowers and informs you. People in the middle ages were influenced by beliefs based on superstition. Even today people who lack education can be strongly influenced by traditional and mythical beliefs.

"Inaction breeds doubt and fear. Action breeds confidence and courage. If you want to conquer fear, do not sit at home and think about it. Go out and get busy."

Dale Carnegie

Fear of Failure

There are three basic kinds of fears which are learned namely; fear of looking a fool, fear of failure and fear of rejection. A barrier to creativity is fear of looking a fool which prevents people from coming up with alternative and novel ways of solving a problem because they fear that they will look stupid in front of their friends and peers. This is not part of the mindset of people like the great inventor, Thomas Edison, who looked on failures as temporary setbacks and thus learning opportunities to find out what went wrong. He regarded failures as people who made mistakes but didn't learn from the experience. He realised that the trick was to get up and try again until you eventually succeed.

In fact the majority of childhood prodigies fail to realise their early promise because they experience success too early and too easily and thus are unable to cope with the disappointment of setbacks and failure when it comes. When they grow up they find it hard to cope with the emotional and economic pressures of adult life and find it difficult to deal with competition, criticism and the normal ups and downs of life. They don't realise that even prodigies have to work hard to gain expertise and recognition. Ability alone is not sufficient.

Some people fail because they happen to be in the wrong job unsuited to their talents or incompatible with their interests. Many famous names we now consider synonymous with success experienced many failures in their lives before they became successful. They accepted that failure was a stepping stone to success. On the other hand a negative reaction to failure and loss can result in a downward spiral of helplessness and hopelessness. In sport a team that feels defeated loses confidence and ceases to be a threat to the opposing team. Michael Jordan one of the greatest basketball players of all time said he failed over and over again and that is why he succeeded.

"Nothing in life is to be feared. It is only to be understood."

Marie Curie

Successful People Who Overcame Failure

The following people became successful in their chosen fields despite failures, setbacks and frustrations which would have destroyed less determined people. Some people don't even enjoy success during their lifetimes but have to wait till after their deaths to gain the recognition they deserved and should have enjoyed while they lived.

- Winston Churchill (1874-1965) did poorly in school and suffered from a speech impediment in his early years. As First Lord of the Admiralty in World War 1, he persuaded the War Cabinet to undertake the Dardanelles Campaign, and the catastrophic allied landing at Gallipoli in 1915. It resulted in a crushing defeat with 200,000 casualties forcing Churchill to resign. This would have destroyed the career of lesser mortals. Nevertheless he fought his way back to become prime minister of the UK in May 1940 at the age of 62 and was instrumental with the belated help of the USA in defeating the Germans in World War 2. Voted out of office in 1945 Churchill showed great resolve in becoming prime minister again from 1951 to 1955. As well as being a great leader and politician he was a gifted orator, talented artist, great writer and won a Nobel Prize for Literature. In a poll conducted by the BBC in 2002 to identify the 100 greatest Britons, he was voted number one.

- Abraham Lincoln (1809-1865) suffered years of personal setbacks, sickness, insults, trauma and defeats on his journey to the presidency. His lack of good looks, formal education and money did not hold him back. It was his perseverance, determination and integrity that brought him through numerous setbacks, personal attacks and criticism. He was able to connect with the public through his marvellous speeches which were spoken with great feelings, honesty and clarity so that the public trusted him completely. He was born in a one-room log cabin in 1809. When Lincoln was 9 years old his 34 year old mother died. He got only about 5 year's formal education but was an avid reader and went on to qualify as a lawyer through self-study. He suffered considerable setbacks and defeats throughout his life. He failed twice in business, lost eight elections and had a nervous breakdown. He had two failed relationships before he married Mary Todd and they had four boys only one of whom reached maturity. In 1843 he was unsuccessful in his bid for the Whig nomination for US Congress. In 1855 Lincoln failed to get chosen by the Illinois legislature to be US Senator. In 1858 he ran against Stephen A. Douglas for Senator and lost but the debates with Douglas won him national admiration, respect and prominence. Two years later he was elected 16th President of the United States. His term of office was consumed by a bitter civil war against the confederate southern states that were in favour of slavery and wanted to break away from the union. During his life Lincoln suffered from numerous bouts of depression but nevertheless managed to live a very productive and successful life becoming one of the best presidents the United States ever had and certainly the most eloquent. He was assassinated in 1865.

- Vincent Van Gough (1853-90) was a Dutch painter who only sold one painting during his lifetime and this was to a friend for a very small amount of money. This painting is titled The Red Vineyard and is now on display in the Pushkin Museum in Moscow. Vincent was the son of a protestant minister and his sister described him as a serious and introspective child. As an adult he was highly emotional and lacked self-confidence. He had two failed relationships with women during his life and worked unsuccessfully as a bookshop clerk, an art salesman and a preacher. Almost unknown while he lived, his fame spread after he died and he is now the most popular of the post-impressionist painters. Van Gogh did not start painting until he was in his late twenties, and most of his best known works were produced during the last two years of his life. He produced about 900 paintings and 1,100 drawings and sketches. Today his paintings are practically priceless. He suffered from anxiety and depression during his life and at one time cut off his own ear. He committed suicide by shooting himself in the chest at the age of 37 in 1890.

To overcome your fear of failure, reconfigure and reframe your mental model of success and failure. Most people see themselves in the middle with success on one side and failure on the other. They do everything they can to move away from failure and towards success. Instead see a continuum of you, failure and success. In other words, see failure as a stepping stone or a prerequisite to success. Don't be afraid of failure as many successful people experience many failures on the road to success. See failure as a learning opportunity and bringing you one step closer to success. You will need to build up reserves of courage to keep going in spite of setbacks.

"We pay a heavy price for our fear of failure. It is a powerful obstacle to growth. It assures the progressive narrowing of the personality and prevents exploration and experimentation. There is no learning without some difficulty and fumbling. If you want to keep on learning, you must keep on risking failure – all your life."

John W. Gardner

Fear of Rejection

Evolution has designed humans to be vigilant about potential rejection as thousands of years ago when we were part of small groups it helped us survive. Scientists have found that rejection hurts just like physical pain. It activates the same brain area that generates our reaction to physical pain. Rejection undermines our feelings of self-esteem and evokes feelings of aggression and even hate which may lead to acts of retaliation and revenge. People who are rejected often feel angry and sometimes seek revenge whether they are jilted lovers, failed job applicants or college entrants, ostracised children, frustrated writers, rebuffed actors or contestants voted off of reality shows. All suffer from loss of face and humiliation.

People who react to rejection with aggression may ruin their own lives and those of others. Feeling rejected is one of the most common reasons why husbands kill their wives with the violence often provoked by real or imagined infidelity. They may even kill their children as a form of punishment, revenge and retaliation against their wives. Fear of rejection is why some of our best writers never send off their manuscripts to the publishers and remain unknown and frustrated. Others with great potential never even take up the writing process so they never find out how good they really are.

People often don't apply for jobs in the first instance because of fear of rejection. Some employed people do not apply for promotional positions because of fear of rejection. Applying for a job makes us very vulnerable as we may not get it and our self-esteem and sense of self-worth plummets. If we don't get the job we create excuses for the rejection as it may be too painful to accept that we might not be good enough and bear some of the responsibility for our mediocre interview performance and lack of success. In order to cope with the pain of rejection we may rationalise that the reason we didn't get the job was outside our control. In psychology this is called cognitive dissonance where we block out upsetting ideas and restore a good feeling about ourselves by placing the reason for the rejection outside our control. Instead you should carry out a post-mortem on the interview to see what you did well and what you did badly so that you learn lessons for the future.

Look for feedback so that you can build on what you did right and take corrective action for what you didn't do well. This means that you will learn from your experience so that the next time around you will do better. To give you the best chance of getting a job only apply for jobs that you are inherently interested in and adequately qualified for, and which match your education, experience, training and skills. Make sure that your application is customised to the requirements of the job you are applying for. At the interview translate your skills into benefits so that your prospective employer will see how your qualifications match the requirements of the job offered.

Prepare thoroughly for the interview by researching information about the employer's business and the challenges facing it. A well informed candidate has a competitive edge over other applicants as you demonstrate interest in the company and an inside knowledge of the business. Ask probing questions that will demonstrate how you will fit easily into the organisation and become part of the team. Your objective should be to minimise the impact of rejection by adopting an approach to the interview that will showcase yourself and your qualifications in the most advantageous and persuasive manner.

People who are fired feel unappreciated, angry, humiliated and depressed. They may feel great emotional pain when a long-term relationship with an employer is severed. In rare cases employees who have been fired have been known to return to their workplace to seek revenge on those who have fired and upset them. This phenomenon is so prevalent in the United States that it has become known as "going postal" because of the number of such incidents which happened in the US Postal Service. However, it is not just confined to the postal service as the incidence in the private sector is much higher. The perpetrators of school and college killings have often been bullied or rejected by their peers. In many of the incidents the victims included schoolmates who had insulted, teased, bullied, or rejected the killer. Children from dysfunctional families who suffered emotional or physical abuse are often highly sensitive to rejections. You will take rejection personally if you don't think you're particularly valuable in the first place. Not all people who suffer rejection act in an aggressive way. Some people may just disengage from the relationship while others may try to improve the relationship.

> "I tell writers to keep reading, reading, and reading. Read widely and deeply. And I tell them not to give up even after rejection letters. And only write what you love."
>
> Anita Diament

Rejection is a Normal Part of Life

Some students who have their hearts set on gaining admission to a particular college are often emotionally upset when they fail to do so. It may be the first time they have experienced a serious setback in their young lives. In Chinese and Japanese cultures college entry rejections are seen as a major loss of face and often result in the applicants taking their own lives. Even Martin Seligman, the prominent psychologist and director of the Positive Psychology Centre at the University of Pennsylvania, was rejected by Harvard. He admits he felt devastated and it took him years to recover from the setback. He graduated a summa cum laude in 1964 from Princeton and has gone on to win world renown as a pioneering positive psychologist as well as producing several bestselling books. He maintains that to become successful in life young people must first experience and overcome failure.

Rejection is part and parcel of being a writer and persistence and resilience is a recommended antidote. Prospective writers should realise that rejection is the beginning rather than the end of the process of becoming a published author. All aspiring writers including this author suffered numerous rejections before being published. The important thing is not to take it personally. Publishers reject manuscripts for numerous reasons other than the quality of your work. Theodor Geisel, who wrote under the pen name of Dr. Seuss, was rejected 27 times before his first book "And to Think I Saw it on Mulberry Street" was published by Vanguard Press. He died in 1991 and left a wonderful legacy of 44 children's books which have been translated into more than 15 languages and sold over 200 million copies, and brought pleasure to children throughout the world. He has received two Academy awards, two Emmy awards, a Peabody award and the Pulitzer Prize for writing.

If you have an ambition to be an actor, be prepared for the inevitable rejection from time to time. Rejection is part of show business. Self-belief in your acting skills is important to keep you going on the road to getting the part that will change your life. The worst thing you can do after a rejection is to mope around, as no one is going to cast someone sitting around their apartment doing nothing. Instead get out there, network and meet people and audition more. Have faith in your ability to eventually get the role you desire. To give yourself the best chance of success make sure you prepare thoroughly for your auditions; arrive early, well groomed, rehearsed and focused on what you have to do. Reflect on your experiences and learn from them so that you will do better the next time. If you were good and you still didn't get the role it probably was because they choose someone whom they considered more suited to the role than you.

Fear of rejection prevents people from asking for a favour, information, assistance, support, money and time. Fear of rejection stops us from asking probing questions and making that difficult but important phone call. Ask and you shall receive and so ask as if you expect a yes. Ask more than once as persistence can pay off in the end. Remember why persistent salespeople are so successful, as it is often on the fifth and sixth attempt that the sale finally comes through. Successful salespeople are not afraid of rejection. These types of salespeople realise that they haven't failed until they give up trying. Ask someone who is capable of meeting your request. It is not the end of the world if you get a refusal. Rejection is a natural part of life and so don't let it get you down. After rejection you haven't really lost anything as things are only the same as before you asked. Rejection is preferable to regret at not knowing what would have happened if you did not try?

"I take rejection as someone blowing a bugle in my ear to wake me up and get going, rather than retreat."

Sylvester Stallone

Rejection and the Matthew Effect

Recognition is usually given to those of considerable repute and is withheld from those who are less well known. This phenomenon has become known as the Matthew Effect based on the quotation from the Gospel of Matthew: "For all those who have, more will be given, and they will have abundance; but for those who have nothing, even what they have will be taken away." It seems to be a case of the rich getting richer and the poor getting poorer.

Some people are ignored by their peers and never get the recognition they deserve or share the fame for their brilliant work. It's a case of the soldiers doing the fighting but the general getting the credit. If you work in an organisation and do sterling work it is usually the manager you report to that gets the credit. Eminent scientists are likely to get all the credit for breakthroughs despite the major or significant contribution of less well known researchers and assistant researchers who support them in their research. The support team that explorers and mountaineers need to get to their destination never get any of the credit and are consigned to anonymity. When a bright graduate student gets their work published in a prestigious academic journal, it is likely that their better known mentor will get most of the credit.

Charles Darwin gets all the credit for the theory of evolution even though a less well known contemporary of his named Alfred Russel Wallace came up with the theory of natural selection at the same time. Edmund Hillary gets the credit for being the first man to conquer Mount Everest in 1953 even though he did so with Tensing Norgay, a Nepalese Sherpa and local mountaineer who seldom gets any of the credit particularly in the western media. Robert Peary and Matthew Henson are usually credited with being the first people to reach the North Pole, though the expedition also included three Inuit. Frederick Taylor, known as the Father of Scientific Management is given complete credit for developing high-speed tool steel even though the discovery was jointly made with his fellow engineer, J, Maunsell White in 1898. The discovery revolutionised metal-cutting techniques and paved the way for mass production methods which revolutionised car production in the Ford Motor Company. The patent earned Taylor considerable sums of money which helped him establish the scientific approach to management and become a world renowned figure in that field.

Francis Crick and James Watson jointly announced the structure of DNA in 1953 and shared the Nobel Prize for Physiology and Medicine in 1962. Rosalind Franklin's molecular structure research findings was used by Crick and Watson and was vital to the discovery of DNA, but was not fully acknowledged until years after her untimely death from cancer at 38. Even the Nobel committee ignored her contribution when the Nobel Prize was presented in 1962 to Crick and Watson.

Famous People Who Suffered Rejection

Most successful people have suffered rejection at some stage of their lives but instead of getting despondent they have shook themselves off and started all over again. Some people may find it very difficult to handle rejection and it may bring on depression and in extreme cases ultimately contribute to suicide and death. The following are some short case studies of rejection.

- The most renowned rock 'n' roll group in history suffered numerous rejections on the road to fame and success but refused to give up. In 1962 the Beatles were rejected by Decca Records executive Dick Rowe, who signed Brian Poole & the Tremeloes instead. They said they didn't like their sound and that guitar music had gone out of fashion and that the Beatles had no future in show business. They must have felt devastation at this put down but nevertheless continued on in their quest for fame and fortune. Their Decca audition tape was subsequently turned down by Pye, Philips, Columbia, and HMV before they eventually went on to great acclaim.

- In 1968 Ronald Reagan lost the Republican nomination for president to Richard Nixon. In 1976 he again lost the Republican nomination for president to Gerald Ford. At this stage most people would have given up but not Ronald Reagan who was elected President of the United States in 1980 and became the first divorced and the oldest US president ever at 69 years of age and possibly the most charismatic.

- William Paul Young a Canadian author born in 1955 is best known for his novel, The Shack. He turned his tragic life into an inspirational spiritual thriller for his family and became modestly rich and famous in the process. He spent much of his childhood with his missionary parents among the Dani tribe in New Guinea some of whose members sexually abused him. Later on he was sexually abused by some of the people his parents preached to when he attended a Canadian Christian boarding school. Years later he got depressed because of the deaths of his younger brother and young niece. He was unfaithful to his wife and this put a strain on his marriage. At one stage his dire financial circumstances led to bankruptcy. He originally wrote the novel for his family and friends to explain to his six children how he coped with tragedy and his struggles with faith and morality and initially only printed off 15 copies. Two of his friends encouraged him to publish it and helped him to edit and rewrite it so that it would be suitable for publication. It was rejected by 26 publishers before going on to become a best-seller, selling 7.2 million copies and appearing for a year on the New York bestseller list. It was the top selling novel and audio book in America in 2008. The unexpected success of his book has modestly transformed Young's life. He traded in his old car for a new one, bought a four-bedroom house, and set up a family foundation, endowing it with $1 million to help literacy and child welfare.

- John Grisham suffered rejection before he became a best-selling author. His first novel, A Time to Kill, was rejected by sixteen agents and twelve publishers. It was eventually published by Wynwood Press in June 1988, who did a run of only 5,000 copies. This was not an auspicious start to someone who had got up at 5am every day and spent several hours writing for three years before going to work in a small law practice. Writing was a consuming hobby and despite this setback he began a new novel. He had greater luck with the next novel and The Firm became a best-seller and was made into a film. Since 1988 Grisham has written one novel a year and all of them have become best sellers. Nine of his novels have been made into films.

- John Kennedy Toole (1937-1969) was an American novelist and English lecturer who grew up in New Orleans. At 16 he wrote his first novel, The Neon Bible, which he thought was juvenile and this was not published until 1989, 20 years after his death. Unfortunately, he got no recognition as a writer during his lifetime and his second but best known novel A Confederacy of Dunces was not published until 1980, 11 years after his death by suicide in 1969 at the age of 31. It is thought that the suicide was caused by the cumulative frustration and pain of many rejections over several years and the resultant depression when he failed to get his book published as he considered it to be a masterpiece. The first publisher he sent his manuscript to, Simon and Schuster, rejected his book saying it wasn't really about anything. This hurtful rejection must have been devastating and humiliating to the aspiring young author who placed such a high regard on his writing skills. It was due to the persistence of his mother after his death that his book was eventually published and recognised as a great piece of literature. He was posthumously awarded the Pulitzer Prize for Fiction in 1981. The book has sold more than 1.5 million copies in 18 languages.

In life we don't get what we want, we get in life what we are. If you want more we have to be able to be more, in order to be more you have to face rejection."

Farrah Gray

Handling Rejection

To deal with the feelings of rejection don't take it personally and realise that you are not alone in feeling this way. Acknowledge that you are angry and that it is okay to feel these emotions. It may take some time for these feelings to subside as rejection is basically a feeling of loss. In the meantime to regain a positive outlook think positive thoughts, take a walk in the park, go to a movie, or meet a friend for lunch. Keep things in perspective as after a few days you may realise that the rejection was more imagined than real, and keep your past achievements in the forefront of your mind to counteract any feelings of inadequacy.

Marcel Proust said: "The real voyage of discovery consists not in seeking new landscapes but in seeing with new eyes." Whenever you are feeling down, try to look at the situation differently. Talk to people with different perspectives so that you get a new reality check on the situation. Feelings are triggered by our expectations, beliefs and hopes and the interpretation we put on our experiences. Change the way you view rejection and your emotional response will change too.

Rejection is often a reflection of the other person's needs, attitudes and values rather than your inherent worth. At Fred Astaire's first screen test he was rejected for being too skinny, balding and being a mediocre dancer. His subsequent career spanned 76 years and he made 31 musical films. He was named the fifth Greatest Male Star of All Time by the American Film Institute. Rejection is part of life and it is the way you react and handle it that is important.

Some people take rejection in their stride while others fall apart. Rejection can spur you on to great things, so learn from the rejection, and keep on trying while realising that you are also good at lots of other things. View your rejections as a badge of honour. Remember that in baseball a batting average of one third is considered good, even though this means that you are not hitting the ball two thirds of the time. If you have lost your job it is important to keep busy so take additional training to enhance your skills and improve your job prospects. Market and economic cycles come and go, so take the opportunity to hone your skills so that you are ready for better times that inevitably will come. In the meantime, read positive and uplifting books such as those on positive psychology and biographies of successful people.

There is no failure except in no longer trying. There is no defeat except from within, no really insurmountable barrier save our own inherent weakness of purpose."

Ken Hubbard

Fear of Success

Some people even fear success and the responsibility and publicity that go with it. The famous psychologist Abraham Maslow called this the Jonah Complex after the biblical character in the Old Testament. The essence of the Jonah Complex is the refusal to exploit ones talents to the full because of a fear of success. Jonah was directed by God to go to the city of Nineveh, now known as Mosul in Iraq, and tell its citizens that God was angry with them and would punish them if they did not change their ways. However, Jonah decided to disobey God and go to Tarshish instead. On the ship there was a fierce storm and the sailors realised that they were in great danger after questioning him. They decided to throw him overboard as they feared the wrought of God, and the storm stopped.

Jonah was swallowed by a whale and after three days he was vomited onto dry land. God reminded him about the request he had made to him and Jonah decided to fulfil God's wish. The people of Nineveh repented and God spared them and Jonah realised his mission. Maslow maintains that there is greatness in every human being waiting to be discovered and exploited. We all have the potential to contribute something special to the world but most of us do not bother to find out our true purpose in life. Only a minority reach their potential, exploit their unique talents, live to their true purpose and become self-actualised.

Successful people are often expected to be role models for others and thus their life styles may come under close public scrutiny through newspapers, magazines, radio and television. It is difficult to live a normal life if your every move is watched, analysed and criticised in the media. Going to the shop for a pint of milk may be unremarkable for most of us but may turn into a media circus for a celebrity who is expected to be presentable and glamorous all the time. Other people may resent and be jealous of their success and real friendships may be hard to come by as they may associate with successful people just because of their celebrity status and what they can gain financially and materially from the relationship. Thus one of the drawbacks of success is that you can never be really sure who your true friends are.

Some women may fear success particularly in traditional male fields like business and politics because of its negative consequences such as competition, unpopularity, rejection and concerns about loss of femininity. In a man's world women may feel they have to behave like men to succeed which can bring on feelings of role ambivalence and anxiety. They may feel they have to work harder to achieve recognition and the burden of balancing a work and home life often falls disproportionately on them. In western society women are brought up to behave in a feminine and ladylike way with an emphasis on caring and interpersonal relationships while men are conditioned to be masculine with an emphasis on autonomy and productivity and so there are societal expectations about gender roles.

> "Always do what you are afraid to do."
>
> Ralph Waldo Emerson

Overcoming fear

To overcome fear, define exactly what makes you fearful. Feel the fear and do it anyway. In psychology this is called paradoxical intention which is the idea that you should face up to the fear and take action to counteract it. For example, a shy person should greet people, get involved with others, express opinions and be more assertive. Adopt the attitude of nothing ventured, nothing gained. As your fear diminishes your self-esteem and confidence will rise. Confront the source of your fears and examine them objectively. Ask the following questions:

- How does the fear hold you back?
- How does it help you?
- What are the benefits of eliminating the fear?

Replace the fear in your imagination with a positive result rather than dwelling on unrealistic catastrophic outcomes. Programme your mind for success. Success can become a self-fulfilling prophecy.

Success depends on mastery of fears and development of courage. Become sensitised to your fears by taking on smaller challenges and gradually work your way up. I overcame a fear of flying by taking numerous short distance flights first before I undertook longer flights. It worked and I now look forward to flying rather than suffering anxiety and panic attacks at the thought.

Summary

People fail because they drift aimlessly through life without any purpose or sense of direction. They neglect to develop their interpersonal relationship skills. They lack the self-belief and confidence to pursue their dreams with persistence and resilience. Instead of seeing the jar as half-full, they see it as half-empty and thus have little hope for the future. They don't believe in the need for lifelong learning and continuous improvement and find it difficult to cope with change. They lack self-discipline and seek instant gratification and adopt self-destructive unhealthy lifestyle habits involving smoking, excessive drinking, drugs and getting into debt. They lack personal values such as honesty and integrity. Procrastination and perfectionism prevents them from reaching their true potential.

Some of our fears are irrational and will never come to fruition. Other fears are rational such as fear of injury, death and poverty and are part of a survival instinct that protects us from imprudent and reckless acts. Fear robs us of confidence, desire, commitment and hope and paralyses us in the face of normal challenges. Insecure people have a fear of change and this keeps them locked in their comfort zone. There are three kinds of fears which are learned.

Fear of looking a fool prevents us from being creative and exploring possibilities. Fear of failure prevents us from taking even calculated risks. Fear of rejection prevents us from carrying out normal everyday activities and undermines our self-esteem. It may prevent you from applying for positions that you are adequately qualified for, asking for a favour or making an important phone call. Some people fear success because of the responsibility that accompanies it. Successful people may become role models for others and thus feel they have to live up to the high standards and expectations of others. To overcome fear, feel the fear and do it anyway. Become sensitised to your fears by taking on smaller challenges while gradually exposing yourself to what you fear.

Five Activities to Overcome Your Fears

1. Overcome your fears by confronting them. Gradually expose yourself to what you fear so that eventually over time you become inoculated against them.

2. Focus on the things you really want to do in your life and embrace every opportunity to do them. Don't come to the end of your life and regret the things you should have done but didn't.

3. To overcome the fear of failure, see failure as a stepping stone to success and resolve to learn from it.

4. Ask and you shall receive. Ask for what you want and expect a yes. Ask more than once as persistence may pay off in the end. Even if your request is rejected you are just in the same position that you were before you asked so that you shouldn't be disappointed as you have lost nothing.

5. After a rejection and you are feeling down, try to look at the situation differently. Change the way you view rejection and your emotional response will change too. View your rejections as a badge of honour. Think of all the famous people who suffered numerous rejections in their lives but yet went on to achieve greatness.

References and Bibliography

Afolabi, Michael. (1993) Application of Johari Communication Awareness Model to Special Libraries Management. Library Management. Vol. 14, No. 1, pp: 24-27.

Agee, Jim. (2005) Literacy, aliteracy, and lifelong learning. New Library World. Vol. 106, No.5/6, pp: 244-252.

Akrivos, Christos; Ladkin, Adele; Reklitis, Panayiotis. (2007) Hotel managers' career strategies for success. International Journal of Contemporary Hospitality Management. Vol.19, No.2, pp: 107-119.

Albrecht, Karl. (2004) Social Intelligence: Beyond IQ. Training. Vol. 41, Issue 12, pp: 26-31.

Alder, Harry. (1991). Seeing is Being: The Natural Way to Success. Management Decision, Vol. 29, No. 1, pp: 25-30.

Arden, John B. (2010) Rewire Your Brain. Think Your Way To A Better Life. New Jersey: Wiley.

Aursnes, Ingunn. (2009) break through the terror barrier to achieve your goals. Supervision. April, Vol. 70, Issue 4, pp: 12-13.

Baker, Arnold B; Demerouti, Evangelia. (2008) Towards a model of work engagement. Career Development International. Vol.13, No.3, pp: 209-223.

Balchin, Jon. (2010) Quantum Leaps. 100 Scientists Who Changed The World. London: Capella.

Banks, Janet; Coutu Diane. (2008) How to Protect your Job in a Recession. Harvard Business Review. Sept, Vol. 86, Issue 9, pp: 113-116.

Barwick, Alexa K. (2009) Personality Factors and Attitude toward Seeking Professional Help. North American Journal of Psychology. Vol 11, Issue 2, pp: 333-342.

Basco, Monica Ramirez. (1999) The "Perfect" Trap. Psychology Today. May/June, Vol. 32, Issue 3, p30.

Bauman, James. (2000) The Gold Medal Mind. Psychology Today. May/June, Vol. 33, Issue 3, p62.

Baumeister, Roy; Campbell, Jennifer; Kruger, Joachim; Vohs, Kathleen. (2003) Does High Self-Esteem Cause Better Performance, Interpersonal Success, Happiness, or Healthier Lifestyles. American Psychological Society. Vol. 4, No. 1, May 2003.

Baumeister, Roy; Campbell, Jennifer; Kruger, Joachim, Vohs, Kathleen. (2005) Exploding The Self-Esteem Myth. Scientific American. Vol 292, Issue 1, pp: 84-91.

Bazerman, Max H. (2006) Decisions Without Blinders. Harvard Business Review. January, Vol. 84, Issue 1, pp: 88-97.

Benady, David. (2004) Look who's talking .. Marketing Week. 12 August 2004.

Bence, Brenda. (2008) Top 10 Secrets to Mastering Your Personal Brand. American Salesman. Dec 2008, Vol.53, Issue 12, pp: 22-25.

Berman, Evan M; West, Jonathan P. (2008) Managing Emotional Intelligence in U.S. Cities: A Study of Social Skills among Public Managers. Public Administration Review, July/Aug 2008.

Bhasin, Roberta. (1997) Feedback: A key to relationships. Pulp & Paper, July, Vol. 71, Issue 7, p49.

Bjorseth, Lillian D. (2007) Ten Principles of Communication. Healthcare Executive, Sept/Oct 2007.

Billings, Lee. (2006) Press for Success. Psychology Today. Mar/Apr, Vol 39, Issue 2, p37.

Birk, Sussan K. (2008) Lessons From Leaders. Planning Your Next Career. Healthcare Executive. Nov/Dec 2008.

Blum, Deborah. (1998) Finding strength: How to overcome anything. Psychology Today. May/June, Vol.31, Issue 3, p32.

Brim, Gilbert. (1992) Ambition. Psychology Today. Sept 92, Vol 25, Issue 5, p48.

Bryant, Liz. (2009) The art of active listening. Practice Nurse. 27/3/2009, Vol.37, Issue 6, pp:49-52.

Canfield, Jack. (2005) The Success Principles. How to Get from Where You Are to Where You Want to Be. London: Element.

Cappon, Daniel. (1993) The anatomy of intuition. Psychology Today. May/June, Vol.26, Issue 3, p40.

Carducci, Bernardo. (2000) Shyness: The New Solution. Psychology Today. Jan/Feb, Vol. 33, Issue 1, p38.

Carr, Albert Z. (1968) Is business bluffing ethical? Harvard Business Review. Jan/Feb 1968.

Casriel, Erika. (2007) Stepping Out. Psychology Today. Mar/Apr, Vol. 40, Issue 2, pp: 68-75.

Chapman, Mary Ann. (1999) Bad Choices. Psychology Today. Sep/Oct, Vol. 32, Issue 5, p36.

Cialdini, Robert B. (1999) Of Tricks and Tumors: Some Little Recognised Costs of Dishonest Use of Effective Social Influence. Psychology and Marketing. March, Vol. 16. No.2, pp:91-98.

Coombes, Frances. (2008) Self-motivation. London, teach yourself, Hooder Headline

Coutinho, Savia. (2008) Self-Efficacy, Metacognition, and Performance. North American Journal of Psychology. Vol 10, Issue 1, pp: 165-172.

Cohen, William. (2009) Peter's Principle. You can rise above failure. Leadership Excellence. March 2009.

Coutu, Diane L. (2002) How Resilience Works. Harvard Business Review. May, Vol. 80, Issue 5, pp: 46-51.

Coutu, Diane L. (2009) Leadership Lessons from Abraham Lincoln. Harvard Business Review. April 2009, Vol.87, Issue 4, pp: 43-47.

Cushnie, William D. (1975) A manager's introduction to transactional analysis. S.A.M Advanced Management Journal. Autumn 1975.

Cuvelier, Monique. (2002) Past Imperfect. Psychology Today. Dec, Vol. 35, Issue 6, p21.

Dalrymple, Theodore (2005). Letting the steam out of self-esteem. Psychology Today. Sept/Oct 95, Vol 28, Issue 5, p24.

Davidson, Thomas W. (2008) Six Principles of Persuasion You Can Use to Influence Others. The Physician Executive. Sept/Oct 2008.

Dawes, Graham. (2009) Mistakes – how can we learn from them? Development and Learning in Organisations. Vol. 21, No.2, pp:20-22.

Dent, David. (2002) Bursting The Self-Esteem Bubble. Psychology Today. Mar/Apr. Vol 35, Issue 2, p16.

Dixit, Jay. (2008) The Art of Now: Six Steps to Living in the Moment. Psychology Today. Nov/Dec, Vol. 41, Issue 6, pp: 62-69

Dixit, Jay. (2009) You're Driving Me Crazy! Psychology Today. Mar/Apr, Vol.42, Issue 2, pp: 66-75.

Dixit, Jay. (2007) Reading Between the Lines. Psychology Today. July/Aug, Vol. 40, Issue 4, pp: 74-79.

Dobbins, Richard; Pettman, Barrie O. (1992) The Psychology of Success. Equal Opportunities International, Vol 11, No. 1.

Doskoch, Peter. (2005) The Winning Edge. Psychology Today. Nov/Dec, Vol.38, Issue 6, pp: 42-52.

Dowden, Craig. (2009) Dealing with the fear of job loss. Canadian Manager. Summer 2009, Vol.34, Issue 2, pp: 16-17.

Dunleavey, MP. (2003) A Rejection Recovery Plan. Good Housekeeping. May, Vol. 236, Issue 5, p142.

Duffus, Lee R. (2004) The Personal Strategic Plan: A Tool for Career Planning and Advancement. International Journal of Management. Vol, 21, No.2 June 2004.

Dweck, Carol. (2006) Press for Success. Psychology Today. Mar/Apr, Vol.39, Issue 2, p37.

Dweck, Carol. (2006) Mindset. The New Psychology of Success. New York, Random House.

Dye, Carson F. (2010) Lifelong Learning. Healthcare Executive. Mar/Apr 2008.

Ellin, Abby. (2010) I Coulda Been A Contender. Psychology Today. Jul/Aug. Vol 43 Issue 4 pp: 70-77.

Eisenhardt, Kathleen M. (1997) How Management Teams Can Have a Good Fight. Harvard Business Review, July/Aug, Vol.75, Issue 4, pp: 77-85.

Emiliani, M.L. (1998) Continuous personal improvement. Journal of Workplace Learning. Vol 10, No 1, pp: 29-38.

Emler, Nicholas. (2001) The costs and causes of low self-esteem. Joseph Rowntree Foundation. November 2001.

Emmons, Robert. (2008) Giving Thanks As A Science. USA Today Magazine. November, Vol. 137, Issue 2762, p7.

Emrich, Cynthia G; Brower, Holly H; Feldman, Jack M; Garland, Howard. (2001) Images in Words: Presidential Rhetoric, Charisma and Greatness. Administrative Science Quarterly, Sept, Vol.46, Issue 3.

Ewing, Dorlesa. (1977) Twenty Approaches to Individual Change. Personnel and Guidance Journal. February 1977.

Farson, Richard. (1996) Managing: The art of the absurd. Psychology Today. May/June, Vol.29, Issue 3, p44.

Fisher, Anne. (1998) Success Secret: A High Emotional IQ. Fortune, 26/10/98, Vol. 138, Issue 8, p293.

Fisher, Helen. (2007) The Laws of Chemistry. Psychology Today. May/June, Vol. 40, Issue 3, pp: 76-81.

Flaum, Sander A. (2008) Get Over It. Pharmaceutical Executive. July 2008.

Flora, Carlin. (2005) Mirror Mirror: Seeing Yourself As Others See You. Psychology Today. May/June, Vol 38, Issue 3, pp: 52-59.

Flora, Carlin. (2005) How to Get Over Status Anxiety. Psychology Today. Oct, Vol.38, Issue 5, pp: 46-50.

Flora, Carlin. (2006) The Beguiling Truth About Beauty. Psychology Today. June, Vol 39, Issue 3, pp: 62-72.

Flora, Carlin (2006) You 2.0. Psychology Today. Nov/Dec, Vol. 38, Issue 6, pp:66-69.

Flora, Carlin. (2007) Dumped (But Not Down). Psychology Today. Jul/Aug, Vol.40, Issue 4, pp: 66-72.

Fracaro, Ken. (2010) Achieving goals and persistence. Supervision. Sept, Vol. 71, Issue 9, pp: 19-21.

Fryer, Bronwyn. (2004) Accentuate the Positive. Harvard Business Review. Feb 2004, Vol.82, Isssue 2, pp: 22-23.

Galpin, Timothy. (1995) Pruning the grapevine. Training & Development. Apr, Vol. 49, Issue 4, p28.

Gamble, Paul R; Kelliher, Clare E. (1999) Imparting Informatiion and Influencing Behaviour: An Examination of Staff Briefing Sessions. The Journal of Business Communication, Vol. 36, No.3, July, pp: 261-279.

Ghoshal, Sumantra. (2003) Going Beyond Motivation to the Power of Volition. MIT Sloan Management Review. Spring 2003. Vol. 44, Issue 3, pp: 51-57.

Gillespie, Jack. (2000) Perseverance is the key to success. Selling. August 2000, p8.

Goldberg, Stan. (2002) The 10 Rules of Change. Psychology Today. Sept/Oct, Vol. 35, Issue 5, p38.

Golen, Steven. (1990) A Factor Analysis of Barriers to Effective Listening. The Journal of Business Communication. Winter 1990, Vol. 27, No. 1.

Gosling, Sam. (2009) Mixed Signals. Psychology Today. Sep/Oct, Vol. 42, Issue 5, pp: 62-71.

Graham, John R. (1996) It's the fear of rejection that keeps you from getting the right job. Canadian Manager. Winter 96, Vol.21, Issue 4, p11.

Grierson, Bruce; Dixit, Jay. (2009) Nine Ways to Fail Better. Psychology Today. May/June, Vol.42, Issue 3, pp: 72-73.

Hager, Paul. (2004) Lifelong learning in the workplace? Challenges and issues. Journal of Workplace Learning: Employee Counselling Today. Vol.16, No. 1/2, pp: 22-32.

Hamel, Gary; Valikangas, Lisa. (2003) The Quest for Resilience. Harvard Business Review. Sept, Vol.81, Issue 9, pp: 52-63.

Handy, Charles. (2001) Tocqueville Revisted. Harvard Business Review. Jan, Vol. 79, Issue 1, pp: 56-63.

Harshbarger, Scott. (2003) Creating A Climate of Corporate Integrity. Corporate Board, May/June, Vol. 24, Issue 140, p10.

Hayashi, Alden M. (2001) When to Trust Your Gut. Harvard Business Review. February, Vol. 79, Issue 2, pp: 59-65.

Honey, Peter. (2008) Learn from your mistakes. Personnel Today. 22/7/2008, p4.

Hughes, Damien. (2009) Liquid Thinking. Inspirational lessons from the world's best achievers. Chichester: Capstone.

Hurley, Amy E. (1997) The effects of self-esteem and source credibility on self-denying prophecies. Journal of Psychology. Nov, Vol.131, Issue 6, p581.

Hutson, Matthew. (2008) Creatures of Habit. Psychology Today. Nov/Dec, Vol. 41, Issue 6, p27.

Hutson, Matthew. (2009) Self-Promote (The Introverts' Edition). Psychology Today. Nov/Dec, Vol. 42, Issue 6, p25.

Jason, Sharon. (2009) Staying positive in negative territory. USA Today. 8/6/2009.

Jay, Joelle. (2005) On Communicating Well. HR Magazine, Jan, Vol.50, Issue 1, pp: 87-90.

Jennings, Gayle R. (2000) Educating Students to Be Lifelong Learners. Review of Business. Fall/Winter, Vol. 21, Issues 3/4, p58.

Jenner, Paul. (2009) confidence and social skills. London, teach yourself, Hodder Education.

Jordan, Martin. (2009) Back to nature. Therapy Today. April 2009, Vol.20, Issue 3, pp: 26-28.

Jones, Ian; Symon, Graham. (2001) Lifelong learning as a serious leisure: policy, practice and potential. Leisure Studies Vol. 20, pp; 269-283.

Kaplan, Robert S. (2008) Reaching Your Potential. Harvard Business Review. July/August, Vol 86, Issue 7/8. Pp: 45-49.

Karbo, Karen. (2006) Friendship: The Laws of Attraction. Psychology Today. Nov/Dec, Vol.39, Issue 6, pp: 90-95.

Kaufman, Scott Barry. (2008) Confessions of a Late Bloomer. Psychology Today. Nov/Dec, Vol. 41, Issue 6, pp: 70-79.

Keiningham, Timothy; Aksoy, Lerzan; Williams, Luke. (2009) Loyalty is Earned. T&D July 2009.

Kendall, Joshua. (2008) Famously Fussy. Psychology Today. Mar/Apr, Vol.41, Issue 2, pp: 43-44.

Kimbrough-Robinson, Carla. (2007) Procrastination: The death of opportunity. Quill, Vol. 95 Issue 2, p43.

Kirkwood, Jodyanne. (2009) Is a lack of self-confidence hindering women entrepreneurs? International Journal of Gender and Entrepreneurship. Vol. 1, No. 2, pp: 118-133.

Kramer, Peter D. (1993) The transformation of personality. Psychology Today. July/Aug, Vol. 26, Issue 4, p42.

Heifetz, Hank & Heifetz, Hank. (1997) The Blonde Leading the Blind. New Republic. 10/2/97. Vol.216, Issue 6.
Lamb, Sue C. (1980) The Use of Paradoxical Intention: Self-Management Through Laughter. The Personnel and Guidance Journal. December 1980.
Lambert, Kelly. (2008) Depressingly Easy. Scientific American. Vol.19, Issue 4, pp: 31-37.
Langer, Ellen. (1999) Self-esteem vs. Self-respect. Psychology Today. Nov/Dec, Vol 32, Issue 6, p32.
Langer, Ellen. (2000) Do Stop Thinking About Tomorrow. Psychology Today. May/April Vol 33 Issue 2, P26.
Leary, Mark R; Twenge, Jean M; Quinlivan, Erin. (2006) Interpersonal Rejection as a Determinant of Anger and Aggression. Personality and Social Psychology Review. Vol. 10, No. 2, pp:111-132.
Leary-Joyce, Judith. (2009) The Psychology of Success. Secrets of Serial Achievement. Harlow. Pearson Prentice Hall Life.
Lovallo, Dan. (2003) Delusions of Success. Harvard Business Review. July, Vol. 81, Issue 7, pp: 56-63.
Law, Jonathan. (1997) The Giant Book of 1000 Great Lives. London: Magpie Books.
Lawrence, Timothy L. (2007) The Keys to Successful Goal Achievement. Journal of Management Development. Emerald Backfiles 2007.
Leary, Mark. (2004) Get Over Yourself. Psychology Today. Aug, Vol 37, Issue 4, pp: 62-65.
Leder, Gilah C. (2003) Successful Females: Print Media Profiles and Their Implications. The Journal of Psychology. Vol. 120, No. 3, pp: 239-248.
Leotis, James D. (1994) What Makes People Fail? Managers Magazine. Vol.69 Issues 6. Page 28.
Lie, S.J; Katz A.E. (1992) Success in the land of the less. Psychology Today. Jan, Vol.25, Issue 1, pp: 74-77.
Linderfield, Gael. (1995) Super confidence at work. Executive Development. Vol 8 No.1 pp: 9-11.
Loftus, Mary. (1995) The other side of fame. Psychology Today. May/June, Vol 28, Issue 3, p48.
Loftus, Paul. (1995) The Pygmalion Effect. Industrial and Commercial Training. Vol. 27, No.4, pp: 17-20.
Lombardo, Tom. (2009) Understanding and teaching future consciousness. On the Horizon. Vol. 17, No.2. pp: 85-97.
Lubin, Shellen. (2001) Weathering the Low Fronts: The Gift of Rejection, Depression and Post Show Crashes. Back Stage. 2/2/2001, Vol. 42, Issue 5, p28.
Macdonald, Eleanor (1986) Confidence – the Source of Inner Strength and External Influence. Women in Management Review. Spring 86.
MacPherson, Mike. (2009) Entrepreneural Learning: Secret Ingredient's for Business Success. July 2009.

Malone, Samuel A. (2005) A Practical Guide to Learning in the Workplace. Dublin: The Liffey Press.

Malone, Samuel A. (2008) Greed, Fraud & Corruption. A guide to Organisational Ethics. Cirencester: Management Books 2000 Ltd.

Malone, Samuel A. (2009) Don't Worry, Be Happy! Finding Happiness at Work, at Home and at Play. Dublin: The Liffey Press.

Malone, Samuel A. (2008) People Skills for Managers. Dublin: The Liffey Press.

Marano, Hara Estroff. (2006) Getting Out From Under. Psychology Today. May/Apr, Vol.39, Issue 2, pp: 41-42

Martin, Roger. (2007) How Successful Leaders Think. Harvard Business Review. June, Vol.85, Issue 6, pp:60-67.

Matour, Susan; Prout, Maurice F. (2007) Psychological Implications of Retirement in the 21st Century. Journal of Financial Service Professionals. January 2007.

Matthews, Virginia. (2006) Spotlight on ...Bad manners. Personnel Today. 12/12/2006, p 33.

McCracken, Martin; Winterton, Jonathan. (2006) What about the managers? Contradictions between lifelong learning and management development. International Journal of Training and Development. 10:1.

McCrimmon, Mitch. (2009) Personal Strengths for Success in Management. Canadian Manager, Winter 2009, Vol 33, Issue 3, pp: 6-8.

McGowan, Kathleen. (2008) Second Nature. Psychology Today. Mar/Apr, Vol. 41, Issue 2, pp: 72-79.

McWhirter, Benedict T. (1990) Loneliness: A Review of Current Literature, With Implications for Counselling and Research. Journal of Counselling & Development. Mar/Apr, Vol. 68, pp: 417-422.

Medintz, Scott. (2010) Clear the Roadblocks in your way. Money. October, Vol.39, Issue 9, pp: 77-84.

Merrell, Susan Scarf. (1996) Getting over getting older. Psychology Today. Nov/Dec, Vol.29, Issue 6, p34.

Miller, Michael Craig. (2003) A Little More Willpower Can Change Your Life. Newsweek. 20/1/2003, Vol.141, Issue 3, p70.

Montefiore, Simon Sebag (2007) 101 Great Heroes. Great Men and Women for an Unheroic Age. London: Quercus.

Moyer, Steven K; Chalofsky, Neal S. (2008) Understanding The Selection And Development Of Life Goals Of Family Business Owners. Journal of Enterprise Cutlure. Vol. 16, No. 1, pp: 19-53.

Mullins, John. (2009) Career planning the second time around. Occupational Outlook Quarterly. Summer 2009.

Murphy, Daragh. (1999) The Pygmalion effect reconsidered: its implications for education, training and workplace learning. Journal of European Industrial Training. Vol.23, No. 4/5, pp: 238-251.

Myers, David G. (2002) The Powers & Perils of Intuition. Psychology Today. December, Vol.35, Issue 6, p42.

Nash, Laura. (2004) Success That Lasts. Harvard Business Review. Feb 2004, Vol.82, Issue 2, pp: 102-109.

Neck, Christopher P. Neck: Bedeian, Arthur G. (1996) Frederick W. Taylor, J. Maunsell White 111, and the Mathew Effect. Journal of Management History. Vol.2, No.2, pp: 20-25.

Neimark, Jill. (2007) The Optimism Revolution. Psychology Today. May/June, Vol. 40, Issue 3, pp: 88-94.

Orlick, Terry. (2000) In Pursuit of Excellence. How to win in sport and life through mental training. United States: Human Kinetics.

Painter, Kim. (2008) Stepping up the gratitude. USA Today. 24/11/2008.

Palmer, Blaire. (2009) The Recipe for Success. What Really Successful People Do and How You Can Do it Too. London, A & C Black.

Palmer, Louise; Foley, Jill; Parsons, Chris. (2004) Principles not values. Industrial and Commercial Training. Vol. 36, No.1, pp: 38-40.

Palmquist, Susan. (2004) Handsome Ambitions. Psychology Today. Aug, Vol 37 Issue 4, p33.

Parachin, Victor M. (2005) Self-Motivation Secrets. American Salesman. January, Vol.50, Issue 1, pp:16-21.

Patten, Dick. (2009) George Washington. Vital Speeches of the Day. May, Vol. 75, Issue 5, pp: 219-222.

Paul, Annie Murphy. (1998) Where bias begins: The truth about stereotypes. Psychology Today. May/June, Vol. 31, Issue 3, p52.

Paul, Annie Murphy. (2001) Self-Help: Shattering the Myths. Psychology Today. Mar/Apr, Vol 34, Issue 2, p60.

Paulson, Terry L. (2010) The Optimism Advantage. 50 Simple Truths to Transform Your Attitudes and Actions into Results. New Jersey: Wiley.

Pearlman, Jeff. (2004) After the Ball. Psychology Today. May/June, Vol.37, Issue 3, pp: 68-77.

Pearlman, Jeff. (2009) Winners +Losers. Psychology Today. Mar/Apr, Vol.42, Issue 2, pp: 92-97.

Pelusi, Nando. (2006) The Right Way to Rock the Boat. Psychology Today. June, Vol. 39, Issue 3, pp: 60-61,

Pelusi, Nando. (2006) Dealing with Difficult People. Psychology Today. Sep/Oct, Vol.39, Issue 5, pp: 68-69.

Pelusi, Nando. (2008) The Ups and Downs of Ambition. Psychology Today. May/Jun, Vol. 41, Issue 3, pp: 67-68.

Persaud, Raj. (1998) The price of fame. Psychology Today. Sep/Oct, Vol 31, Issue 5, p12.

Perkins, Anne. (2009). When self-love is out of control. Guardian, Monday 27 July 2009.

Pinker, Susan. (2009) Extra Credit. Psychology Today. Nov/Dec, Vol.42, Issue 6, pp: 39-40.

Posen, David B. (2008) The Beliefs That Run Our Lives. National Underwriter Life & Health. 30 July 2008.

Pychyl, Timothy. (2009) Ending Procrastination – Right Now! Psychology Today. Sep/Oct, Vol. 42, Issue 5, p79.

Qubein, Nido R. (1997) Stairway to Success. The Complete Blueprint for Personal and Professional Achievement. New York: Wiley.

Rayl. A.J.S. (2007) The High Price of a Broken Heart. Psychology Today. July/Aug, Vol.40, Issue 4, pp: 96-102.

Regester, Mike; Green, Neil. (2007) Learning From Others' Mistakes. New Zealand Management. August, Vol. 54, Issue 7, pp: 78-79.

Roberts, Paul. (1994) Risk. Psychology Today. Nov/Dec, Vol. 27, Issue 6, p50.

Robbins, Stever. (2009) Seven Communication Mistakes Managers Make. Harvard Management Update, February 2009.

Rodgers, Joann Ellison. (2006) Altered Ego: the new view of personality change. Psychology Today. Nov/Dec, Vol. 39, Issue 6, pp: 70-75.

Ross, Randy. (2009) Overcoming Self-Limiting Beliefs: A Personal Challenge for You and Me. Infonomics. July/Aug. 2009.

Russell, Robert F. (2001) The role of values in servant leadership. Leadership & Organisation Development Journal. Vol. 22, No.2, pp: 76-84.

Saxbe, Darby. (2003) Small World, After All. Psychology Today. Nov/Dec, Vol.36, Issue 6, pp: 1-2.

Sayre, Kent. (2008) Unstoppable Confidence, How to use the power of NLP to more dynamic and successful. New York, McGraw Hill.

Schraeder, Mike; Freeman, Willie; Durham, Charles. (2007) A Lexicon for Lifelong Learning. The Journal for Quality & Participation. Winter 2007.

Schrof, Joannie M; Schultz, Stacey; Koerner, Brendan I; Svetcov, Danielle. (1999) Social Anxiety. U.S. News & World Report, 21/6/99, Vol. 126, Issue 24, p50.

Segerstrom, Suzanne C. (2009) the Glass half-full. How optimists get what they want from life and pessimist can too. London, Robinson.

Seitz, Victoria A; Cohen, William A. (1992) Using the psychology of influence in the job interview. Business Forum. Summer 92. Vol.17, Issue 3, p14.

Seitz, Jay A. (1993) I move..therefore I am. Psychology Today. Mar/Apr, Vol.26, Issue, 2, p50.

Shearer, Branton C; Luzzo, Anthony Darrell. (2009) Exploring the Application of Multiple Intelligences Theory to Career Counselling. The Career Development Quarterly. September, Volume 58.

Shermer, Michael. (2000) Psyched Up, Psyched Out. Scientific American Presents, pp: 38-43.

Siegal, Daniel J. (2010) Mindsight. The New Science Of Personal Transformation. New York: Bantam Books.

Sieger, Robin. (2004) Natural Born Winners, How to Achieve Happiness and Personal Fulfilment. London, Arrow Books.

Sieger, Robin. (2005) You Can Change Your Life Any Time You Want. London. Arrow Books.

Sills, Judith (2006) Criticism: Taking the Hit. July/Aug, Vol.39, Issue 4, pp: 61-62.

Sills, Judith. (2006) How to Become Your Own Boss. Psychology Today. Sept/Oct Vol 39 Issue 5, p65-66.

Sills, Judith. (2008) Take This Job and Love It. Psychology Today. Nov/Dec, Vol.41, Issue 6, pp: 58-59.

Slowman, Leon; Dunham, David W. (2004) The Matthew Effect: Evolutionary Implications. Evolutionary Psychology. Vol.2, pp: 92-104.

Smith, Nick. (2008) Mountains of motivation. Engineering & Technology. 9 August – 5 September 2008.

Smith, Sara Anne; Kass, Steven J; Schneider, Sherry K. (2006) If at First You Don't Succeed: Effects of Failure on General and Task Specific Self-Efficacy and Performance. North American Journal of Psychology. Vol.8, Issue 1, pp:171-182.

Somes, Liz. (2008) Unwitting Wits. Questioning Your Place On The Pedestal. Psychology Today. Mar/Apr, Vol.41, Issue 2, p30.

Spackman, Kerry. (2009) The Winner's Bible. Rewire Your Brain for Permanent Change. Pittboro, NC. USA: The Winner's Institute.

Spellman, Ruth (2003) Ernest Shackleton. Personnel Today, 2/11/2003,

Streib, Lauren. (2009) Miraculous Success. Forbes, 22/6/09, Vol.183, Issue 12, pp: 96-97.

Sullivan, Jim. (2009) Studying mistakes with humility, discipline reveals the lessons that make great leaders. Nation's Restaurant News. 8 June 2009.

Svoboda, Elizabeth. (2007) The Real Insiders. Psychology Today. Mar/Apr, Vol.40, Issue 2, pp: 43-44.

Szalavitz, Maia. (2003) Stand & Deliver. Psychology Today. August, Vol. 36, Issue 4, p50.

Szegedy-Maszak, Marianne. (2004) Rejection Lessons. 30/8/2004, Vol. 137, Issue 6, pp: 86-87.

Tasso, Kim. (2009) Step out of the comfort zone and take a risk. Estates Gazette. 25/7/2009. Issue 929, pp: 94-95,

Taylor, Eugene. (1995) Oh Those Fabulous James Boys! Psychology Today. Mar/Apr, Vol.28, Issue 2, p56.

Thompson, Geoff. (2006) the elephant and the twig, the art of positive thinking. Chichester, Summersdale Publishers Ltd.

Tombaugh, Jay R. (2005) Positive leadership yields performance and profitability. Development and Learning in Organisations. Vol.19, No.3, pp: 15-17.

Tracy, Brian. (1993) Maximum Achievement. The proven system of strategies and skills that will unlock your hidden powers to succeed. New York: Simon & Schuster.

Tracy, Brian. (2008) Success Is No Accident. T&D, June 2008.

Tracey, Brian. (2009) Flight Plan, The Real Secret of Success. San Francisco, Berrett-Koehler Publishers.

Ungerieider, Steven. (1992) Visions of victory. Psychology Today. July, Vol.25, Issue 4, p46.

Waitley, Dr Dennis. (1984) The Psychology of Winning. Ten Qualities of a Total Winner. New York: Berkley Books.

Webber, Rebecca. (2010) Make Your Own Luck. Psychology Today. May/June, Vol.43, Issue 3, pp: 62-68.

Weihrich, H. (1976) MBO Goal Setting Through Transactional Analysis. Industrial Management. May/June 1976,

Weisser, Cybele (2005) Afford the Life You Want. Money. February, Vol.34, Issue 2, pp: 62-68.

Weisser, Cybele. (2010) The Crisis is (Mostly) Over. Now What? Money. April, Vol.39, Issue 3, pp: 58-63.

Wheeler, Patricia, A. (2005) The Importance of Interpersonal Skills. Healthcare Executive. Jan/Feb 2005.

Wheelwright, Verne. (2003) Ageing: a personal futures perspective. Foresight. Vol. 5, No.6, pp: 61-68.

Wilson, JR, Robert Evans. (2009) The Un-Comfort Zone. Information Executive, April, Vol 12, Issue 4, P14.

Wood, Joanne. (2009) Words of wisdom. Economist. 13/6/2009, Vol 392, Issue 8635, p84.

Wright, Karen. (2008) In Search of the Real You. Psychology Today. May/June, Vol. 41, Issue 3, pp: 70-77.

Yemm, Graham. (2006) Can NLP help or harm your business? Management Services. Summer 2006, Vol.50, Issue 2, pp: 43-45.

Yemm, Graham. (2008) Influencing others – a key skill for all. Management Services. Summer 2008, Vol.52, Issue 2, pp: 21-24.

Yerys, Arlene. (1982) How to get what you want through influential communication. Management Review. June 1982.

Index

Also Available from Glasnevin Publishing:

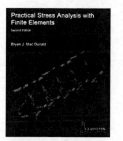

Practical Stress Analysis with Finite Elements
2nd Edition (Hardback)
Bryan J. Mac Donald
2011
ISBN: 978-0-9555781-7-5

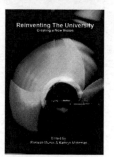

Reinventing the University: Creating a New Vision
Ronaldo Munck & Kathryn Mohrman
2011
ISBN: 978-0-9555781-5-1

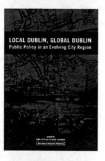

Local Dublin, Global Dublin: Public Policy in an Evolving City Region
Deiric O'Broin & David Jacobson
2010
ISBN: 978-0-9555781-4-4

Industrial Clusters in Local and Regional Economies
Helen K. McGrath
2008
ISBN: 978-0-9555781-1-3

Visit: *www.glasnevinpublishing.com* for more titles and information

Lightning Source UK Ltd.
Milton Keynes UK
UKOW021344241011

180863UK00001B/21/P